JUDGMENT
MISGUIDED

JUDGMENT
MISGUIDED

Intuition and Error
in Public Decision Making

Jonathan Baron

New York   Oxford
Oxford University Press
1998

Oxford University Press

Oxford   New York
Athens   Auckland   Bangkok   Bogota   Bombay
Buenos Aires   Calcutta   Cape Town   Dar es Salaam
Delhi   Florence   Hong Kong   Istanbul   Karachi
Kuala Lumpur   Madras   Madrid   Melbourne
Mexico City   Nairobi   Paris   Singapore
Taipei   Tokyo   Toronto   Warsaw

and associated companies in
Berlin   Ibadan

Copyright © 1998 by Oxford University Press, Inc.

Published by Oxford University Press, Inc.
198 Madison Avenue, New York, New York 10016

Oxford is a registered trademark of Oxford University Press

Library of Congress Cataloging-in-Publication Data
Baron, Jonathan, 1944–
Judgment misguided : intuition and error in public decision making /
Jonathan Baron.
p.   cm.
Includes bibliographical references and index.
ISBN 0-19-511108-7
1. Public administration—Decision making.   2. Policy sciences.
I. Title.
JF1525.D4B365   1998
352.3'3—dc21   98-11138

1 3 5 7 9 8 6 4 2

Printed in the United States of America
on acid-free paper

Preface

This book presents my current thinking about what is important in the psychology of thinking and decision making and how it relates to questions of public interest. I try to provide sufficient references so that an academic reader could track down the source of these ideas. The ideas here are a continuation of those presented in an article I wrote for *Behavioral and Brain Sciences* in 1994, titled "Nonconsequentialist Decisions."

I would like this to be read by everyone concerned with public affairs or the psychology of thinking and decision making. That is, of course, too much to expect.

In attempting to reach a somewhat wider audience than usual for me, I have tried to simplify the presentation by eliminating some of the usual academic qualifications, such as "It could be argued that X" when I really mean to say that I think X is true. I have also put references in endnotes so as not to clutter the text.

I am grateful for specific comments and general advice in the early stages of this project from Paul Rozin, Martin Seligman, and Karen Steinberg. Helpful comments on specific chapters came from Willett Kempton, Howard Kunreuther, Howard Margolis, Jay Schulkin, Karen Steinberg, and Peter Ubel. Judy Baron, David Baron, Deborah Frisch, Joshua Greene, Robert Jervis, and Joan Bossert and Nancy Hoagland (at Oxford University Press) provided helpful comments on the whole book. Mark Spranca convinced me of the importance of the intuition of naturalism, and Howard Margolis strengthened my belief that intuitions can affect public outcomes. Before and during the writing of this book, my research has been supported by the National Science Foundation. David Baron helped with typesetting, which was done with LaTeX2e in Adobe Palatino font.

Contents

CHAPTER 4

Nationalism and Group Loyalty   69

CHAPTER 5

My-side Bias and Violent Conflict   83

CHAPTER 6

Do No Harm   95

CHAPTER 7

Risk   109

JUDGMENT
MISGUIDED

CHAPTER 1

Introduction

———————

One way to make decisions is to weigh our options on the basis of their expected effects. We would favor options that we expected to have better outcomes. We do not always make decisions this way. Instead, we apply various intuitive rules to our decisions, rules that do not refer to outcomes alone. We also apply these rules when we evaluate the decisions of others, including government officials.

For example, we often consider the harm caused by our actions to be more serious and more to be avoided than harm caused by our omissions. We avoid positive options that have negative side effects, even if the positives outweigh the negatives. The resulting bias against helpful action is often reinforced by similar biases in favor of the status quo, of what is natural, or of what others have autonomously chosen. When we think about decisions affecting large groups of people, we tend to favor groups we belong to — such as nations or races — at the expense of outsiders. We judge fairness within these groups, attending less to the larger groups that contain them. Our judgments of fairness and justice are based on a kind of balancing — an eye for an eye — even when we could foresee that this attitude would make things worse on the whole.

The point of this book is that we should not be surprised when these intuitions — played out in the public sphere through the actions of individuals and government officials alike — lead to outcomes that are worse than the best we could have, often substantially worse. After all, these intuitions are not based on the principle of achieving the best. Sometimes they may lead to the best despite their apparent design, but this is not typical. If we want a better world, one relatively inexpensive way to get it is to improve the way we make decisions. We need to think more about their effects, and less about the rules that might guide them.

Consider again the intuitive bias against causing harm through action, as opposed to omission. As a result of this intuition, some people avoid taking protective measures that might cause harm, even though the same measures are more likely to prevent harm. When a vaccine — such as the DPT vaccine (diphtheria, pertussis, and tetanus) — causes rare but serious side effects or death, people resist using it because they want to avoid these effects, even though the vaccine can prevent a disease that is more likely and equally serious and deadly. Government officials resist requiring the vaccine. It is not that the government officials are wise but capitulate to public demands. They make the same intuitive judgment.

The intuition that distinguishes acts and omissions is a principle that people apply to their decisions. It has, through its effect on many people, brought about outcomes that nobody wanted, in particular, epidemics and deaths from preventable diseases. This is the pattern that I explore in this book. People follow intuitive principles of decision making that are not designed to produce the best consequences in all cases. Predictably, these principles sometimes lead to unhappy results that could have been avoided if people had focused more on how to produce the best results. So our intuitive principles have a cost. I focus on cases in which the cost is borne by many people — that is, public outcomes. Some of these people may not even agree with the principle that made things worse for them. The question I raise is why we should keep paying that cost.

Intuitions

People have an intuitive moral rule "Do no harm" or, more specifically, "Do no harm through action." In some cases, this rule is sensible. If Tom pushes Dick into the lake and Harry fails to rescue him, we punish Tom more than we punish Harry. Harry, after all, might have thought that someone else would rescue Dick or that he might be sued if he tried and failed. In other cases, like vaccination, this rule is potentially harmful. It leads us to neglect things we could easily prevent, like disease and death. This has happened in whooping cough epidemics in England and Japan. If parents or pediatricians had questioned the do-no-harm intuition at the outset — asking whether they should just try to minimize children's risk — then many of these deaths might have been avoided.

Some parents resist the DPT vaccine for their children even when they know that the total risk is lower with the vaccine than without it. They do not want to see themselves as the *cause* of harm to their children; better that the harm should come from "nature," even if they could have prevented it. Once people have made this judgment, however, they adjust their other beliefs to conform to it. They come to believe that vaccinating really *has* more risk than not vaccinating.[1] Although the original intuition was not based on consequences, people convince themselves that following it will always lead to the best results anyway. My main point here is that this is not true. Intuitive principles that are *not* based on consequences do not always produce the best consequences, and we should not be surprised by this.

The do-no-harm intuition also affects the decisions of judges and juries when people sue the makers of the vaccines for brain damage and other long-term effects. These consequences are awful, but so are the consequences of not making any vaccine at all. Yet drug companies do not get sued for the injuries caused by their failure to make a product. So pharmaceutical companies take these lawsuits into account when deciding to invest research and development resources into more, possibly risky vaccines versus yet another drug to lower cholesterol. The same intuitive rule makes people resist government policies that help many people while hurting a few.

Intuitions and Morality

Notice that bad results come from well-intentioned intuitions about what is right. These intuitions play some role in a great variety of human tragedies. Wars — both military and trade — result because citizens support the belligerent stance of their government against the immoral behavior of another nation. People oppose regulations or agreements that could protect the environment because these regulations seem to violate some principle, such as autonomy or the right to self-determination. As a result, they get results that they do not want.

This is a kind of paradox because many of the opinions in question are moral beliefs and judgments. The capacity to form and espouse moral beliefs is one of the wonderful features of humanity. People do not feel they are doing wrong when they act on these beliefs, but these beliefs repeatedly cause trouble.

The basic problem is that many of our beliefs, like the distinction we make between acts and omissions, do not concern consequences or results. We could try to follow just those principles that bring about the best results, but our principles are not designed this way. So we are constantly facing conflicts between the intuitive principles that we all follow and the results we all want.

The Costs of Expressing Intuitions

The problem is most serious when we can follow the principle without much risk of facing the consequences ourselves. In vaccination, for example, the risk of the disease and the risk of a serious reaction to the vaccine are both very low. If we ourselves were faced with a choice between certain death from a disease (which we would get if we failed to vaccinate) or a fifty-fifty chance of death from the side effects of a vaccine, we would probably think harder about the consequences, and we would not worry so much about the intuitive distinction between acting (vaccinating) and not acting.

One area where the risks of facing the consequences seem low is our political behavior. This includes voting, speaking to each other, making contributions and working for causes, and other things we do to try to influence public policy. It is difficult to think about the consequences of this behavior because we see it two different ways. In one view, because so many other people affect the outcome, the contribution of each person's action to the overall outcome is tiny. Thinking about public issues, and acting on these thoughts, is "cheap." You don't have to pay for it by accepting the consequences of your mistakes. Even if your candidate for office turns out to be a disaster, you can console yourself by saying that your vote wouldn't have mattered. Even government officials and elected legislators may feel that their main task is to express their moral intuitions, for their vote is just one among many. Thus, the political sphere is one where intuitions tend to have free play.

In the other view, public action of many people — whether through voting, speaking, or doing a government job — affects so many people that the effect of everyone's behavior together is enormous. If a billion people together, through their political action, affect the outcome of a billion people (perhaps the same billion, perhaps not), then, on average, the effect of each person's action is just as noticeable as if that person were making a personal decision. Political action no longer seems so cheap when we take our effect on others into account. It may seem that voting is an exception here because each vote is rarely decisive; elections are hardly ever so close. Yet the margin of a vote is often important, aside from the outcome. The margin tells elected officials about the extent of their mandate and the actions that will make them popular, and it informs them and other candidates about prospects for the next election. Elected officials in modern democracies are, in general, highly sensitive to public opinion.

The same arguments apply to other expressions of political opinions and moral views, such as writing letters to representatives and newspapers, posting messages to news groups on the Internet, and just talking to people. These things ultimately have consequences. They are part of the total body of opinion that guides the behavior of nations and other institutions. In sum, we cannot ignore the potential consequences of our political action so long as we care about our effects on others. Yet the first view, that our voice has little effect, often encourages us to express our intuitions without even thinking about the consequences.

Our Acceptance of Intuitions

Some intuitive beliefs are held blindly. People do not know what gives them their authority, and often nothing does. This ignorance does nothing to weaken people's commitment. The abortion debate in the United States is a good example. One side thinks of the fetus as a human being with a right to life and protection of the law. The other side thinks that prohibition of abortion infringes on the rights of women to control their bodies. Extremists on both sides do not think that their views are amenable to argument or reason. Commitment flows from the strength of feeling, from a raw perception of rightness. People even pride themselves on the strength of their ability to resist reasoned arguments from the other side. Debates take the form of repeated assertions. Each side tries to wear down the other rather than to persuade it.

Part of the problem is that one particular intuition makes us believe more strongly in the others. This is the intuition, discussed later in more detail, that what is natural is good. We tend to see our intuitions as the product of some natural force that, in some sense, understands more than we do. It has a kind of authority, like the authority that religious leaders sometimes have, that allows it to make pronouncements to us, which we then accept without knowing fully the reasons for them, trusting that the reasons are there. I shall argue, however, that many of these intuitions arise in a much simpler way. They are the application of principles that *are* often consistent with bringing about good consequences but that are applied in cases where they do not do this. They are, in the language of psychology, overgeneralized.

My use of the term *intuitive* is meant to include both blind feelings and also more reflective beliefs. The term is meant only to capture the idea that the fundamental basis of these beliefs or principles is that they appeal to some judgment other than consequences.

Intuitions and Other Causes of Misfortune

Intuitive principles are surely not the only cause of human misfortune, even if we limit ourselves to human behavior as a cause. Bad events happen sometimes when individuals simply pursue their self-interest rationally. Financial markets crash when thousands of investors all try to get their money out of a falling market: the market crashes because everyone wants to sell and few want to buy. Other bad events result from the violation of moral standards that limit the pursuit of self-interest at the expense of others' interests. Some people seem to have very weak standards of morality to begin with, so they are easily swayed toward immoral behavior by the example of others or by a bit of benefit they might obtain. Some people knowingly violate their own standards of morality. Perhaps violent criminals do this, or soldiers who rape or torture their prisoners of war. Sometimes these violations result from social pressure, which itself results from other factors such as weak standards.

I certainly do not want to deny these other behavioral causes of harm. But they are the usual suspects when we talk about the human causes of human misfortune: self-interest, weakness of will, absence of self-restraint, lack of principles, and social pressure. We know about them already, and we have been trying to control them for centuries. Perhaps by working a little harder on a somewhat neglected cause of trouble — our intuitions — we can gain a kind of leverage over the human condition. Even if the effects of our intuitions are small in the grand scheme of things, we might get a handle on them more easily than we can on other causes of harm. And even a small benefit can help a lot when its effects are accumulated over great masses of people.

Moreover, our intuitions affect our ability to deal with the other causes of trouble. If, for example, we believe in the morality of retribution and in group responsibility for the acts of individuals, we may support excessive retaliation for clearly immoral acts against groups whose members were at fault, punishing the innocent along with the guilty, even though we know that such excesses will only lead to a cycle of escalating violence, as we have seen in the Middle East, the Balkans, Northern Ireland, Eastern and Central Africa, and India in recent years. Our beliefs in retribution and group responsibility are not the basic problem. But they exacerbate the original problem, making it worse than it would be if we took other goals into account, such as the goal of making a peace agreement.

In sum, intuitions may have only small effects on big outcomes, but they may also be more controllable than some of the other forces, especially because they have not been seen before as a source of trouble. Reducing the negative effects of intuitions might thus be a cost-effective way of improving the human condition. Such improvement gives us a kind of leverage. Although the effect is small, it is broad.

How Intuitions Play Out

Harmful intuitions show up even in situations where one would think that self-interest was paramount. Consider the decline of fisheries in the Atlantic Ocean off the coasts of New England and Canada. Between 1963 and 1993, the number of flounder, haddock, and cod declined by more than 90%, mainly as a result of overfishing. It took almost 10 years for effective regulations to be imposed. Now the regulations must be so drastic that some fish cannot be caught at all until the stocks come back. Thousands of people are out of work.

Part of the problem was that each person pursued his or her economic self-interest. It was not in anyone's interest to cut back fishing, regardless of what others were doing. But democratic mechanisms were in place to impose limitations on fishing. Every time some regulation was proposed, many people thought that it was wrong, and they opposed it. The personal cost of supporting the regulation — or of assenting silently — would have been low, and almost all of the regulations would have been better for each person in the long run than no regulation at all. So we cannot explain this opposition in terms of the same simple self-interest that makes fishermen unwilling to cut back spontaneously. As I will argue in the next chapter, the fishermen opposed the regulations on the basis of their intuitions concerning personal autonomy and fairness, abetted by wishful thinking: that the decline in the fish population resulted from everything else aside from overfishing.

This pattern is repeated in a variety of social misfortunes examined in this book. People are gripped by some idea, a principle that has much to be said for it but that ignores some equally valid principle on the other side. On the basis of such principles, people commit themselves to one side of a debate. They want their side to be right, so they engage in wishful thinking to convince themselves that both the facts and the arguments support their view. They make up additional arguments on their side and fail to try to think of arguments on the other side. Some of the arguments they make are ones they would recognize as weak if they were not already committed to their positions.

Actively Open-minded Thinking

Intuitions can be useful when we correctly perceive them as *part* of the story rather than as the whole story. They become dangerous when we think in a way that protects whichever idea grips us first. How can we keep these intuitions in check? For a start, it may help to be *actively open-minded*, to put our initial view to the test by seeking evidence against it as well as evidence in its favor. It may also help to ask whether there are possible answers other than our own, and whether we are ignoring certain goals or values — even the values of others — that would make some alternative answer seem more reasonable. When we find alternatives or counterevidence, we must weigh it fairly. Of course, there may sometimes be no "other side," or it may be so evil or foolish that we can dismiss it quickly. But if we are not open to it, we will never know. When large groups of people fail to think in a way that is actively open-minded, social discourse breaks down.

Actively open-minded thinking must often be quantitative. When good arguments are found on both sides of an issue, we must often find a way to compare the arguments quantitatively. In the DPT vaccination example that began this chapter, an argument for the vaccine is that it prevents disease and resulting death. An argument against is that it causes side effects, which may also result in death. A simple quantitative comparison is to count the resulting deaths from vaccinating or from not vaccinating. A more complex quantitative comparison would take into account the severity and frequency of the symptoms and side effects other than death. This could be done informally, or formally by assigning numbers to everything. The important point is that we must be willing to think of decision making as a kind of balancing, with each argument put onto the scales and weighed.

Some Intuitions of Interest

I have suggested that intuitions can get us into trouble if we follow them blindly. So let us look at the most common ones that do this, intuitions that most of us apply frequently (and usually appropriately). The boundaries of each are fuzzy, some can be subdivided further, and some important ones are doubtless missing. But some list is probably better than no list. None of the intuitions in question is crazy or evil. That is the point. We all hold these, and most of the time they are reasonable or at least harmless compared to other ways of making decisions.

- *Do no harm.* We worry more about the harm we do through action than about the harm we do through failing to act.

- *The status-quo effect.* The burden of proof is on the side of changing the status quo. Those who want to keep the status quo do not need arguments.

- *Naturalism: Nature knows best.* It is wrong to go against nature. Of course, there is a valid point here: evolution set up a kind of order that can fail in surprising ways when we tamper with it. But we *do* tamper with it, and often we improve on it by doing so (e.g., with vaccines).

- *Autonomy and individual rights.* People should be allowed to make their own decisions, to control their own bodies, their own property, and so on. It is wrong to interfere, to coerce. A right is usually a protection of someone's autonomy in a certain domain, such as property or speech. In general, people do know what is best for them. Their autonomy should be protected in general and strongly protected in certain domains (such as free speech). But protections need not be absolute. Sometimes we can violate autonomy and be sure of doing more good than harm, as when we protect children from their own immature decisions.

These first four principles form a group because they often work together. Inaction tends to favor the status quo, which is often what is natural. Violations of autonomy often require active interference as well. The remaining principles concern distribution of benefits and burdens among different people or groups of people.

- *Group loyalty.* I should be loyal to groups I belong to, whether I chose them or not — my nation, my race, my religion, and so on. This principle is a kind of unselfishness because it obliges people to be concerned with others. But it sharply limits this concern, even to the point of supporting harm to outsiders, when groups compete. Again, there is a point here. We know our own groups best, but this has limits. Sociobiologists have called this phenomenon "tribalism" because it may be related to the fact that people evolved in tribes. Group loyalty may have other causes aside from biological ones, however, and even if some biological factor is at work, we might be able to redirect the biological drive toward the "tribe" of all people.

- *Retribution.* The idea of retribution is that we should retaliate in kind: "an eye for an eye." Punishment has a role in deterring harmful behavior, but we exact retribution even when this role is not served. The tendency to seek retribution is particularly dangerous when combined with group loyalty and with our tendency to magnify the harms against our own group. As Gandhi put it, "An eye for an eye makes the whole world blind."

- *Fairness.* Fairness is, of course, a good thing. The trouble is that we have so many different conceptions of what makes something fair: equality of opportunity; equality of results; equal benefit per person; equal benefit per dollar or per share; to each according to contribution; to each according to need; honoring prior contracts and rights; protecting the common good; and so on. Each principle of fairness can become a strong intuition. Often, people choose principles that favor themselves or their group.

Common Patterns

All of these intuitions are reasonable rules of thumb. Using them often leads to the best outcome, for good reason. For example, we should usually favor the status quo because we are not so good at anticipating the effects of changing it. Likewise, people usually know what's good for them better than other people do, so autonomy is a good idea, other things being equal. And evolution has created a kind of purposive design for living systems, one that is best left undisturbed — again, other things being equal.

The intuitions cause trouble because we conduct our thinking as if they were more than this, in several ways.

1. *The intuitions become absolutes.* Instead of thinking of these principles as rules of thumb, we elevate them to the level of absolute constraints on action. The do-no-harm principle, for example, becomes an

absolute prohibition on hurting some people in order to help others, even when the help is great and the hurt is small. Thus, a trade agreement among nations, which will cause some workers to lose their jobs, may be rejected because of this, despite preventing many other people from losing jobs, as well as making more goods available at lower prices.

When absolutes conflict, compromise becomes more difficult. For example, a trade agreement involves economic benefits and increased autonomy on the one hand, but on the other, greater difficulty in enforcing environmental regulations (which are often challenged as restraints on trade). People who care about both the economy and the environment will be sensitive to the magnitude of each effect. Environmentalists who also care about economics might decide to accept the risks of a trade agreement because the environmental costs are small relative to the economic benefits. Other international environmental agreements might have great environmental benefits and small economic costs, and it would be better to work on getting these adopted rather than on opposing the trade agreement. When principles are held absolutely, compromise and logrolling are difficult. The end result is that, instead of either agreement, we end up with neither, and both economics and the environment may suffer.

The intuitive principles that people follow — autonomy, not going against nature, nationalism, preserving the status quo, etc. — are often good rules of thumb. In general, it is better to honor them than not to honor them. People usually know what is good for them, so autonomy leads to better decisions. Tampering with nature is risky. Citizens know more about what is needed in their own nation than in other nations. But these are rough guidelines — rules of thumb that are not always true. They become most problematic when people elevate these useful rules of thumb to inviolable principles, neglecting the big picture in favor of a small piece of it.

2. *Intuitions define aspiration levels.* Intuitive principles almost always define acceptable levels of some good. Once an acceptable level is defined, the principle obliges us not to fall below that level, but does not oblige us to rise above it. Thus, for example, we are obliged not to harm people through our actions, but we are not obliged to help people through our actions. The level of aspiration here is whatever results from doing nothing.

This sort of intuition is very strong. When I play tennis, I often open a can of tennis balls on the court. I feel a strong obligation to throw away the metal top to the can I just opened, rather than leaving it to litter the court. So I do this. But I often leave behind several tops left by others, which I could easily pick up and throw away. My intuitive sense says that I am obliged not to make the situation worse, but I am not obliged to improve it.

Such principles are convenient because they limit our obligations in our daily lives. If I felt just as obliged toward every lid, I would have no clear rule for stopping. I would have to judge, each time, whether the effort of picking up another lid was worthwhile. But the same intuition can be applied in matters of policy. If we are talking about governments regulating pollution instead of tennis players picking up their lids, we should ask how we can get the most pollution reduction for a given expenditure, and it may turn out that it is better to make companies clean up someone else's pollution rather than their own, regardless of our intuition to the contrary.

The status quo often defines an aspiration level. We are more upset about losing what we have than about failing to get what we do not have. Imagine the reaction if someone in the U.S. government proposed a new subsidy for tobacco growers. Yet the opposition to the current subsidies is so muted that nobody thinks they are threatened. Likewise, when a new law helps many people but hurts a few, relative to the status quo, we are reluctant to support the law because we take the harm more seriously than the gain. But if the law were already in effect, we would not want to repeal it because those who benefit from it would then be hurt.

In the vaccination case described earlier, the aspiration level is inaction, the result of doing nothing. (This is not the status quo because nobody is sick yet.) In other cases, the aspiration level is defined by some principle. One principle we shall see repeatedly is that of autonomy. Thus, interfering with autonomy is considered a great loss, although creating additional autonomy where it does not exist is seen as less important. Likewise, destruction of what is natural is particularly harmful, more so than failing to return something to its natural state. Finally, a distribution seen as fair can define an aspiration level. If it seems fair for two boys to get 10 peanuts each, and if one gets 12 and the other 8, then the 8 will be seen as a loss of 2, which will seem more serious than the gain of 2 for the other.

Once an aspiration level is defined, losses relative to it are taken more seriously than gains. This is called "loss aversion."[2]

3. *Wishful thinking.* People tend to believe what they want to believe, which is often determined by their immediate self-interest. Credit-card interest rates are extremely high compared to other rates for borrowing, and banks try hard to sell credit cards because this interest is so profitable for the banks — several times the profit they make on other activities. According to economic theory, the interest rates and the profit ought to come down because of competition. It seems that this does not happen, in part because card users tend to think that they will not borrow on their cards, so the high rates are irrelevant to them. Card holders do not even admit to themselves the amount of borrowing they are doing: they drastically underestimate the amount that they already owe.[3]

Likewise, most drivers believe that they are safer and more skillful than average, and most people believe that they are more likely than average to live past 80.[4] There are limits on this. We can't convince ourselves of anything. But we can trick ourselves into believing what we want by paying attention to the evidence that supports a belief, ignoring the evidence against it and not worrying too much about what our beliefs might be if we were more objective.

Once we are gripped by an intuitive principle, wishful thinking sets in. As we shall see, when scientists told fishermen that they were overfishing and should cut back, the fishermen did not want to hear this particular news, so they looked for reasons why the scientists were wrong.

4. *My-side bias and overconfident belief.* Although people usually employ wishful thinking so that they believe good news and disbelieve bad news, the opposite can happen. Chicken Little misinterpreted the evidence to support his pessimistic view that the sky was falling. People suffering from clinical depression often try to convince themselves that they are to blame for some bad chance event, and sufferers from anxiety exaggerate their fears. It is thus sometimes more sensible to speak of "my-side bias" rather than wishful thinking. Even Chicken Little wanted his side to be correct, despite, we assume, wishing that it were incorrect. Once people have committed themselves to a belief, they tend to look for evidence in its favor and reject evidence against it, even if the belief makes them unhappy. This is called "my-side bias" because it favors the thinker's side of the argument.

My-side bias results in overconfidence, in unwillingness to listen and to compromise, in breakdowns in cooperation.[5] The overconfidence in the rightness of the principles in question is, of course, one reason that people treat them as absolutes that cannot be compromised.

The mechanism of my-side bias is often subtle, involving several people. An interesting case concerns the question of whether global warming is resulting from human activity, particularly the burning of coal, oil, and gasoline, which produces carbon dioxide, which traps the sun's heat in the atmosphere. The mechanism of warming has been understood for some time, and computer models predict that considerable warming will occur over the next few decades. Although temperatures have increased slightly over the past century, most scientists who worry about global warming are more impressed by the computer models than by the warming so far, which may be the result of random fluctuation (although the most recent evidence says that even the observed trend is real). In 1990, an article in *Science*[6] demonstrated that precise measurements of atmospheric temperature could be made from satellites by measuring microwaves. Such measurements had been made from 1979 through 1988, and the article remarked incidentally that during this 10-year period no overall warming was observed. The authors were concerned with the accuracy of their measurements. In press accounts, they acknowledged explicitly what they should have said in the article, that 10 years is simply too short a time to detect a trend, so their finding "does not prove that there is not a global warming." Still, despite this clarification in the text, the headlines emphasized the lack of trend: the *Washington Post* account of March 30, 1990, was titled "NASA satellites find no sign of 'greenhouse' warming." An anti-environmentalist congressional staff member, however, sent out a letter to members of the U.S. House reprinting a key graph from the article and saying, "The NASA study offers strong evidence that there is *no* 'greenhouse effect.'"[7] It is easy to understand this event without assuming any deliberate attempt to deceive. The staff member involved saw the headline and the graph and, given that these supported his view, saw no need to look very hard for evidence on the other side, such as a disclaimer by one of the authors of the original study. Moreover, the staffer's confidence in his conclusion took no account of the fact that he had failed to look for such a disclaimer. He was as confident as if he had looked and failed to find it.

5. *Belief overkill.* Many controversial issues are controversial because there are good arguments on both sides. A rational decision would involve balancing the arguments in a quantitative way, a way that takes into account their strengths or the magnitudes and probabilities of the possible results. But people find ways to avoid this balancing. Through wishful thinking, they convince themselves that all the good arguments are on one side. Robert Jervis provides many examples of this kind of overkill in judgments about foreign policy.[8] In discussions of a ban on testing nuclear weapons, "People who favored a nuclear test-ban believed that testing created a serious medical danger, would not lead to major weapons improvements, and was a source of international tension. Those who opposed the treaty usually took the opposite position on all three issues. Yet neither logic nor experience indicates that there should be any such relationship. The health risks of testing are in no way connected with the military advantages, and a priori we should not expect any correlation between people's views on these questions."

Attitudes about capital punishment provide a good example of overkill.[9] It is possible in principle to believe that capital punishment is morally wrong yet effective as a deterrent against serious crimes, or morally acceptable yet ineffective. Yet almost nobody holds these combinations of belief. Those who find it morally wrong also think it is ineffective, and vice versa.

Here is an example of the process at work, from a subject in a study of reasoning, asked his opinion about animal experimentation: "We actually have no right to do such things. It's not even necessary. If it was necessary, maybe there would be a reason for it, but, there's no need for it, I don't think. We're sort of guardians here." The subject's intuition was that animals have a right to our protection. He could believe this and still also think that we could gain some benefit from experimenting on them, a benefit that we ought to forgo. But, instead, he convinces himself that no benefit exists.[10]

The Role of Psychology

The idea that intuitions cause trouble is part of a relatively recent tradition in psychology, the study of heuristics and biases. In the past three decades, psychologists have discovered dozens of cases in which people use principles of thinking in ways that lead to errors. The principles themselves, heuristics, are typically good rules to follow in certain situations, but people use them where they are not so good. As a result, people display biases away from the best judgment. Biases are not just errors. Errors could go in either direction, but biases are in one direction.

The status-quo principle is an example. In this case, the heuristic principle is "stick with what you have." The bias is that people tend to change less often than they should if they want to achieve their goals as much as possible. For example, in several experiments, half of the college students in a room were given a large candy bar and half were given a college mug. These objects were put on their desks, but the students could not touch them. Then the students were asked if they would trade the object they were given for the other one: a mug for a candy bar or vice versa. If the students had been asked in advance, before they were given anything, we would expect half of them to prefer the object they did not get. After all, the objects were assigned at random. Typically, in the experiments, only about a quarter are willing to trade. Here is a clear case where no arguments can be made for the status quo — the object each student has — yet people maintain it anyway.[11]

One explanation of this effect is that the status quo defines a psychological aspiration level. If you have a mug — even if you would otherwise slightly prefer a candy bar — a trade will involve losing the mug in order to gain the candy bar. A basic principle, the principle of loss aversion, says that losses loom larger than gains. So the loss of a mug seems too great to justify the gain of the candy, even though the gain of the candy would be preferred to the gain of the mug.

This status-quo effect, and other effects, may also result from the misapplication of principles that are useful in many situations. In general, other things being equal, it is in fact better to keep the status quo, for many reasons: in organizations, constant changes make it difficult for people to learn how things work; it is good to be predictable; and the status quo was often chosen for good reasons that are now unknown. But people honor this principle even when all these arguments are carefully removed.

The reason for this kind of misapplication of principles is not fully understood, but it seems to be a general feature of learning. In arithmetic, for example, many children faced for the first time with "17 − 9" answer "12." They apply a principle that was useful up to that point: when subtracting within a column, subtract the smaller number (7) from the larger (9). If they understood the purpose of this rule, however, they would realize that it does not achieve its purpose when the smaller number is "on top." Perhaps the ultimate reason for this misapplication of principles is that we do not always fully understand the purposes of the principles we use.

The term *heuristics* is understood as equivalent to *rule of thumb*. I prefer the term *intuitions* here because I argue that the principles in question are not always used as rules of thumb. They are elevated to a higher status because they are perceived as being absolutely correct. When decisions affect many people, these intuitions take on moral force. We feel that they are more than just personal rules; rather, they should be accepted by everyone. When others go against them, that is a reason for righteous anger.

Effects such as the status-quo effect are often called biases because they move people away, in a systematic direction, from what is optimal. The interesting finding of the mug experiment was not that the students made random errors, sometimes one way and sometimes the other. (The experiment would not have revealed such errors in any case.) It was rather that responses were systematically biased toward the status quo more than they would be if the students chose what they would have preferred before being given anything. Thus, in general, biases often result from the use of heuristics.

I am going one step beyond most past psychology by extending this heuristics-and-biases approach to moral intuitions, as well as non-moral principles of decision making. This extension has a problem. In the study of personal decision making, we can usually specify a "right answer" and then show that subjects aren't giving it. In the mug experiment, for example, we cannot give the right answer for each subject, but we can say that, if subjects had responded in terms of their real preference, half of them would have switched. In matters of morality, however, it is more difficult to specify a right answer.

Consequences, Consequentialism, and Utilitarianism

I shall assume here that the right answer is the one that can be expected to yield the best consequences. More generally, the best principles to follow are those that lead to the best consequences. This claim is called *consequentialism* or (in one form) *utilitarianism*.[12] So people are making errors, in a sense, if they do not follow these consequentialist principles. Although I cannot fully defend this assumption here, I adopt it because my main purpose is to show that intuitions often make consequences worse and to ask why we should make this sacrifice to the intuitions that do this.

The vaccination case provides an example. The lower the death rate, the better the result; this is the main consequence of the decision. So it is better to vaccinate as long as fewer deaths will result from it, even if the vaccine itself will directly cause some deaths. The do-no-harm intuition argues against vaccinating, so it leads to worse consequences. This does not imply that the people who follow it have bad intentions. Indeed, the interesting thing is that they make their choice exactly because they think it is morally right. But it turns out to be wrong according to the consequentialist standard. Thus, intuitions that are not justified in terms of consequences often result in consequences that we do not like. We pay a price for following our intuitions, and sometimes it is a heavy one. In view of this situation, we might want to reexamine the reasons we have for our intuitive judgments.

If we correctly follow the principles that lead to the best outcome, we will achieve the best outcome possible. If anyone argues for an alternative principle — such as "respecting the right to autonomy even when it allows people to harm themselves" — that person must explain how the harm is justified. This explanation must be addressed to those who do not accept the intuitive principle, so it cannot appeal to the principle itself. The whole issue is whether the principle can be justified. We do have reasons to oppose the principle, namely, that it produces results that we do not like. For example, if I put the long-run health of fisheries and those who work them ahead of the autonomy of fishing people, then, if you want to prove me wrong you must explain to me why we should let the fisheries die for the sake of autonomy, even though all the other costs of honoring this principle exceed the benefits, in terms of what matters to people.

One explanation is that, in the long run, it is better to respect autonomy because, that way, people learn to make decisions for themselves, and they make better decisions. Even if, along the way, some harm results, this harm is outweighed by better consequences. Notice, however, that this argument is made completely in terms of consequences. It is an argument *within* utilitarianism, not an argument against it, whether it is correct or not.

Utilitarianism is based on the idea that decisions in general should produce the best consequences. It extends this idea from ordinary decisions that affect mainly one person to decisions that affect many people. This principle, applied to ordinary decisions, explains why the status-quo effect is an error. If you judge that the candy bar is a better outcome for you than the mug, and you still keep the mug, then you are producing a worse result. You are adhering to a principle that, in this case, does more harm than good.

Similar things happen in the domain of moral judgment. One example is honoring autonomy even when people use it to hurt themselves. Another example concerns punishment. We have a moral principle that harm doing should be punished. This rule usually yields good consequences because punishment deters future harm doing. But when we punish — through lawsuits — the makers of beneficial and well-made vaccines because of harmful but rare side effects, we discourage companies from making such vaccines, so we do more harm than good. Many people do not think about justifying punishment in terms of its consequences, so they are willing to punish a company even when they believe that no good will result. This is even true of judges.[13] The utilitarian principle here is that two wrongs do not make a right, unless the second wrong prevents another, greater, wrong.

The nonutilitarian moralist will argue that these bad outcomes are simply the price we pay for morality. If a regulation infringes upon the autonomy of fishermen, for example, then it should not be put into effect, even if its absence leads to a worse outcome for the fishermen themselves. If a vaccine harms some, we should not use it, even if many more will suffer from our omission. But why would we want moral principles that lead, over and over, to unwelcome outcomes? Where do these principles get their authority to override our interests? Of course, many have tried to answer these questions, and it would take at least another book to deal with all their arguments. I raise these questions here not to settle the issue but to hint at why I think the task for the other side is formidable.

To apply utilitarianism, we need a thorough accounting of consequences. We need to consider emotional effects, such as the bitterness that results from perceived unfairness or from the regret that comes from harming someone through an action. We need to consider the effects of our decisions on other decisions taken later: when people break a rule for the greater good, they make it more likely that they and others will break the same rule in the future, for what seems at the time to be the greater good but isn't. Sometimes it is best just to follow the rules, despite appearances to the contrary: don't lie under oath, don't commit adultery, and so on. But we can understand that we do this because following the rules *does* serve the greater good, not because morality is separate from consequences. When we make decisions quickly, when we have a strong self-interest, when our information is compelling but unreliable, and perhaps in other cases, we must take into account the possibility of error as part of our judgment. We must override the judgment we would make without taking error into account, exactly because that judgment is likely to lead us away from the best consequences.

Most moral systems make some room for consequences. The arguments here are not totally alien to anyone. Even those who admit some other principles aside from attention to consequences might come to feel, on the basis of looking at the effects of moral intuitions, that *more* attention to consequences is warranted.

Many of our problems and their solutions are rooted in our psychological makeup. Others have made this kind of argument before, but they have pointed to different aspects of human nature. The problem is not a matter of evil motivation, false consciousness, sexual repression, neurosis, or psychosis. Rather, our problems come — paradoxically — from some of the best aspects of our nature: our desire to be moral and virtuous. We are well intentioned, but our intentions go awry because we do not always think well. This is a hopeful view because the solution to our problems can be found, in part, in the standards of thinking that we adopt for public discourse.

Summary and Outlook

The intuitive principles that cause trouble are not just the results of greed or impulsiveness. The trouble results from people acting on principles that they themselves believe to be right, if only because people have convinced themselves of the principles' rightness. The problem of concern here is not evil, but if anything, an overconfident morality that results from an excess of self-deception. Most people take stands on public issues on the basis of gut feelings or intuitions about what is right. These feelings often capture part of the issue — like the blind men and the elephant in the fable — but they miss the whole.

Of course, people sometimes do act out of bad intentions, knowing that what they do is morally wrong by their own standards. This is surely true of many criminals, especially those who attack and rob strangers. Even bad public outcomes, like disease epidemics and the decline of fisheries, are often blamed on some sort of malice on someone's part — greedy fishermen, corrupt officials or legislators, and so on — as if the intentions had to fit the outcomes. This is almost the standard story in news media and private discussions about such outcomes. And perhaps it is sometimes true. Yet many commentators neglect the possibility that these outcomes arise from actions fully congruent with the intuitive beliefs of the actors, and that the intuitions in question, though held through no malice, are misapplied.

The intuitions that drive us are often related to goals that we do not think about. For example, autonomy is a good principle because it usually helps to achieve better consequences. People usually know what is good for them better than other people do, and social support for autonomy helps people learn to make better decisions. So we can justify autonomy in terms of our goal that people should make good decisions. But when people think about autonomy as a value in its own right, rather than as a means to another end, they cannot easily make tradeoffs between autonomy and other values.

To see the whole, we must think more about consequences for everyone. The autonomy of fishing people *is* a good thing, other things being equal; it allows them to plan their work efficiently. But overfishing destroys the fish. Each side — fishermen and conservationists — transforms one of these consequences into a near absolute, and a compromise that respects both values becomes difficult.

Thus, our well-meant and deeply felt intuitions about what is right often prevent us from achieving the results we want. We should not banish these intuitions, for they are often important reminders of things we need to consider. But we should relegate them to a secondary role. Primarily, we should base decisions that affect the common good on our understanding of consequences, results, effects. This simplifies decisions, in a way. We usually ask about consequences *and* other principles. I am suggesting that we can omit the second step, although we might have to be more careful in how we think about the first.

The following chapters examine a number of issues in which intuitions lead to bad effects in the public domain. They consist mainly of a series of case studies, organized into chapters according to the type of intuitions involved in people's arguments. Each chapter has a substantive theme as well. For example, Chapter 2 is about social traps, such as the fisheries problem just discussed. That problem serves as the major case study, but other, related problems are discussed, too. A final chapter will include recommendations for action.

In most cases, the biases discussed are mainly on one side of a controversial issue. The main argument does not depend on which side is right. The examples I have chosen are just examples. They are not the entire set of possible examples. The reader should not assume that the presence of bias makes the side in question wrong. People can be right for the wrong reasons. But it is important to know what the right reasons are, for they affect future decisions. The point here is to get clear on the distinction between good and bad reasons for our attitudes. If we get rid of all the bad reasons, we will all be better off.

It may seem that a change in our way of thinking and talking will not have much effect. After all, the future of humanity depends mostly on economics, scientific progress, or the limits of the earth, not on the quality of our thinking. But small changes can help a lot. All of our major problems can be seen as races between constructive and destructive forces. Whether population growth outstrips food production, for example, is a matter of a fraction of a percent in the growth rate. A small change in an attitude toward birth control on the part of a mere billion people can make a big difference. Likewise, a small increase in world trade could allow some poor nations to change direction, if ever so slowly at first, from deepening poverty to economic growth. When we are dealing with long-term trends, small changes in rates are amplified after many years. When the rate of growth of world food production is about the same as population growth, a small change in one or the other can lead to famine or plenty. Our attitudes toward decision making act like a lever. With a place to put it, we can move the world.

CHAPTER 2

All the Fish in the Sea

<hr>

Some warnings are worth heeding. In the 1980s, scientists such as Vaughn Anthony of the National Marine Fisheries Service in Woods Hole, Massachusetts, began saying that the fish off the coast of New England and Canada's maritime provinces were disappearing because of overfishing.[1] Fishing has been a major industry in these areas for centuries, and nothing like this had happened before. People did not act fast enough. Now the numbers of cod, haddock, and flounder are so low that it is not worth fishing for them.

Around the year 1500, the explorer John Cabot described the Grand Banks area as so "swarming with fish that they could be taken not only with a net but in baskets let down with a stone."[2] Fishing was a mainstay of the economy of the colonies, and then, after the Revolutionary War, of the United States and Canada. It stayed that way because the basic technology did not change that much.

The problems began in the 1960s, when giant "factory trawlers" from Japan, Poland, and other countries began fishing off the New England coast. Often these ships fished in teams, taking all the fish from one area and then moving elsewhere. In 1976, as part of a larger series of international changes, the U.S. government passed the Magnuson Fishery Conservation and Management Act, which extended coastal waters to 200 miles, evicting the foreigners. It also set up a system for regulating fisheries, which depended on eight regional management councils, consisting of representatives of fishers as well as others. The Commerce Department controlled the whole system. In 1977, to restore stocks of cod, haddock, and yellowtail flounder, the New England Council adopted quotas. Five years later, it dropped the quotas because the fishermen thought that they were no longer needed. The U.S. government then made low-interest loans available to fishermen — in part to take up the slack left by the departure of the foreigners — and the number of boats increased. Between 1982 and 1986, the cod catch in Georges Bank dropped by 50%.

At this point, scientists such as Anthony urged the regional council to take drastic action, but fishermen thought that a series of milder steps would do the job. The Environmental Law Foundation sued the Commerce Department, and the New England Council began to develop a regulatory plan. Hearings were held. Agreement on the magnitude and methods of regulation was elusive. Meanwhile, the fishing kept on going.

Now the cod are nearly gone, and the halibut and haddock are "commercially extinct." In 1993, the Canadian cod fishery was closed, causing the loss of more than 40,000 jobs. In 1994, U.S. quotas for haddock and cod were cut almost to zero off the New England coast, including, of course, Cape Cod, which was named for the once-plentiful fish. The fish are disappearing from overfishing.

This is a world phenomenon.[3] In the past few decades, the world's people have acquired the technology to extract all the edible fish from the ocean in a few years, and population growth has increased the economic incentive to use the technology. More fishing is done for export rather than for feeding the fishing communities. Governments even try to subsidize fishing as part of a program of economic development. In Kerala, India, for example, the government tried to promote economic development by subsidizing fishing. First it subsidized large trawlers. Then, after protests from small fishermen, it began subsidizing their purchases of outboard motors and modern equipment. In both cases, overfishing resulted. The officials involved did not think of the fishery as limited, because it had seemed inexhaustible to the traditional fishing folk who had worked it for centuries.[4]

In the Phillipe and Tongan Islands of the South Pacific, fishermen now pour bleach into the reefs — or even use dynamite — to make the fish come to the surface, where they are easy prey. This destroys the reefs, the habitat of future fish as well as places of great beauty. But once some fishermen do it with impunity, those who refrain will only lose out. The reefs, and ultimately the fish that live in them, will be destroyed by others.[5]

This chapter will discuss these problems of fishing as examples of a general type of problem, typical of environmental problems of all sorts.

The Tragedy of the Commons

The main problem is that each person overfishing is best for him and worse for all the other fishermen. In other words, each would want all the others to stop overfishing. This kind of case is known as a commons dilemma. It goes by many other names and takes many forms: social dilemma, public goods problem, resource dilemma, free-rider problem, collective action problem, negative externality, n-person prisoner's dilemma, and so on. Scholars from psychology, economics, philosophy, and political science have recognized the importance of these dilemmas, and each discipline has taken a slightly different point of view on what the relevant situations are and what they should be called, hence all the different names.

In a commons dilemma, many people face the same pair of options: cooperation or defection. Defection (fishing as much as possible) is better for each individual, and cooperation (restraint) is better for everyone else. The term *commons dilemma* comes from Garrett Hardin's classic article, "The Tragedy of the Commons," which used the problem of overgrazing cows on a common pasture as an example.[6] Defection can involve taking from a common pool, as in the case of overfishing and overgrazing, or it can involve failing to contribute to the pool, as in shirking on the job. Such dilemmas exist when people cut down too many trees for firewood, have too many children, use too much water in a water shortage, cheat on their taxes, violate contractual agreements, or exaggerate their losses when they make insurance claims. Hardin argued that the natural course of a commons dilemma was to end in overuse of the commons: "ruin is the destination toward which all men rush. . . . Freedom in a commons brings ruin to all." The only solution is "mutual coercion, mutually agreed upon." Those involved must regulate themselves through collective institutions such as government.

Overfishing is a classic commons dilemma. For each person, catching fish helps him and hurts others. A single fisherman might think, "I could fish only enough so that, if everyone else did the same, we could all continue to fish the same amount in the future, and I would benefit from this in the long run." But the future benefit from what a single fisherman does will spread around everyone else who fishes the same waters. The total effect of what a single person does will be so small that each individual would not notice. Unless the person has some sort of social bonds with the others, which make them all cooperate, the future benefit would be too little to make the person want to restrain his catch to the sustainable level.

An additional feature of some commons dilemmas is that the benefits of defecting are immediate and the costs to others are in the future. This makes the dilemmas more difficult to deal with. When this feature is present, the situation is called a "social trap." Overfishing is a social trap because its effects are exerted in part by slowing the rate of reproduction of the fish, which affects the future. Fishermen themselves understand the problem quite well: "Fishermen are hard pressed economically right now. They have to look at the short-term reality, that they have to feed their families like everyone else. It's tough to be an altruist and say, 'Let's let the fish rebuild.' It is politically unpopular."[7]

The problem is more difficult when the short-term advantages of fishing are a matter of life and death. Shrimp fishermen on the West Coast of Mexico and their families were seriously malnourished for parts of the year because of regulations against fishing at those times.[8] (In part, the problem came about because more shrimp were being exported for cash than were being eaten by the fishermen and their families.) Violation of the regulations was thus more tempting. This was so even with full and rational understanding that overfishing could deplete the shrimp. For children who might die from their weakness, the future was unimportant if they could not make it through the year. Under such conditions of high risk, neglect of the future is rational. The situation may sometimes be truly hopeless, but that is not the usual case.

Another source of difficulty is that it is sometimes in a person's rational self-interest to ignore the future. Older fishermen who plan to retire soon and who do not care about those who take their place have every selfish reason to take what they can while they can. If interest rates are sufficiently high, even younger fishermen may think that they could make enough money in a short time to retire early from fishing and live partly off the interest. But then the resource is lost to other fishermen, not to mention people who eat the fish.

We might think that all commons dilemmas would lead to ruin, but this is not so. Many have been solved because people have come to recognize them and come to some kind of collective agreement. In Alanya, Turkey, in the 1970s, the fishermen faced a situation of declining stocks and increased competition. Their local cooperative, after several trial-and-error efforts, adopted a set of rules that solved the problem. The rules, which are still in effect, involved identifying all the licensed fishermen in the area and assigning each one to a fishing location by lot. Because some locations are better than others, the fishermen rotate through all the locations, taking a new location each day throughout the fishing season. The technology ensures that plenty of fish will be left: it is impossible to take them all from any given site. The fishermen enforce the system themselves through formal and informal penalties.[9]

Elinor Ostrom and her colleagues have described this and other examples of spontaneous solutions, not only in problems of fishing but also in use of scarce water resources (in southern California, for example) and agricultural land (in Switzerland, Japan, and elsewhere).[10] They have contrasted these successes with other commons dilemmas that went unsolved, like that of the North Atlantic fisheries. The successful cases tended to be those with clearly defined boundaries (so that defectors could not enter after an agreement had been made), rules appropriate to local conditions (e.g., the assignment of locations would not work in an ocean fishery), democratic participation in modifying the rules, arrangements for monitoring and enforcement, gradual sanctions (not too severe for the first defection), mechanisms for conflict resolution (e.g., local courts), and noninterference from outside governments.

Ostrom's cases all involved small communities of up to a few hundred people, in which most people were known to other members of the community. This made enforcement easier, because defectors would lose their reputations. Other dilemmas, such as the North Atlantic fisheries, involve larger communities in which exclusion of outsiders is difficult without the cooperation of national governments. Yet many of these larger dilemmas have been solved too, even those that involve the whole world. A major international success story is the Montreal Protocol, in which the nations that produced chlorofluorocarbons (CFCs) such as Freon agreed to phase out their production. (CFCs destroy the protective layer of ozone in the upper atmosphere, leading to increased ultraviolet radiation, which has a variety of effects on plant and animal life, most of them harmful.) Other examples are international trade agreements and United Nations peacekeeping efforts.

The problem in the North Atlantic is thus not just that the fishermen overfished. It is unreasonable to expect them to do otherwise, in the absence of some agreement. If a single fisherman decided to stay home in order to help the fishery rebuild instead of going out and working as hard as all the other fishermen, his action would have very little effect on the fishery but a pronounced negative effect on himself. Only a saint without a family would do this.

But this was not the only choice. The fishermen are represented by various organizations. A second decision that each one faced is whether to try to influence these organizations one way or another, or not at all. Unlike cutting back on fishing in the absence of rules, such attempts at influence are not going to ruin anyone's livelihood. It does not take a saint to make the effort. Of course, if enough people make the effort and succeed, there will be cutbacks for all, but all fishermen will also benefit because of cuts made by others. Here is another example of how political action is effective, relative to its cost, because its benefits are spread over many people.[11]

What happened was that many of these organizations opposed any regulations proposed by others and made little effort to design better regulations. Jake Dykstra, a fisherman involved in regulatory issues over a long period, said, "The fishermen are indicating rather strongly that if they could get a management program that they believe in, they have a willingness as never before to self-enforce it." But, according to Paul Schneider, it "became apparent that constructing an effective groundfish plan that the fishermen of New England 'could believe in' was going to be extraordinarily difficult, and not only because of their understandable disinclination for a 'stick in the eye.' For every suggested policy option, somebody — fisher, conservationist, or enforcer — had a reason why it just wouldn't work. For every measure amenable to the fishermen of one port, there were fishermen in another port who claimed they would be put out of business."[12]

An individual fisherman can ask those who represent him to fight regulation, or to lobby in favor of reasonable regulations proposed by others or constructively proposed changes that might be acceptable to all involved. It is perfectly reasonable for a fisherman to do this while, at the same time, fishing as hard as he can. Similarly, people concerned about their nation's budget deficit might write letters asking for a tax increase while, at the same time, filling out their own taxes carefully to pay the minimum legally required. Writing a letter to your representative surely has less cost to you than sending in an extra check for the taxes that should be collected, yet the benefits might be as great in increasing the chance of a change that will benefit everyone.

So why did the fishermen oppose regulations? I suggest that two intuitions were basic causes of their opposition: perceived unfairness and a belief in the rightness of autonomy. Once these intuitions had dictated a position, other reasons were recruited to justify it. These intuitions and others like them may characterize other commons dilemmas. Although these dilemmas arise because of the conflict between self-interest and the interest of others, the solution to them may sometimes have more to do with thinking differently, so that mutual regulation can be achieved, than with simply becoming less selfish.

Unfairness

When people must cut back, it is important that the pain be fairly distributed. Unfairness becomes an excuse for defection and for opposition to the proposed scheme. Each group evaluates fairness in its own favor.

A psychology experiment has made this point clearly.[13] Subjects were instructed to fill out questionnaires until told to stop. They expected to be paid but did not know how much. Each subject was given either three or six questionnaires (depending on the experimental condition) and was told to stop after either 45 or 90 minutes. When a subject finished, she was told that there had been another subject who had had to leave before he could be told that he was supposed to be paid. The experimenter, who also said he had to leave, gave the original subject $7 (in dollar bills and coins) and asked her to send the other subject his money (in the stamped, addressed envelope provided). The subject was told that the other subject had put in either more, the same, or less time and had completed more, the same, or fewer questionnaires.

At issue was how much money the original subject would send to the "other" subject (actually a confederate of the experimenter). Subjects who *either* worked longer *or* completed more questionnaires than the "other" gave the other *less* than $3.50. It just cannot be true that, if they had been asked before the experiment, the subjects who worked longer would have thought that time was more important and subjects who did more would have thought number of questionnaires was more important. Subjects apparently seized on any excuse to see themselves as deserving more. When the original subjects were equal to the other subject on *both* dimensions, they sent almost exactly $3.50, on the average. Only when subjects did worse on *both* dimensions (time and number of questionnaires) was there a slight tendency to send more than $3.50 to the other.

This experiment may tell us something very interesting about human nature. People are not simply selfish; they want to do what is right. Almost all subjects took the trouble to give the other subject half of the money when they had no reason to do otherwise. When people behave selfishly, then, it is likely because they have deceived themselves into the belief that they are behaving fairly. More relevant here, this experiment shows how people can convince themselves that, when different standards of fairness are available, the correct one is the one that favors them.

In 1981, the National Marine Fisheries Service proposed a regulation for striped bass. Fishermen in regions where the bass spawned would be allowed to catch relatively small fish, as short as 14 inches. The length limit for other fishermen was much larger. This was a compromise designed to protect the former group. Larry Simms, a Maryland fisherman who had led the successful opposition to previous attempts to raise the limit from 12 to 14 inches, said, "You take [the 12-inch rule] away from us and you take away a million dollars. . . . We don't want to be the only ones sacrificing . . . . The fish swim away after they reach 14 inches."[14]

Undoubtedly, the Maryland fishermen thought it was fair to base limits on past catch levels, while others probably thought that the same length limit should apply to everyone. Other disputes involve groups who think that fairness involves some special provision for them. For example, many Japanese viewed proposed restrictions on the bluefin tuna as "an outrage aimed at Japanese fish-eating habits, . . . a part of our national food culture."[15]

Unfairness is still the major argument against proposed regulations. Recent opposition to a quota system in the United States has come from small fishermen, who object to basing quotas on past catches, which they see as favoring large ships. They are supported by some en-

vironmental groups, particularly Greenpeace.[16] Alaska Governor Tony
Knowles has opposed the U.S. National Marine Fisheries Service efforts
to save the chinook salmon by declaring it an endangered species and
limiting Alaskan fishing severely. Knowles argued that the salmon declined because of hydroelectric dams on the Columbia River in Washington state, and that the restrictions would benefit Canadians, who would
not be subject to them. Likewise, Connecticut's congressional delega-
tion is working to change the quotas for fluke (flounder), which are now
based on past catches. Connecticut had lower catches than other states
and now wants quotas to be divided equally among the states.[17]

The perception of regulation as unfair is particularly acute when
those who bear the brunt of the regulation do not see themselves as the
cause of the original problem. Often, in fact, their perception is correct
— they are not the cause. But they may still be the cure. This is particularly common with small-scale fishermen, whose fisheries are invaded
by large factory trawlers, often from other nations.[18] Pollution also flows
into the ocean and can ruin a fishery, just as it has almost destroyed the
famous oysters in Chesapeake Bay on the East Coast of the United States.
When fishermen or crabbers are told that they must cut back to preserve
what remains, they feel justifiably angry. But those who are truly at fault
cannot bring the fish or the crabs back. In the Chesapeake Bay, the problem occurred before most people were aware of the effects of pollution.
Laws have now been passed to prevent more pollution, but the damage
has been done. Likewise, in the 1970s, most nations prohibited foreign
fishing within 200 miles of their coasts, but again the damage to coastal
fisheries had already been done, and small-scale fishermen were asked
to cut back. Those who took the fish cannot put them back, and most of
the damage was fully within existing international law. Until the 1970s,
nations accepted the idea that the seas were a common resource open to
all.

In other cases, the unfairness is less blatant. Restrictions on seal
hunting caused the seal herd to increase, and seals eat fish. In many
cases, fish stocks declined for unknown but entirely natural reasons. Yet
the same fishermen must bear the brunt here too, and it still seems somewhat unfair that they should suffer for what they did not cause. It seems
even more unfair when another human being caused it and cannot be
made to suffer. Yet from a utilitarian point of view, restraints on the fishermen are the best solution, if not the only possible solution. We cannot
control natural fluctuations. In the case of the seals, it would be at best a
short-term fix to kill the seals in order to help restore the fish.

A fundamental intuition about fairness is that those who cause
harm should pay and those who do not cause harm should not pay. This
intuition establishes an aspiration level for the payments made by each
of the parties involved. When this intuition is necessarily violated, as it
is here, anger results. People may then seek some other outlet for that

anger in the form of some other way in which they are being treated unfairly, such as the imbalance between regions, between large and small fish, or between commercial and sport fishing. They will tend to insist that the imbalance against them be rectified before they accept regulation. Because most fishermen are able to find some way in which they are being treated unfairly, a majority will resist practically any regulation.

Autonomy

Perhaps the most important cause of the failure to demand regulation is that fishermen want autonomy. Small-scale fishermen may be particularly protective of their autonomy because of the nature of their work, and citizens of the United States are steeped in a political culture that emphasizes autonomy, yet this attitude is found in fishermen the world over,[19] and, to some degree, it seems likely that nobody likes to be given commands, even in the most collective cultures. This desire for independence, which may be particularly strong in East Cost fishermen, is aggravated when the rules seem the slightest bit neglectful of the details of the local scene. "The head of one East Coast fishermen's group called the proposed NMFS [National Marine Fisheries Service] attempt to curtail Georges Bank overfishing 'moronic little bureaucratic games' and accused the agency of 'a desire to take control of every aspect of the business.' "[20]

This intuitive attitude toward autonomy leads people to oppose coercive solutions, yet commons dilemmas such as overfishing require such solutions. We cannot depend on the goodwill of fishermen. The immediate benefits of excess fishing to the individual are too great, and the long-term benefits from a single fisherman's restraining himself are spread over so many people that no single person would even notice. Even if all current fishermen just happened to be saintly enough to cooperate on their own and reduce their catches voluntarily, we can be sure that others would move in to take advantage of the situation if there were no penalty to prevent them.

In a small fishing community without outside interference, the coercion may be subtle, taking the form of social disapproval or withdrawal of support (e.g., failing to help in an emergency), but it is coercion still. And the number of communities that can regulate themselves in this way is dwindling.[21]

Some people have advocated "market solutions" to the problem of overfishing and other social dilemmas. For example, a market could be set up for the right to fish. This could take the form of a transferable license to fish some amount. The question of what "amount" to use is a technical one: it could be number of fish per year, pounds of fish, days fishing, number of boats, area of the sea, length of coastline, or some combination of these and other quantities. The number of licenses sold would be set so as to preserve the fish, to make fishing sustainable. Then the licenses could be bought and sold freely, just like any other productive property, such as land for agriculture. Although such schemes may work well, the idea that they are somehow based on freedom — because the market is "free" — is a play on words. Some authority must decide how many licenses to sell and, most important, must enforce the rules against taking more fish than the license allows and against fishing without a license. Such enforcement can be costly. And it is still inescapably coercive.

Yet many people resist the idea of coercive solutions in any form. Perhaps some people just have not heard of commons dilemmas (under any name). Their thinking about social issues is influenced by the examples they can think of, which happen to be cases in which a free market works best, and in which the support of property rights is so much in the background that it is not seen as coercive. Or people understand the concept of a commons dilemma but do not happen to think of it. More likely, they have heard of such situations but do not want to believe that overfishing, or whatever dilemma they are in, is one of them. They engage in wishful thinking.

Wishful Thinking

Perceived unfairness and intuitive support for autonomy often lead us to wishful thinking. The fishermen were no exception. They convinced themselves that the proposed regulations were not needed, and they did this in several ways.

Wishful Thinking about the Scientific Facts

Fishermen wanted to believe the fisheries scientists were wrong when the scientists said that overfishing was causing a decline and that regulation was needed. Joseph Brancaleone, a former fisherman who chaired the New England Council, defended the council's moderate (and ultimately ineffective) controls in terms of scientific uncertainty: "The data that we have are so slim that we can't put a number on [the effect of the controls]. By the third or fourth year, we'll have the data."[22] Another fisherman put it more bluntly, speaking to government scientists: "You fellows seem to have a lot, I don't know what you call it, somebody asks you a question and we ask you a question, 'Well, I — I don't really know.' And you base everything you tell us on what you really don't know. It kind of bothers us fishermen. We're going to be told we've got to do all this stuff, but nobody really knows anything. Doesn't make much sense.

You guys have got some jobs, but I don't think we're going to have any if you keep on. Save the fish, but what about the people?"[23]

Uncertainty is used here as an argument against regulation. The default or status quo is assumed to be correct in the absence of clear evidence against it. (The status-quo bias is also at work here. If the regulations were already in effect, the arguments against them would probably be less vehement.) But uncertainty could go either way. The use of uncertainty to support the status quo is like not having bypass surgery because you might die from the operation. Decisions under uncertainty are all calculated risks. For both the fishermen and the surgical patient, both action and inaction are risky. Uncertainty leaves room for wishful thinking, but the world is deaf to our wishes.

Fishermen have an opportunity for wishful thinking in the fact that fish stocks fluctuate for reasons unrelated to overfishing, such as the weather or ocean currents. When stocks decline, fishermen can usually find some other explanation aside from overfishing, and they are often correct. But the stocks would still be higher without overfishing than with it, and they would recover more quickly.

Such wishful thinking is easier when people do not understand how expert knowledge comes about, through critical inquiry. Scientists and other experts frequently hedge their pronouncements with caution. They know they are talking about objective matters and could be shown to be wrong. Their opponents do not take this critical stance toward their own beliefs, so they express high confidence.

Many writers have pointed out that fishery regulation can work without changing human psychology if the proper administrative procedures are set up.[24] Many fisheries throughout the world have been regulated on the basis of scientific advice, so this is humanly possible. Still, we are not doing nearly as well as we might, so some change in human thinking could help, too. All of the sources of resistance to particular regulations operate as well when changes in the law are proposed. Fishermen oppose these changes, too.[25]

Blaming Others

Fishermen also argued that proposed regulations were the result of political influence, not science. In one case, the political influence of sport fishermen was blamed.[26] Of course, such influence is possible, but the fishermen's degree of confidence that the scientists were wrong was unwarranted because the scientists had been correct repeatedly.

Wishful thinking led to blaming others, with the implication that regulation of fishing was not needed: "The finger is being pointed at commercial fishermen for overfishing, and it's not our fault. The real fault is pollution."[27] Some fishermen and politicians blamed the decline on the environmentalists, who were successful in banning the annual

Canadian seal hunt in 1983, leading to an increase in the seal population, which then competed with the fishermen for the fish.[28] Others argue that violations of existing rules are the problem.[29] Sometimes the blame was placed on nature: declines were the result of year-to-year variations or spontaneous increases in the number of predators.[30]

In general, when a policy goes against some intuition, such as support for autonomy, blame and mistrust of others can justify advocacy of other solutions. Either the facts are wrong or someone is doing something even more insidious.

The Utopian Fallacy as Wishful Thinking

Another type of wishful thinking is what we might call the utopian fallacy: if a proposal is not ideal, then it should not be adopted. The wishful thinking is in believing that the ideal is possible. Of course, this is a good attitude if the ideal is possible, but typically it is not. In this way, the utopian fallacy resembles many intuitions I discuss. By adopting the ideal as an aspiration level, it views the proposed rule as a loss. But the real choice is between an imperfect rule, which will save the fish, and no rule at all, which will not. In the case of fisheries, the utopian fallacy is particularly clear because of the cost of delay: as regulators hold more hearings and strive for perfection, the fish continue to decline.

Wishful Thinking about the Need for Coercion

People support their intuitive desire for autonomy by convincing themselves that no coercion is required. They think that the goodness of people, suitably focused, will make coercion unnecessary. We see this in some followers of Ayn Rand, in radical free-market advocates, and in leftist communitarians. For example, an anonymous posting on several Internet news groups advocated the abolition of income taxes and of all money on the ground that

> the restoration of economic freedom by no longer requiring people to use money . . . would establish the best possibilities for a civilized world . . . All right and sustainable societal change can be brought about by "moralsuasion" and a good character based economic life . . . If personal taxes are eliminated then people [can] set up a natural, more efficient and more truly profitable barter system which has at its center good character and personal trust . . . This type of civilization evolves locally self-sustaining inter-networked human eco-systems with naturally balanced resource distribution systems — i.e., the planet naturally works for 100% of humanity.

When people think about solutions to commons dilemmas, they frequently think of voluntary solutions; coercion is an option that rarely springs to mind. For example, in one study with Bill Hale (a student), I asked several college students about seven different examples of commons dilemmas: declining soil productivity, air and water pollution, depletion of fossil fuels, global warming, population growth, loss of animal and plant species, and overfishing. After we described each item, we asked subjects what actions might help the situation and who should take the actions, and we asked why the actions have not been taken yet. (We emphasized that we wanted all the actions that might be taken, not just one.) Several subjects failed, in one or more cases, to note the possibility of collective action as a solution. In answer to the question about what actions should be taken, they mentioned only individual restraint. For example, on the problem of soil productivity, "The companies that own the land should use the land for grazing and producing for only a short time and then let the land regain its nutrients for a time." Or, on the global warming item, "Logging companies can take steps to gradually reduce acreage of cut forests."

I noticed a similar assumption in a video presentation on automobile pollution put on by the Franklin Institute Science Museum in Philadelphia. The presentation allowed an audience to respond to questions by pushing buttons on their seats, and their responses were immediately displayed. After warning of the dangers of pollution, the video asked, "Would you use public transportation to commute to work?" and other such questions. Of course, the audience answered yes because the wording of the question allowed them to fill in whatever "if only" conditions they chose (e.g., if only it weren't so expensive, if only it were more convenient). The presentation implicitly assumed that the solution was an increase in voluntary use of public transportation. Of course, for most commuters who drive, considerable personal sacrifice would be required for this solution to work. A significant change in transportation use requires significant incentives, in the form of making public transportation more attractive, making driving less attractive, or both.

Even Lester Brown, head of the Worldwatch Institute, does not seem immune to this kind of thinking. In an article on population, he says, "If people know that maintaining current family size will reduce cropland area per person by a third or half during the next generation, they can see what this will mean for their children. If they know that large families almost certainly will bring more hunger and even mass starvation, they may well decide to shift to smaller families."[31] Unfortunately, each family's food intake is determined mostly by *other* people's children. It would be nice if mere awareness of a social dilemma could solve it, but that is not always the case.

The Morality-as-Self-Interest Illusion

A special form of wishful thinking about the sufficiency of voluntary solutions is apparent when the benefits of cooperation are in the long run, a
situation called a *social trap*. People may think that cooperation is in their
long-run self-interest, even though they understand that it is not in their
short-run interest. In a small group of people who interact regularly, this
may of course be true for a variety of reasons: cooperators gain a reputation for cooperating, which makes them more desirable; and they also
really do influence the tendency of others to cooperate, so they benefit
somewhat from the later cooperation of others. But in large-scale social
dilemmas involving thousands, millions, or billions of strangers, both of
these effects are unlikely to pay off. People may still think cooperation
pays off because they understand that *collective* cooperation pays off in
the long run, and they apply this conclusion to the acts of individuals.
In essence, they think about individual action without holding constant
the actions of others. As a result, they believe that cooperation is in a
person's long-run self-interest, so that no coercion is required. Instead of
coercing people with rules, it is sufficient to explain to them where their
real interest lies.

I looked for this belief in another questionnaire study, in which I
told people about various social traps, including one involving a water
shortage and another involving overfishing.[32] I made it clear that people
could overuse the water or overfish without anyone knowing about it,
so that their reputations would not be affected and so that they could
not set an example — good or bad — for anyone else. To check their
understanding, I asked subjects whether it was in their immediate self-
interest to restrain themselves, and most said that it was not. I then asked
if it would be in their long-run self-interest to restrain themselves, and
about half — more or less for various items — said that it was. I found
this result even in a fishing scenario in which I asked whether cutting
back would increase a fisherman's long-run income, so that it was clear
what "self-interest" meant.

Subjects' explanations seem to confuse the effect of one person's
actions with the effect of everyone's. They speak as if they were making the decision for everyone, not just one person: "By not cutting back
on my current level of fishing I would more than likely be hurting myself in the future, for sooner or later the fish population would dwindle
down to zero, leaving me with absolutely no income. I am willing to give
up short-term financial growth for long-term financial stability." "For
the short term I'd bring in more money [by fishing more], and be better
off. But the more and more of this particular fish I caught, the less there
would be breeding in the ocean. Eventually, they will die out and I will
be left with *none* . . . ." "It would not increase directly, but in the long
run you will end up with more money over the years." "We shouldn't

be selfish. We should look to the long term instead of the short term .... In the long run, it may [increase my income] because the fish would be less frenzied, and there would be more of them, and they would have time to reproduce more so there may be more fish to catch in the future." The last response illustrates the wishful thinking inherent in the idea that virtue is its own reward. If only this were true.

Many responses explicitly referred to the group even though the question was about the individual: "In the long run, the water shortage would eventually affect me too. If everyone thinks the same way, . . . everyone will water their garden and the water shortage will continue and worsen, which will highly affect me."

Thus, people confuse their own interest with that of the group, especially when the long-run is at issue. This confusion has advantages. It may make people more willing to cooperate spontaneously or even to take political actions such as voting, which are actually somewhat costly to them even when the selfish benefits are considered.

But it also has dangers because the confusion of self and group may work both ways. People may see their own interest as identified with a *particular* group that they are in, such as Cape Cod fishermen or Rhode Island fishermen (or Americans). They may thus think that their support of *this* group is justified in terms of their self-interest, even when the interest of this group goes against the interest of some larger group that also includes them, such as fishers as a whole (or all people). In such cases, it might be better for people to understand that actions on behalf of the smaller group are just as much against their narrow self-interest — if only because of the effort involved in taking action — as are actions on behalf of the larger group. If they understood that the good reasons for action were based on the benefits to others in both cases, they might be more willing to act on behalf of the larger group. Such action would smooth the path to agreement among groups, and it would do more good on the whole than would action for the smaller group only.

Ozone and Freon

There is hope. Some fisheries have been saved by regulation — either by local indigenous groups of fishermen or by governments — and they are thriving. Even at the world level, agreements to protect dolphins and whales have had some success. Regulation of forests has at least reduced the rate of their destruction. Rich nations have taken other successful steps to protect their internal environments, such as laws that have reduced air and water pollution.

One of the great success stories of recent years is the Montreal Protocol of 1987, in which countries around the world agreed to phase out the production and use of chemicals that were harming the upper atmosphere. Ozone in the stratosphere reduces the ultraviolet light from the sun that reaches the earth. Increased ultraviolet light would cause higher incidence of skin cancer and many other effects on animals and plants around the world. In 1970, the chemist Paul Crutzen called attention to the deleterious effects of nitrogen oxides on ozone. This argument was one source of political opposition to the building of supersonic transport airplanes in the early 1970s. In 1974, F. Sherwood Rowland and Mario Molina found that chlorofluorocarbons (CFCs) were transported to the ozone layer, where they could also destroy the ozone. CFCs are inert chemicals that do not break down spontaneously, so their effects are long lasting. They were used in aerosol cans, in plastic manufacture, and in refrigerators and air conditioners. (Freon is a CFC.) Many countries soon banned their use in aerosol cans. In 1985, a pronounced reduction of the ozone layer over Antarctica was observed.

In 1987, representatives of 24 nations and the European Economic Community met in Montreal and agreed to reduce production and use of CFCs and other ozone-destroying chemicals. The agreement made provisions for developing countries, which were allowed more time and given some assistance in converting to CFC substitutes. It also called for frequent reviews based on scientific evidence. These have occurred, resulting in several more agreements and some speeding up of the process. The treaty is working. Declines have been found in ozone-destroying chemicals (those containing chlorine), and although others were still increasing (those containing bromine), the problem at least appeared to be getting no worse, and a reversal is within reach.[33]

The agreement is interesting for several reasons. First, it is a solution to a commons dilemma that involves the whole world. Commons dilemmas are easiest to solve when they involve small communities; this was no small community. Second, the problem of fairness was solved by compromise. The poorer countries had some relaxation of the rules, but not as much as they would have liked. Third, the agreement was made on the basis of scientific evidence, before any epidemic of skin cancer or extinction of species from ultraviolet radiation actually occurred.

Some special factors contributed to this success: the problem was clearly delimited; the costs of solving the problem were manageable because there were substitutes available for most of the chemicals involved; and these chemicals were made by a relatively small number of companies, so that monitoring was relatively easy. The scientific evidence was also fairly clear about the harmful effects of CFCs. However, the U.S. government supported the agreement even before its cost-benefit analysis was completed (although it was clear what the results would be). Part of the support for the agreement among government officials came from the intuition I've called naturalism: "Don't fool with Mother Nature."[34]

Of course, success is not perfect.[35] Moreover, despite the fact that Crutzen, Rowland, and Molina won the 1995 Nobel Prize in chemistry for their discoveries, wishful-thinking opponents of government regulation continue to question the science. Tom DeLay, the Republican majority whip in the U.S. House of Representatives, called ozone depletion a "media scare."[36] And the state of Arizona in 1995 passed legislation declaring itself exempt from the federal law implementing the Montreal Protocol; Governor Fife Symington declared the ban on Freon production to be based on "hokey science."[37] Still, despite these problems, we must count the Montreal Protocol as a success.

Global Warming

Much less successful have been the world's efforts to prevent global warming from human activity. It seems likely that the earth's surface is going to get warmer over the next few decades. At least part of this warming will result from the production of carbon dioxide (CO_2) and other gases such as methane and CFCs. These "greenhouse" gases reduce radiation from the earth into space without reducing the effectiveness of the sun at warming the earth, making the atmosphere more like a greenhouse.

People influence production of these gases in many ways, but mostly by burning fossil fuels such as oil, coal, and natural gas, which are oxidized to form water and CO_2 when they burn. Burning wood does not have any effect unless we fail to let it regrow. We can think of trees and other plants as reservoirs of carbon, keeping it out of the atmosphere. So if the total mass of plants is reduced — including the residues of plants in the soil and the oceans — then atmospheric carbon must increase, and that happens through increases in CO_2. Massive deforestation without replacement of the trees is thus part of the problem too.

The expected warming will have many consequences for us, some positive but more negative. Oceans will rise and coastal areas will become uninhabitable. Dikes will be needed to protect cities and some agricultural land. Some coastal countries, such as Bangladesh, will be particularly hard hit. Changes in weather patterns will make some land dryer and other land wetter. Current predictions suggest that the net change will be for the worse for food production. Even if it is not, time will be required to change the organization of agriculture. People will have to move away from areas that become too dry to provide sufficient drinking water.

All these effects are highly uncertain. The predicted effects could not occur at all, or the effects could be much worse. In the case of ozone, the chemistry was well understood, and action was taken only after reduction of ozone was observed. The predictions of global warming are based on computer models of global climate, models that are not fully based on theoretical understanding, although they do predict current seasonal weather patterns fairly well. Uncertainties have to do with things like how much carbon can be absorbed by the soil, how much of the sun's energy will be reflected away by increased air pollution from industry, and how arctic ice sheets will respond to whatever warming occurs. Specific predictions about particular regions, such as the North American grain belt, are even more uncertain.

The potential problems are exacerbated by other trends, particularly the increase in population. If population were stabilized, we would have a better chance of producing sufficient food. As it is, however, agricultural production is barely keeping pace with population growth, and global warming could upset the balance. Although much malnutrition results from inadequate distribution rather than inadequate supply, we cannot assume that the problems of distribution will be solved by any given time. To say that "population growth is not the problem because the real problem is distribution" is to engage in the utopian fallacy, if, as seems likely, controlling population is more feasible than redistributing wealth.

Another trend that creates problems is the economic growth of some countries out of poverty — for example, China, India, and the countries of Southeast Asia. This trend is to be welcomed, of course. But development brings increased use of fossil fuels, and more CO_2. China, in particular, has vast deposits of coal, on which it depends for future development.

In sum, unlike the problem of the ozone layer, that of global warming is complex, uncertain, and linked with many other changes and policy questions.

Given these trends, we have several options, many of which may be combined with other options. First, we could do nothing special now. When the oceans start to rise, people will build dikes. When land becomes arid, people will move. When population outstrips food production, we could stave off mass starvation for a while by switching from meat to grains, and this might give us time to control population. Given the uncertainties, and given that the warming process is probably slow, this might be the best approach.

Second, we could prepare for the consequences. We could direct new development away from coastal areas and areas that are likely to become dry. We could try to reduce population growth. We could develop plans for gradual resettlement of those who would have to move. The trouble here is, of course, the very uncertainties that make the first approach attractive. We could take the wrong steps and waste resources doing so. Even planning requires resources.

Third, we could reduce the production of greenhouse gases. Some of the steps required to reduce greenhouse gases could be beneficial for other reasons. For example, increases in energy efficiency could be cost-effective in their own right. Such beneficial steps would — given the laws of economics — be taken anyway, eventually, but it might be worth putting some resources into speeding them up. Even here, the resources required, such as incentives and taxes, are not trivial.

Other steps are more costly still. Substantial reduction of CO_2 production would weaken the economy of any country that tried it. Large amounts of resources would go into rebuilding and redesigning everything, from automobiles to the layout of residential patterns. Changes in social behavior would be required. For example, substantial energy savings could be realized by concentrating residential patterns, with more people living in highly concentrated developments (perhaps surrounded by nearby "green belts"), linked by convenient systems of mass transportation. Such a step would require overcoming the reluctance of many people in developed countries to live in urban areas, a reluctance stemming from the current social decay of cities in many countries.

Fourth, we could try to remove CO_2 from the atmosphere. We could do this by "natural" methods such as planting trees — thereby rebuilding the massive forests that people have destroyed in the past few hundred years — or by "unnatural" methods such as "fertilizing" the Antarctic Ocean with iron so that microscopic plants could grow there in abundance, sucking CO_2 out of the atmosphere.

Fifth, we could try to change the course of development of those countries that would rely on increased use of fossil fuels, such as China. We — that is, the international community — could try to induce these countries to develop in other ways. Such induction could involve bargaining, in which we offer some benefit in return for cooperation.

Any of these actions to counter the problem require cooperation of the sort that occurred in the Montreal Protocol. Unlike what happened in the North Atlantic fisheries, people would have to be willing to accept the idea that some agreement is better than no agreement, even if it seems unfair and even if it threatens national and individual autonomy. I am not sure that any action is needed. The problem is that, if action *were* needed, and if that were to become clear to scientists, we would not be able to take it.

All the elements for an impasse are in place. Unlike the situation with stratospheric ozone, the magnitude and nature of global warming are highly uncertain. We know that increased CO_2 must lead to warming eventually, that CO_2 has been increasing, and that warming itself will have some of the effects listed earlier. We do not know how fast this will happen, or even whether the warming effect will be countered by opposite cooling effects such as those that caused past ice ages. Quantitative predictions are difficult because they require the use of computer models of the global climate, and the best models still do not work well. Most models require fudge factors just to explain the current temperature level in a way that is consistent with other data. They predict that greater warming should have occurred than what has been measured, so they seem to be taking insufficient account of some factor that is slowing things down. Or, alternatively, the data on past warming aren't really good enough to say that the models are wrong. The models also fail to incorporate various mechanisms that could lead to a *sudden* increase in warming.

Even as these uncertainties are resolved, the public and their representatives will be skeptical. Uncertainty provides room for wishful thinking, and it causes resistance to new evidence. Those opposed to international agreements or government intervention have found, and will probably continue to find, plenty of scientists who will tell them about the uncertainty, and that is all they need. Science is always uncertain. Rush Limbaugh, a popular and very conservative radio talk-show host, has argued that scientists disagree, so we need do nothing.[38] Limbaugh's evidence comes from opinion polls of scientists, which show considerable disagreement on the question of whether human-caused warming has *already occurred*. This is, of course, a different question from the more important one, which is whether it *will* occur, or, even more to the point, whether it is *likely enough* so that we ought to worry about it. Thomas Schelling, in a very wise essay about global warming, argues that our real concern should be preparing for unexpected effects that are larger than what the models predict. "There isn't any scientific principle according to which all alarming possibilities prove to be benign upon further investigation."[39]

The BTU Tax

Signs of problems to come are already present. Following the example of the Montreal Protocol, the United Nations Conference on Environment and Development took place in Rio de Janiero in 1992. Among other agreements made, the Rio Declaration on Sustainable Development, signed by 150 countries, committed the signers to reduce CO_2 emissions to 1990 levels by 2000. As I write this in 1997, a conference just held in Kyoto, Japan, let to a tentative agreement to reduce CO_2 and other greenhouse gases, but the agreement in its present form seems unlikely to be approved because the United States wants developing countries, such as China, to accept binding reductions and they do not think it is fair for them to deny themselves what the developed countries had in the past. Let us ask, though, what developed countries like the United States could do to reduce greenhouse gases.

One thing that might be effective is a tax on the carbon content of fossil fuels. This would discourage, in the most direct way, the emission of CO_2. It would leave people and businesses free to decide, within this constraint, what is most efficient for them. Some might move from oil to natural gas. The latter has relatively more hydrogen (which produces water when burned) and relatively less carbon (which produces CO_2). Some might replace fossil fuels with other sources of energy such as nuclear power, wind energy, or "biomass" (wood or other plants that are burned but then replaced). Even moving from coal to oil would help.

More generally, the idea of taxing whatever causes bad effects is economically efficient. It is more efficient than "command and control" regulation because it allows these bad effects to occur when there is enough benefit in return. (True, the test of "benefit" is what people can pay for. Although this test is crude, it is not so crude as to be useless.) If energy cost more because of the tax, people would still use it — they would just waste less of it. They would buy more efficient cars and refrigerators, for a start. Some economists have suggested that taxes of this sort could ultimately bring in enough revenue as to replace most other taxes.

In 1993, the newly elected Clinton administration proposed a complex tax on energy for the United States, a BTU[40] tax with exemptions for solar, wind, and renewable energy sources. The tax was designed to reduce both the U.S. government's budget deficit and greenhouse emissions. The administration had already considered and given up the idea of a carbon tax and a gasoline tax. As Vice President Al Gore explained: "A gas tax . . . is unfair to those in the rural areas and western states who drive long distances. A carbon tax . . . which might make sense for other reasons, hits especially hard the coal states. . . . A BTU tax . . . is fair in its impact to every region of this country."[41]

Although the BTU tax was designed to minimize perceived unfairness from the outset, the perception persisted, and the tax ultimately died. Energy producers claimed that some sources of energy would be hit harder than others, particularly coal, oil, and natural gas. The American Trucking Association complained that truckers would pay relatively more than other energy users because of the formula adopted.[42] Senators from farm states — which rely heavily on diesel fuel for farming — and from oil-producing states ultimately formed a coalition to defeat the proposal in the Senate. Of course, any tax will hit some people harder than others and is thus subject to interpretation in terms of unfairness; indeed, a majority of Americans seem to agree that a "fuel tax would be an unfair way to reduce fuel consumption because some people are forced to use more fuel than others by their business or personal needs."[43]

The farm-state senators were not, by themselves, enough to defeat the tax. The public was largely against the tax, perhaps because people are against taxes in general, but perhaps also because they they thought that it was unfair.[44] Of course, those who were especially hurt by the tax screamed the loudest, but if fairness were not the issue, and if this was indeed the fairest possible tax increase that would reduce both greenhouse emissions and the deficit, then it should have won majority support. We do not know for sure, but the lingering perception of unfairness might have led to its demise. This was especially likely if each senator attended most to those constituents who were hurt relative to others. The situation is analogous to that of the fishermen, with each group applying a concept of fairness that favors itself, each group finding any agreement unfair, and no agreement coming about.

Also, like the case of the fisheries, the costs of the tax were immediate and the benefits — both economic and environmental — delayed. This made people more prone to wishful thinking, trying to find reasons for delay or inaction.

Some of the perceived unfairness was essential to the goal of reducing CO_2 emissions. Any tax that does this will penalize those who emit more CO_2 more than it will penalize other energy users. The idea is to shift the economy away from activities that cause emissions and toward other activities. This was perceived as unfair because it "punished" people for something they could not foresee. As Senator Max Baucus put it, "Either we have an energy tax where everybody pays evenly, or we have no energy tax."[45] Of course, such a tax would be impossible in principle: some people use more energy than others; and if the tax were equal for everyone, it would not provide any incentive to reduce energy use. Senator Baucus's intuition of unfairness worked against the greater good.

In the end, the administration settled for a 4.3 cent per gallon tax on transportation fuels and more budget cuts. (Senator Baucus, from the sparsely populated state of Montana, was able to kill a larger gasoline tax.) This left the United States with the cheapest energy in the developed world (except for Canada), despite importing half of its oil, and with little more incentive to reduce emissions. Worse still, in 1996, the price of gasoline began to rise, and Congress voted to repeal this small tax for one year, with the president's promise of support. Editorial opinion was largely against the repeal, but on grounds of budget balancing or fairness (noting that U.S. gasoline prices were low relative to other countries). I could find only one editorial that even mentioned the effect of gasoline use on the atmosphere, and that mention consisted of two words in a list of effects.[46]

This, of course, is what happens within a single nation. Played out at the world level, distorted perceptions of fairness and wishful thinking will only be worse, if we do attempt to reduce global warming by reducing output of greenhouse gases. But we may have another way.

The Geritol Solution

Marine phytoplankton, the little organisms that populate the oceans and provide food for other creatures, contain carbon. The limiting factor on the growth of these plankton is the iron content of the water.

If you put some ocean water in your bathtub and add iron, plankton will grow. In 1990, a panel of the U.S. National Research Council recommended that dumping iron in the ocean be studied as a possible solution to the problem of global warming. The plankton would suck CO_2 out of the atmosphere. The scheme was called the "Geritol solution" after a patent medicine, an iron supplement for "tired blood." As the late John Martin, one of the scientists who developed the theory, put it (half in jest, it seems), "You give me half a tanker full of iron, I'll give you another ice age."[47] As it turned out, the experiments were done. The iron did increase the growth of plankton, but it disappeared too quickly. Much more than half a tanker would be needed — in fact, so much as to make the solution impractical.[48]

Many people, including scientists, were appalled at the idea of tinkering with nature: "Environmental intervention on a global scale, no matter how well-intentioned, could prove worse than the global changes already in evidence. We simply do not understand the global ecosystem well enough to attempt large-scale quick fixes."[49] Scientists' comments were echoed by others. A U.S. congressional staff member said, in an interview, "Some scientists are suggesting that you could put 500 tons of iron into the ocean to make plankton bloom. The plankton would soak up carbon. It's obviously bullshit. On the face of it, it's ridiculous."[50]

But the idea won't die. In 1995, Kenneth Coale and his colleagues modified the procedures for adding iron, and the experiment yielded much more promising results. But Coale himself is worried: "We are conducting research that may be used toward geoengineering and that does make me feel a bit uncomfortable. I don't feel we have the same dilemma as the scientists who worked on the Manhattan Project [building the first atomic bomb], but there are some similarities." He, and a few others, think that research should proceed.[51]

How can the skeptics be so sure that the idea won't work? It seems that they started with their moral intuition against "tinkering with nature" and simply assumed that the scientific facts would bear them out by showing that the idea would fail. It may even be true that scientists gave up the idea too quickly because they did not try hard enough to make it work — to find ways of making the iron stay in place longer, for example.

What if the experiments succeed? Or what if some other idea, such as farming seaweed on a large scale, seems more promising? Of course, the uncertainties of tinkering are enormous, but so are those of doing nothing. It is true that the safest solution is to reverse course and decrease the production of CO_2 and other gases, but suppose that turns out to be politically impossible or economically unjustifiable, as seems likely. The question is whether we will then be inhibited by a reluctance to risk harm through action, like those who will not vaccinate children even though the risk of vaccination is smaller than the risk of the disease.

Such inhibition could be exacerbated by the belief that the solution in question is not ideal, even though the ideal is impossible. This was a problem for fishermen too.

Here the problem is particularly acute because the tinkering is with nature. Reluctance to tinker with nature is a strong intuition, little understood by those who are in its grip — or by anyone. It is widespread in modern society: many people oppose any attempt to modify the weather;[52] many others strongly prefer to drink a glass of natural spring water rather than a glass of distilled water with chemicals added to make it chemically identical to the spring water.[53] The same consequences are evaluated differently depending on whether people bring them about: "I don't mind natural extinctions, but I'm not too enthusiastic about extinctions that are directly caused by man. I feel that a species has a right to survive and be able to survive on its own and be able to change and evolve without the influence of whatever man does. I don't want to see man kill [any species]. If it's going to happen, it should happen naturally, not through anything that man has an influence on."[54]

The Geritol solution to global warming is one of a host of proposals for solving environmental problems through active manipulation of nature. Alfred Wong has proposed that about 20 panels made of zinc, each the size of a football field, carried into the stratosphere by balloons, could inactivate the chlorine atoms from CFCs that are the root cause of ozone loss.[55] Happily, for those not wanting to tamper with nature, this too was shown to be a bad idea.[56] The idea that what is natural is good can influence the debate about global warming in more subtle ways, as well. For example, some of the debate about global warming is about the extent to which it is caused by human activity, as if it must be benign if it were naturally caused. In the long run, what matters are its effects, whatever its causes.

This bias toward the natural is puzzling because of its haphazardness and inconsistency: people have been tinkering with nature throughout history, through fishing, hunting, tree cutting, agriculture, construction, medicine, paving, mowing, and cosmetics.[57] Perhaps the bias toward the natural expresses itself only when some *new* way of tinkering is proposed, so that it really operates mainly in conjunction with biases toward the status quo or toward the default option (toward doing nothing, omission as opposed to commission). The bias, of course, is not an absolute or else no forests would ever have been cleared for agriculture and no ears would have been pierced for earrings. Such things may have happened sooner if not for the bias toward nature.

Chapter 9 will discuss a particularly strong manifestation of the bias toward nature: its expression in matters having to do with creating, ending, or modifying life, such as abortion and genetic engineering.

Conclusion

In sum, many of the world's problem have the form of social dilemmas. The option that is best for each person is different from the option that is best for everyone else. Fishing is a clear example. The problem here is not one of selfishness and greed; self-sacrifice of the sort required cannot be expected. The solution thus depends on some sort of force imposed on individuals by the group, through either social custom or the state. Such solutions are often reached, but not always. When they are not, the problem can often be found in moral intuitions, particular those concerning autonomy and fairness. These intuitions are abetted by wishful thinking, which leads to belief overkill. People come to think that force is not needed.

CHAPTER 3

Benefits and Burdens

Most national politics is about fairness in distributing benefits and burdens. Who should be rich? Who poor? How poor should we allow the poor to be? Who should be punished for what? How much? Who should be compensated, by who, for what injuries? More specifically, is medical care a right? If so, how much care? Should we compensate people who become sick from pollution? Who should pay for the compensation? Should we compensate people when their property loses value because it is declared a protected wetland? Should we punish people for crimes when they themselves were the victims of criminal abuse? These issues may seem disparate, but they are all related.

   This chapter first discusses how we might answer these questions by thinking about consequences. Then I discuss a number of cases related to law, rights, and the environment in particular. The next chapter discusses fairness among nations and national loyalty.

The Utilitarian Approach

One answer to question of distribution — within and among nations — is that we should try to do the best we can for everyone, in total. We can ask how much we achieve the goals of each person, and we can distribute things so that the total goal achievement is as great as possible. Suppose we call the amount of goal achievement "good." We thus want to make the total amount of good as great as possible. But this by itself is not enough. We need various principles to help us apply this general principle.

Equality

The first principle says that we should try to distribute things equally, unless we have some good reason not to. Imagine twin sisters, both struggling artists, who together suddenly inherit $200,000 and you, the executor of the estate, must decide how much to give each of them. The condition of the will is that they must spend the money; they cannot save it. (This isn't terribly important, but it makes for a clearer example.) Your intuition probably says to give them $100,000 each. But can you explain why?

The idea of the greatest total good can explain it. Suppose you start with this idea of equal division. Can you increase total good by departing from it? That is, can you make things better? Suppose you propose to give $110,000 to Alice and $90,000 to Betty. This probably will decrease the total good. This is because we usually spend money on things we value more before we spend it on things we value less. Suppose each sister will spend the first $90,000 on the same things — a new studio. The next $10,000 will go for supplies, and the next $10,000 after that will go for additional furniture. Both sisters seem to get more good out of the supplies than the furniture, because they would buy the supplies before buying the furniture. Suppose the supplies have 5 units of good and the furniture has 4 units for each sister. With equal division, both will get the supplies and get 5 units each, for a total of 10 units (beyond the units in the first $90,000). With unequal division, Alice will get the supplies and the furniture, and Betty will get neither, so Alice will get 9 units and that will be the total. By giving Alice the extra money, you will, in effect, take the supplies from Betty and give Alice the furniture, which is less valuable. Because both sisters prefer the supplies to the furniture, you would have done more harm (taking the supplies) than good (giving the furniture). Hence, departing from equal division will probably make things worse.

In real life, things are less certain than this. One sister could already be wealthy. Or the other could have no interest in the things that money can buy beyond the minimum. If you know which sister is which, you can try to take these things into account. But if you do not know, these possibilities could go either way, so they cancel out. You are left with equality as the best policy. Equal division of money is generally the best policy when other things are equal in this way. This is because, as in the twin sisters example, people choose the most important things first. When money is divided equally, they all get to buy the things that are most important, and unequal division permits some people to buy unimportant things while others lack important ones. The same principle applies for goods aside from money. Most goods are more valuable, per unit, when you have only a few of them than when you have a lot.

Moreover, if you decide to take some factor into account and give one sister more, this opens the way for the other sister to accuse you of bias — to employ the kind of wishful thinking that makes people think that fairness works in their favor. Equal division avoids such conflict.

Perhaps because equality is such a useful heuristic for dividing benefits and burdens, we react emotionally to inequality. We sympathize with those who are dealt a poor hand, and on the destructive side, we envy those whom we see as getting all the high cards through luck of the draw.

Incentive and Deterrence

We depart from equal division, of course, and we usually do not consider it wrong. We pay some people more than others, and we make other people suffer punishment or pay penalties. One reason for this is that we use goods to reward people for doing things that help others and, conversely, we punish people for doing things that hurt others. People are motivated by reward and punishment. These things provide incentive for people to do good things deterrence against doing harm.

Most countries use the tax system to try to strike a balance between equality and incentive. We tax the rich and help the poor. If we do this too much, so that people are too close to being equal, then we reduce the incentive to work. Any benefits of moving toward equality are outweighed by the loss of production. If we move too far away from equality, then we make things worse in a different way: the poor lose important goods such as housing and food, and, in return, the rich gain access to fashionable clothing and nice vacations, which are less important even though they may cost more.

The issue here is not how to balance incentive and equality, or which country has done it best. The issue is how people think about this question in public discussions. If there is some truth here about where the optimum is, we are more likely to find it if we are not biased by our intuitions.

A code word for one side of this issue is "responsibility." Those who favor the incentive principle say that they want people to be "responsible." The question of punishment is part of the same issue, and the same code word is used. Popular thinking about punishment is confused. The utilitarian approach to this issue — and I believe the correct one — is to ask how we can deter harmful behavior without inflicting more harm (through excessive punishment) than we prevent. Thus, the question of whether an abused person is "responsible" for a crime converts itself into another question. If we excuse people because they were themselves victims of abuse, will more such victims commit crimes as a result? (Or will more people successfully pretend to be abused?) Or, alternatively, are victims insensitive to punishment, compelled to do what they do regardless of the consequences, so that letting them off will have little effect on others? This is not how most people think about this issue. They rely instead on principles for balancing harm by harming the one who commits it, and principles for making up the losses of those who lose. The former principles typically lead to anger and the desire for retribution; the latter, to sympathy and the desire to help.

Compensation and Insurance

People who suffer some loss can benefit from certain resources more than other people can. If your house burns down, the utility of money increases for you because you need it to get a new house. (Before that, your needs were not so urgent.) We can increase the total good by taking a little money from lots of other people to enable you to build your new house. The money we take consists of insurance premiums. This is how house insurance makes for better consequences on the whole. The same argument works for two other kinds of compensation: social insurance and damage payments in tort cases.

People's feelings about compensation are tied up with particular institutions, particularly the idea that injurers should compensate victims. Thus, people get millions of dollars from lawsuits if they are injured by a vaccine, even if the vaccine is approved and properly manufactured. But people who suffer the same injury from the disease that the vaccine is supposed to prevent do not get compensated. We make an enormous distinction between injuries caused by people and those caused by nature. This sort of thing has happened with DPT vaccine, other vaccines, birth control, the Superfund law in the United States (which requires cleanup of wasted deposited by people at great expense, when naturally occurring hazards could be reduced with less expense), and compensation for unemployment caused by trade agreements as opposed to the ups and downs of business.

We are not stuck with this predicament. New Zealand has instituted a system in which people who suffer medical misfortunes are compensated according to a schedule, according to the misfortune but without regard to the cause. Those who negligently cause such injuries pay fines to the government rather than to the victims. This system is fairer to victims and less expensive to operate, since fewer legal fees are involved. (Like any insurance system, however, it is sometime abused.) Japan has a similar system.

The rest of this chapter discusses some intuitions that loosely fit the consequentialist scheme just presented but that have taken on a life of their own, leading to decisions that bring about worse outcomes than could be achieved by thinking about consequences alone. The next chapter considers more examples of this sort, involving distributions between insiders and outsiders of nations and other groups.

Can Equality Go Too Far?

I explained how equal division can be justified in terms of utility in the twin sisters example. The intuition favoring equal division sometimes detaches itself from this justification, so that it favors equality at the expense of utility. The simplest case — not always so simple — is that of "not having enough to go around." If we have one piece of hard candy (too hard to cut in half) and two children, we may decide to give the candy to neither child rather than give it to one. We can make the situation seem somewhat fairer by flipping a coin, so that each child has an equal chance before the flip. And this does seem more acceptable to many people. Of course, after the coin flip, the unfair inequality reappears. All we have done is to put the responsibility on the coin rather than on ourselves. Inequality seems more tolerable when it is not intentionally imposed, but we still may think that it is better not to give either child the candy, even better than flipping a coin. (A less pleasant example of the same principle is the theme of William Styron's novel, *Sophie's Choice*, in which a woman in a concentration camp in World War II is forced to choose which of her two children will live; she chooses, but is wracked by guilt.)

One issue in the candy decision is envy. If both children are present, the loser will envy the winner. The loss in utility from the experience of envy might be greater than the gain in utility from getting the candy, so our decision to do nothing might truly be best. Perhaps this is why envy is considered (by some) to be sinful; it prevents what would otherwise be the best outcome. People would be better off, at least in cases like this one, if envy did not exist. Then we would not have to take it into account, and we could freely make decisions to bring about the greatest good, whether the distribution was equal or not. In this case, we could flip the coin and give one child the candy. But the badness of envy itself is no reason for us to ignore it. Envy is a consequence, and we must count all consequences. At the same time, we can try to discourage it, of course. One way to discourage it is to ignore it, but this is justified only if such neglect is successful enough, in the long run, to make up for its immediate harm.

People sometimes prefer equal division even when it makes the consequences worse. In one study, people were asked to choose between two hypothetical programs for colon-cancer screening for a population covered by government health assistance for the poor. In program A, there was enough money to give everyone in the population a screening test. The test would save 1,000 people's lives. In program B, the test cost twice as much, so it would be given to only half of the people, chosen at random by their Social Security numbers. But the test was so much more effective that it would save 1,100 lives instead of 1,000. Most subjects favored program A, thus expressing willingness to sacrifice 100 lives for the sake of giving everyone an equal chance. These results are also found in similar situations where envy is absent because the intervention is given without anyone knowing who gets it.[1]

A real case with a similar issue concerns some experiments being done in Africa of new therapies for AIDS.[2] The experiments were initiated because most pregnant African women with AIDS cannot afford the usual treatment — a complex sequence of administrations of the drug AZT — given to prevent their children from catching the disease. The experiments involved comparing new drugs and shorter courses of AZT with a control group. The problem was that the control group was to be given only a placebo, an inactive drug. The idea of using no treatment as a control is that this is the fastest way to learn whether the new treatment is effective. (The placebo reduces the psychological effects of knowing whether one is getting treatment or not.) In the United States, in such studies, it is typical not to use placebo controls but, rather, to use the best available alternative treatment. But the best available alternative treatment in Africa is no treatment at all. Moreover, it would be pointless to compare the newer treatments to the usual form of AZT treatment given in the United States, since the new treatment would, very likely, be somewhat less effective and the standard treatment could not be used in Africa anyway because of its cost. If the new treatment were found to be a little less effective than the standard treatment, it would still be nearly impossible to tell whether it was sufficiently better than nothing, without a placebo control group.

The situation was thus very much like the candy example or the screening-test example (but more extreme than that). It was a choice of giving the treatment to half the subjects, or to none at all. Still, Public Citizen, a consumer-advocacy organization in the United States, protested the trials because they were "unethical," and some members of Congress seem to agree. This is a clear case of a moral intuition about fairness getting in the way of people's good. No good at all would result from canceling the experiment. But the experiment itself could save the lives of many children, and it could lead to knowledge that would save the lives of many more.

Intuitions about fairness and equal division sometimes operate within political units. An example is hurricane insurance in Florida. The east coast of Florida is hit by frequent hurricanes. One of them, Andrew in 1992, came close to bankrupting some major insurance companies. The companies have, since then, repeatedly asked state regulators to let them charge much higher rates to property owners living on the east coast. This would have the beneficial effect of discouraging further construction of buildings that might be destroyed, at great expense to other policyholders around the state and, indeed, the country. In terms of consequences, it is better on the whole if fewer buildings are built in hurricane-prone areas. It is simply wasteful to build things that probably will not last. Regulators, however, have resisted these requests on grounds of fairness. They think that everyone in Florida, or everyone in the United States should pay the same rates regardless of the risk.

Of course, this may be the better solution in terms of consequences. It may turn out that people are too unresponsive to such incentives as insurance premiums. (Most experts consider this unlikely.) The regulators have apparently avoided asking this question, however, by consulting their intuitions and those of their constituents.

Taxation as Theft?

If we think about taxation in terms of its consequences, I have argued, the situation is complicated. We need to strike a balance between incentive and redistribution. In addition, taxes help pay for public goods, such as military defense, law enforcement (including laws protecting private property), roads, education, and scientific research. Provision of such goods in the absence of government raises the same kinds of problems discussed in chapter 2. Preservation of fish and other natural resources is also a common function of government. Taxes can also be used to change behavior through deterrence: a tax on pollution can make people look for alternatives that pollute less.

Many people have intuitions that oppose this view. A widespread theory is that taxation is an infringement of rights. A letter appearing in the *New York Times*, defending proposed cuts in the U.S. budget, stated that "the pending budget cuts will be a small step in the direction of returning to productive individuals their right to spend their money on what they value, and protecting such individuals from being compelled by legislation to support groups and organizations they're either not interested in or regard as anathema."[3] Another letter in *Christian American* argued that "the income tax is intrinsically wrong — that is, the very concept of a tax on income is wrong in and of itself .... Any tax on any type of private property — and the money we earn is one type of personal property — is an assault on the very concept of private property, whether we are talking about wages, homes or whatever. By imposing such a tax, civil government is claiming that our property is not really ours — it really belongs to the government.[4] Taxation for the purpose of helping the poor, for example, is seen as coercing what ought to be voluntary — namely, charity. By this view, taxation, at least for some purposes, is a kind of theft.

These intuitions — like most discussed in this book — have some basis. Letting people earn money and spend it "on what they value" provides incentive for people to work productively, and this benefits others. The invisible hand of people pursuing their own interests works to increase overall good. But this freedom is a means to an end. It makes sense to allow it because of its beneficial effects. Some redistribution of income from rich to poor also increases overall good because the poor value the money so much more than do the rich. To bring about the most good, these two principles must be pitted against each other. Without taxation of the rich to help the poor, total good is reduced. And taxation serves other functions aside from redistribution. For example, it helps to enforce cooperation in commons dilemmas and pays for the defense of private property itself.

Elasticity: Taxes to Change Behavior

Global warming is one of many environmental problems that involve unintended effects of ordinary activities. By heating our homes and driving our cars, we contribute CO_2 to the atmosphere, making widespread future harm to others more likely. A similar problem is air pollution, which is caused by industries, small businesses such as dry cleaning, and drivers. The pollution is an unintended by-product of things that people do to achieve their goals, things that would otherwise be almost entirely beneficial.

One solution to this problem is to make people pay for their effects on others so that people will take these effects into account in making personal decisions. For example, we can tax gasoline so that the tax represents the value of these unintended effects. (Economists call them externalities.) Then people will take these effects into account when they decide whether to buy a fuel-efficient car or whether to take the train to work. It may turn out that it is best for some people to drive to work, even paying the extra cost. But if the tax were just right and if everyone responded to it so as to maximize his own interest, nobody would drive to work when it would be best on the whole, counting the pollution, to take the train, or vice versa.

Economists like this idea because it allows flexibility. People who still benefit from driving can do so. The idea is better than alternative schemes such as absolute prohibitions on gas guzzlers or rationing, in which everyone gets the same amount of gasoline whether he wants it or not. Moreover, as I noted in chapter 2, taxes of this sort could be used to reduce other taxes, which often create negative incentive effects of various sorts.

The BTU tax that I discussed in the last chapter was an example of this kind of tax. People would still be able to use the fuels, however, if it were important enough. They would just have to pay the tax. If the tax were set so as to fully represent the harm done by the excess carbon, then everyone would make the ideal decision. If driving an extra mile did more harm than good once the global warming were considered, then people would not do it. If, on the other hand, the benefits to them were greater than the harm to the world, they would be willing to drive the extra mile even though they had to pay the tax. They would simply be "internalizing" the harm they were doing to others, paying for it directly. Because the tax allows beneficial uses of fuel to proceed in this way, it is better than other solutions such as rationing or banning the use of certain products, such as gas guzzlers.

We have already seen one source of opposition to such taxes. People think they are unfair because they hit some people harder than others. This is in part an example of the do-no-harm heuristic, built into an absolute. We should indeed worry about fairness, about some people being so much richer than others. But we can attack that problem directly; for example, we can increase the tax on income for the rich, decrease the tax for the poor, or even subsidize the poor with direct grants. By preventing gasoline taxes on grounds of fairness, we lose the environmental benefits. (On the other hand, rigidly sticking to the argument I just made is an example of the utopian fallacy. If redistribution from rich to poor is needed and somehow impossible, then the fact that a gasoline tax worsens this need is an argument against it.)

A second source of opposition is that people do not believe that taxes will have any effect on behavior. Anthropologist Willett Kempton and his colleagues asked people what they thought about a 100% tax on certain fuels. Some responses were: "It wouldn't stop people. It wouldn't stop me. . . . I commute to work, so I have to have gas. It's not a good idea. It wouldn't accomplish its object." "I wouldn't be interested in that proposal, and I wouldn't use less gas. . . . That would really anger me if I were taxed on my gas. . . . Just so I can take my children to school and visit my mother." "My job [is] to call on accounts, and most of the time you can't do it by phone, I mean I do some work on the phone, but most of the time I'm out on the road so, whether it costs me $200 [or] $400 for gas, I'm gonna have to do it, I guess."[5] In a survey, about half of the respondents thought that their own use of fuel was insensitive to its cost. Almost none of the people interviewed thought of getting a more efficient car as a way to reduce the use of gas, as many people did when fuel prices increased in the 1970s. Because many people did not see the possibilities for reducing fuel use, they saw the tax as particularly unfair, as a punishment that would be applied to some people for behavior they could not help. So this perception of lack of control increases the perception that taxes are unfair.

Economists have the concept "elasticity" to describe the extent to which behavior changes in response to changes in incentives, such as the price of a good. Typically, when the price or cost goes up, fewer people are willing to pay that price, and demand goes down — that is, people buy less. Sometimes it takes time to adjust. Short-term elasticity may be lower than long-term elasticity. People may continue to use the same amount of gasoline until they buy their next car, or sell their second car and start using public transportation. Economic research has confirmed that almost everything has *some* price elasticity. In the case of fuel use, the elasticity is quite high. People in countries with very high fuel taxes, such as most European countries and Japan, drive more efficient cars than people in countries with low taxes like Nigeria, Venezuela, Kuwait, and the United States.

People often think wrongly that behavior is inelastic, perhaps because it is difficult to imagine the possibilities for adjusting to changes in price. Probably people are more likely to perceive *in*elasticity when it serves as an argument against some policy that their intuitions tell them is wrong, such as an increase in fuel taxes.

The belief in inelasticity is seen elsewhere. People who want to raise the minimum wage paid to workers sometimes say that it will not cause low-wage workers to lose their jobs. A current debate in the United States concerns welfare payments for children. One group wants to cut payments for *additional* children in order to discourage childbearing by poor, unmarried, teenagers, but their opponents argue that childbearing is inelastic. They say that people will have children regardless of whether they get extra welfare payments for each child. Other debates concern penalties for crimes. Advocates of stricter penalties say that crimes will decrease; opponents sometimes say that the penalty will have no effect.

In fact, some decisions *are* more elastic than others. Some of them may be so inelastic as to make some incentive effect too small relative to other factors. It may be that the slight loss of jobs resulting from increasing the minimum wage is worth the benefits, or that the benefits of welfare for children outweigh the costs of slightly higher teenage childbearing (or vice versa). Increased criminal penalties and tougher laws may have too little effect to justify the extra suffering of criminals or the increased number of erroneous convictions. (In the case of capital punishment, there may even be an opposite effect in which murders increase because of the message that killing is a good way to rid the world of evil people.)

Self-destructive Behavior

Intuitions about inelasticity seem to deny incentive effects, but other intuitions exaggerate these effects, or the conclusions that would flow from them. In both over- and under-estimation of incentive effects, people tend to adopt positions that fit their other intuitions. They are engaging in belief overkill. People like decisions to be simple. They do not like to have to compare two effects pointing in different directions, such as the effects of welfare payments on the birth rate and their effects on the development of children. They would rather think that one of these two effects is completely absent, so that they can convince themselves that their favored policy has only benefits, no costs.

Some people feel that we should not help people who have hurt themselves. Thus, we should not give liver transplants to people who have destroyed their livers by drinking too much alcohol. (There is less sentiment for denying major heart surgery to those whose heart disease resulted from too many calories and too little exercise. Perhaps this situation is more common.) Senator Jesse Helms is unenthusiastic about spending government money on AIDS research, as opposed to heart disease (from which he happens to suffer). He says, "We have got to have some common sense about a disease transmitted by people deliberately engaging in unnatural acts."[6] (The "unnatural" part here is an example of naturalism, the equating of what is good with what is natural. We can, of course, argue with Helms about what is natural, and we can also argue about whether naturalness matters.)

The health professions are generally opposed to this kind of thinking. They think that research priorities should not depend on whether a disease is self-inflicted or not. If they are ever willing to consider alcoholism as a reason against a liver transplant, it is because the prognosis for recovery is lower if the patient continues to drink.

But Helms has a point. If we stop helping people who hurt themselves, we increase the incentive for them not to do it. Perhaps more alcoholics would reduce their drinking if they knew that it would prevent them from getting a liver transplant. Perhaps people would take fewer risks of getting AIDS if they were less optimistic about the possibility that research would ultimately find a cure. The standard arguments for ignoring the causes of illness may be an example of belief overkill: denying the possibility of incentive effects for the sake of making a decision easier.

On the other hand, these may really be cases where the incentive effects are so small that it is better to ignore them. Other advocates of holding people responsible for their mistakes might exaggerate the extent to which such a regimem will affect what people do. This applies to insufficient effort in school, unhealthful behavior, taking drugs, and unintended pregnancy. Forcing people to bear children that they conceived by mistake may have some incentive effect on such errors, but quite possibly not enough to justify such a policy (putting aside other arguments concerning abortion, of course).

Taking Property

The Fifth Amendment to the U.S. Constitution says that "private property [shall not be] taken for public use, without just compensation." A political movement in the United States now wants to include the effects of environmental regulation under such "takings." The movement wants to do this through legislation, since courts have ruled that the Fifth Amendment does not apply in these cases. Proponents cite examples like that of Margaret Rector of Austin, Texas, who put her retirement money into a piece of land that was then declared, under the Endangered Species Act, to be a protected habitat for a species of warbler. The value of the property declined from $830,000 to $30,000.[7] It seems coldhearted, hearing such a story, to say that she should have known better than to put her money into land if she wasn't willing to take this risk.

Proponents feel that people have an inherent right to their property. Many of them recognize the practical difficulty of compensating large numbers of people for small losses in value, so they have limited proposed laws to losses greater than a certain magnitude. Still, the intuitive idea of property rights is strong. As one Colorado real-estate developer put it on a television news program: "There are examples ad infinitum of takings, of the deprivation of private property rights, without fair compensation by limiting the uses of the property. There are all kinds of egregious examples of wetlands abuses and other types of . . . deprivation of values imposed upon individual property owners. And I don't think that there is anything more sacred to the future of this nation than the protection of private property rights. They're at the root of liberty and freedom and opportunity."[8]

The intuition of an inherent right to property may exist in all cultures, since cultures all have some form of recognized association between people and things, which gives the people some sort of rights to the things in question. Some rules of this sort are surely necessary for smoothing interpersonal relations, like the rules of etiquette. However, cultures differ extensively in the type and extent of property rights. In cultures with extensive use of these rights, especially, the belief in their inherent goodness may separate itself from any understanding of the function of property rules in making life better.

We can, however, think about property rights, and limitations on these rights, in terms of their consequences. Regulations are one way of preventing people from doing harm. Another segment of the same news show discussed the case of the Gerbaz brothers, who built a dike on a river to correct damage caused by a neighbor modifying the course of the same river, with government permission. In the process, they disturbed the work of landowners downstream and largely ruined a trout fishery. They felt that the government should have compensated them for the original damage.

The point is that things that people do to their "own" property have effects on other people, if only on people who care about warblers. If the value of property to its owner declines because the harm to others has been prevented, who should pay? If I let a bridge on my property fall into disrepair, I can be sued if the bridge collapses while a stranger tries to cross it. This legal principle encourages me to take care. I must bear the cost of fixing the bridge myself. I cannot ask all the potential bridge crossers to chip in for it. So it is not an absolute principle that I am free to do what I want with my property. I am not free to harm others. And I must take care to prevent harm if it is easy to do so.

Who *should* bear the cost of avoiding harm? Under certain conditions, it doesn't make any difference.[9] Suppose that the Gerbaz brothers' dike would harm only one neighbor. And suppose the magnitude of the harm is greater than the benefit to the brothers. Then they should not build the dike. One way for the law to ensure this outcome is to require the neighbor to compensate the brothers for the cost to them of *not* building the dike. The neighbor pays, and the brothers agree not to build. (The law must enforce this contract.) Another way is to require the brothers to compensate the neighbor for damages if the dike is built. The first way assigns a property right to the brothers; the second assigns it to the neighbor. Both cases require the force of law: the first involves a contract; the second, a potential lawsuit.

But things are not this simple in the real world, as in the case of my bridge. It would be hard for all potential pedestrians who will want to cross it to get together and pay me to fix it. Guido Calabresi has suggested that the one who should pay is the "least-cost avoider," the one who can avoid harm with the least cost.[10] In the case of the bridge, that would be me. Such a regime would also lower the value of bridges in general, but that is as it should be. It is simply a way of recognizing that bridges must be maintained and that doing so has a cost.

Let us return now to the owner who finds that her property is home to the mauve-tufted warbler, an endangered species and a rare find for birders. It isn't so clear how this fits in. Should the government pay her on behalf of the birders (if not the bird)? Or should she herself pay to protect the bird? If she pays, then the value of property like hers will be lower because of the dangers of harming endangered species. Perhaps this, too, is as it should be. It is disturbing that property owners bear a large risk now. But this problem could be solved if insurance companies would just sell policies against loss of value from endangered species. If Margaret Rector had been able to buy such insurance, then she might have done so, and if she didn't we would feel less sympathetic. (Once again, the utopian fallacy rears its head if insurance companies refuse to provide such insurance. I have discussed this with a few insurance executives and have found them resistant to the idea, for no good reason I can discover. Possibly they believe that property rights are absolute, and they make up reasons why such insurance would not work, when their real objection is that they prefer to maintain absolute rights.)

In the movement to force compensation, we see an elevation of the principle of private property to an absolute right. Property is a good idea. Assignment of property rights to land and buildings gives owners an incentive to care for their property so as to maintain its value — for their own use while they own it, for its resale to someone else, or both — and this benefits other users and future owners, perhaps even those not yet born. A right to property also allows people to make plans that involve that property. So the institution of private property can have good effects. For this reason, governments collect taxes and pay police to protect property. But an absolute right to private property, whatever the consequences, will, in fact, sometimes lead to worse consequences than some limitation on that right. If we are going to do something that leads to worse consequences on the whole, we should have some good reason. Perhaps we should not think of property as a God-given right, but rather as a means to certain ends.

As in other cases, though, people have failed to understand that the assignment of property rights can be justified by their effect on the common good. When this justification does not apply, particularly when some use of property has secondary effects on others, we should limit property rights. Thus, the principle of property, like the similar principle of autonomy, is a good heuristic, but people may follow it blindly, with full commitment but without understanding its purposes, even when reflection would reveal that it could not be justified terms of its effects.

Of course, environmentalists who always oppose compensation resulting from environmental regulation may be elevating some other principle to an absolute, such as the rights of nature. If we, through our taxes, must compensate property owners, we are forced to recognize the tradeoffs between protection of the natural environment and other goals. Such recognition is likely to mean less protection. Those who think that nature has absolute rights will thus oppose compensation under all conditions.

Changing the Rules of the Game

When the value of your property is reduced because it turns out to be part of someone's habitat, people feel that the rules are being changed in midstream. This is especially true if the law in question was passed after you bought your property.

Governments have many reasons for such retroactive laws. The clearest example is that of civil courts — those that decide lawsuits. The courts, through their decisions, set precedents that influence the behavior of others. In one classic case decided in 1932, two barges sank in a storm on the way from Norfolk to New York City.[11] If the tugboats that were towing the barges had been equipped with working radios, the tugs' captains would have learned of the storm and pulled the barges to safety. Most tugs did have radios at the time, but it was not considered "customary" to have them. The barge owners sued the owners of the tugs, and the barge owners eventually won. In awarding damages to the barge owners, Judge Learned Hand held that "a whole calling [tug boat owners] may have unduly lagged in the adoption of new and available devices [radio receivers]. . . . Courts must in the end say what is required; there are precautions so imperative that even their universal disregard will not excuse their omission." The result was, of course, that tugs started using radios routinely. But the losers in this suit most likely felt that nobody told them that they needed to do it. In effect, the court decision created a new customary practice by penalizing someone who did not follow that practice, even though it was not legally required before the decision.

When the U.S. government passed the "Superfund" law in 1980 to clean up and prevent the dumping of hazardous waste in places that could contaminate groundwater, it had to find ways to pay for cleanup. The basic principle was that "the polluter pays." This principle applied not only to companies that dumped their waste after the law was passed but also to other companies that dumped their waste years or decades earlier. Such "retroactive liability" was one of the most objectionable features of the law. Many people saw it as unfair.[12]

The consequences of such retroactive liability — whether imposed by new laws or by court decisions — are not obviously bad. These laws and decisions send messages to people. One message they might send is, "Don't feel smug. No matter how good you think you are, you may wind up in court for something that you did without any bad intention at all, perhaps even without any thoughtlessness on your part." This is what people feel they are hearing when they object to retroactive liability. But another message is, "Think about how your behavior affects others. If you are careful to do the right thing, regardless of the law at the time, then in the end the law will support you." The question here is whether, if people had been careful in this way, they would not have dumped the waste that they later had to pay to clean up. In some cases, the answer seems to be that they would have dumped it anyway. Some of the waste involved was considered completely harmless when it was dumped.

On the other hand, lots of others were just not doing the research to find out whether the stuff they were dumping was hazardous or not, perhaps not even going to the library to look it up. By failing to ask whether it was potentially harmful, they may have deceived themselves into thinking it was harmless. If most of the dumpers were of this type, then retroactive liability may be sending the right message. It may be telling people to think, to be moral, even if the law does not seem to require it.

Opinions about retroactive liability are unlikely to be based on a judgment of its consequences, on whether the message it sends is a good one or a bad one. It seems that they depend somewhat on the position of the person making the judgment. Corporation executives were more opposed to the retroactive liability of the Superfund law than were environmentalists.[13] This does not mean that people are insincere. It may simply mean that, when they think about fairness, they attend to arguments that suit their self-interest, and then they adopt attitudes consistent with the arguments they know, without considering that the selection was biased at the outset.

Fair Distribution: Health Insurance and Genetics

Many social institutions are concerned with rules for distributing some particular good, such as transplanted organs, scholarships, college admission, or insurance. Arguments about these rules appeal to a great variety of intuitions about fairness. Some of these intuitions involve consequences, but many do not.

Of course, the effort to figure out the best distribution in every case is usually self-defeating. Consider the case of distributing one or more children among divorcing parents. Family courts try to make such decisions about child custody on the basis of many relevant factors, including the best interests of the child. Often, though, the cure is worse than the disease. The court proceedings drag on and have such negative emotional effects on parents and children alike that cases might be better decided by simpler, more mechanical rules. Even flipping a coin might be better.[14]

Likewise, doctors rely on formulas rather than attempting to make case-by-case judgments about recipients for organ donations.[15] When kidney dialysis was first invented, committees were set up — called "God squads" — to decide who would get dialysis for kidney disease and, therefore, who would die as a result of not getting it. There weren't enough machines to go around. Ultimately, the process of deciding became so intolerable to everyone involved that, in the United States, the government decided simply to ensure that everyone who needed dialysis would get it, even though this meant that money was spent on dialysis that could save more lives if spent elsewhere.[16]

Other examples abound, from distributing access to the copying machine, to office space, to pieces of a pie. Simple rules avoid the costs of making decisions. But people sometimes think of the rules not as mere conveniences but rather as inviolable moral principles. When people disagree about which rules should be used, real trouble results.

Most rules take the form of matching inputs to outputs, "To each according to his . . . ." The definition of the input is where a lot of the trouble is. "Contribution" is one kind of input, and "need" is another. Equality rules count each person as one unit of input, in a sense. Voting is an example. (But stockholders get one vote per share, and sometimes the rule is unclear. In a department with some half-time members, should these people get half a vote?)

One major means of distributing goods is the free market. By this mechanism, goods go to those who are willing and able to pay the market price. Markets cater to individual differences in tastes. People can buy what they most value, rather than what others choose to distribute to them. Capitalistic market systems in which people, in essence, sell their labor in order to buy the products of others' labor, also create incentive to work. Market systems, however, often lead to situations that conflict with other principles of distribution, both intuitive principles and utilitarian ones.

A good example of how this happens is health insurance, which is a contentious issue in the United States. Health insurance is distributed partly through the market. But the laws encourage large employers to provide equal access to subsidized insurance to all their employees, so the employees have little choice about whether to get it or not. Those without insurance, about 15% of Americans, usually go to emergency rooms when they get sick, which is more expensive than standard care, and hospitals have been covering the costs of the uninsured from other income, a situation that is becoming more difficult for them. Worse, insurance companies face a conflict between, on the one hand, keeping their premiums low, which makes insurance more affordable to more people, and, on the other hand, making insurance available to all, regardless of their risk.

Health insurers — except those that insure employees of large institutions and those that are regulated by some recent state laws — can now ask questions that help determine a person's individual risk. They can exclude people with diabetes, heart disease, cancer, AIDS, or even those at risk for these conditions because of family history, habits such as smoking or heavy drinking, or some prior occurrence of disease (e.g., of cancer). Those excluded must either pay more or go without insurance altogether. Many have criticized this system as unfair. The situation has recently become more pressing because of the discovery of new genetic tests that can predict much more accurately a person's individual risk for certain diseases, such as Huntington's chorea or breast cancer. Insurance companies do not insist on testing of applicants, but some of them argue that they ought to be allowed to use such information, just as they use family history.

At issue are two intuitive principles of distribution. One — equality — says that people should be treated equally, regardless of their risk.

Insurers call this "community rating" because fees are set for a large community, such as employees of a large company or government. The other says that they should pay according to their risk. This is called "risk rating." (A third principle, "experience rating," says that policy holders should be divided into groups, with each group paying for itself by adjusting its premiums to cover past illnesses. In principle, experience rating could be more like community rating or more like risk rating, depending on how the groups are formed, but in practice it is more like risk rating.)

From a utilitarian point of view, insurance is beneficial because it prevents large losses. As in the earlier example of fire insurance for houses, medical insurance redistributes money each year from the many people who pay premiums to the few who need expensive medical care (with, of course, a cut for the insurance company and its stockholders). Because of the declining marginal utility of money, large losses reduce utility disproportionately (even when the company is considered), and total utility is increased by this redistribution. The kinds of losses in question are either the financial hardship of paying for major medical care, such as major surgery, out of pocket or else the health effects of going without care, which could include pain, disability, and early death. The ill effects of these losses do not depend in any obvious way on the individual risk. In a system in which everyone is insured, community rating — charging everyone the same fee — seems better than risk rating because the benefit of decreased costs for some is smaller than the harm from increasing costs to others.

The situation is more complex when some people choose to go without insurance. Unless insurers use risk rating, those with the greatest risk will be the most likely to buy insurance. Insurers must then pay their costs of care, so individual premiums will have to be higher than if everyone were insured. As a result of these higher premiums, more low-risk people will choose to take the risk and not buy insurance. The tradeoff here is between insuring more people by excluding those with the greatest need or insuring fewer people and making sure that those with the greatest need are covered. The answer cannot be deduced from utilitarian first principles. We need data on people's willingness to pay as a function of their risk. Of course, other reforms are possible, such as making insurance universal. But the specific issue of whether insurers should use risk information might have to be answered in the absence of such reforms. The fact that the best choice depends on facts and involves competing principles does not prevent people from trying to answer the question with simple, intuitive principles.

Of greatest interest are the rationales provided by insurers, which often consist simply of asserting the principle: ". . . policyholders with the same expected risk of loss should be treated equally. . . . An insurance company has the responsibility to treat all its policyholders fairly by establishing premiums at a level consistent with the risk represented by each individual policy-holder."[17] Or,

> Clearly, individuals with certain genetic traits may have risk characteristics that would result in increased claim costs. . . . The main goal of insurance risk-sharing is to allow individuals subject to an unpredictable risk to pool resources, so that the individuals who, on a random basis, may suffer the effects of the insured event will receive the benefit of the pooling mechanism, which will in turn be appropriately paid for by other members of the class. If all the insured in a class face a roughly comparable probability of loss, they will be willing to pay a premium equal to their expectation of loss."[18]

Similar views are expressed by people unconnected with the insurance business, such as the following comment by a law student posted to an electronic discussion group: "Insurance premiums should reflect the ex ante expected cost of one's health costs over a lifetime. . . the probabilities of certain events happening, times the health care costs of those events happening. If you want to adjust away from that scheme, in my mind, definitionally you are not talking about insurance anymore. That is, if you want to charge people the same premiums even though some will have rather higher expected lifetime health care costs, you are talking about effecting a cross-subsidy between those with lower expected health care costs and those with higher ones."[19]

The "ex-ante" probability of something is the probability before some piece of information is available, such as whether the person will get cancer. The difficulty here is that there is no single ex-ante probability. Probability is a function of what is known. If you do lots of genetic tests and look carefully at health habits and family history, you will assign very different probabilities than if you know only a person's age, sex, and race, for example. It is arbitrary to say that genetic test results are relevant to this probability but that the final outcome is not. If it is acceptable to define two classes of people depending on whether they have a certain cancer gene and then charge them different rates, then it should also be acceptable to define two classes according to whether they get cancer or not, and charge accordingly. In the limit, we could define each "class" of patients according to their medical bills. Then nobody would subsidize anyone else, but this would no longer be insurance. True insurance always involves a subsidy: those who do not get sick in any give year subsidize those who do.

This case is interesting because it applies the principle of proportionality — each class of people paying in proportion to its needs — to arbitrarily defined groups. The principle seems intuitively strong to those who accept it. But except for this acceptance, it should be possible to apply the same principle in very different ways to reach very different conclusions. Again, the utilitarian conclusion is not obvious, but intuitive principles make people think the answer is very simple.

Unrealistic Optimism

The greatest sources of inequality, as I mentioned, are the wide distribution of income both within nations and among them. Why is so much inequality tolerated by so many? Later we shall see that intuitions concerning nationalism limit support for foreign aid to the needy in other countries or other steps that would reduce international inequality. Within countries, much of the opposition comes from the sources already mentioned, such as the intuition that taxation is a kind of theft. In all cases, a do-no-harm principle applies, by which moral concern is limited to harms caused through actions rather than harms caused by failing to help.

A curious political phenomenon is that poor people often vote for right-wing candidates who oppose the redistribution of wealth from rich to poor. Perhaps this should not be surprising. The poor may be voting according to their political ideology. And yet we might think that their situation would make them more sensitive to the plight of other poor people.

Why does this sometimes not happen? Perhaps one source of this attitude is unrealistic optimism, a kind of wishful thinking. People overestimate their chances of becoming rich, and the chances of others like them. One of the saddest examples of this phenomenon is the hope of many inner-city boys of becoming stars in professional sports. So few will make it, but so many hope.

Ironically, unrealistic optimism is helpful for the success of capitalism. If it were not for this bias, far fewer startup companies and small businesses would be formed. Here is an example of a bias being good for everyone, except those who have it. Most new businesses fail, but those who start them are forever optimistic. They roll the rock up the hill over and over.[20]

Conclusion

Over a century ago, John Stuart Mill described our intuitions about justice in this way:

> The feeling of justice might be a peculiar instinct, and might yet require, like our other instincts, to be controlled and enlightened by higher reason. If we have intellectual instincts,

leading us to judge in a particular way, as well as animal instinct that prompt us to act in a particular way, there is no
necessity that the former should be more infallible in their
sphere than the latter in theirs: it may as well happen that
wrong judgments are occasionally suggested by those, as
wrong actions by these."[21]

This chapter has tried to point out where some of these "instincts" might
cause trouble today. People often take some simple principle, such as
equality or proportionality, and elevate it to an absolute. They also adopt
principles on the basis of wishful thinking, especially about how the
morally best principle affects their own interests. Once they have a favored principle, they convince themselves that following it requires no
sacrifice. Compromise or discussion becomes difficult.

Mill argued that the solution, the "higher reason," was to think
in terms of consequences. If we do this, principles of distribution rarely
reduce to anything simple. We can, of course, adopt simple rules to avoid
the difficulty and the errors of trying to make case-by-case decisions, but
we then should recognize that this is what we are doing.

This chapter has put aside some of the biggest questions about
fairness, which concern the distribution of goods among nations. The
facts are disturbing, and the situation is getting worse. In 1960, people in the richest countries that contained 20% of the world's population
earned 31 times as much as people in the poorest countries with 20% of
the population. In 1991, people in the richest countries earned 61 times
as much as people in the poorest.[22] This is not entirely a mirage resulting
from exchange rates. In poor countries, people die young from diseases
that are treated or prevented easily in rich countries. They suffer from
dangerous levels of pollution. They are weakened by malnutrition from
the lack of grain, while the rich nations use grain to fatten animals. It
is difficult to see any justice here. People do not choose where they are
born.

Do people have a right to food, education, or medical care regardless of where they live? Whose responsibility is it to provide such things?
What, if anything, should be done about international discrepancies in
material well-being? If anything should be done, who should do it? How
should current inequality affect the way we deal with future problems
such as global warming? Should the rich nations let the Chinese use
the abundant resources of Chinese coal for economic development in the
same way that England, Germany, and the United States did over the
past century?

In the next chapter, I suggest one answer to the question of why
such questions are so rarely addressed — nationalism — which draws a
line around our moral concern.

CHAPTER 4

Nationalism and Group Loyalty

Where should we draw the line in our moral concerns? Most of us think about our concerns in terms of expanding circles. We care first about our-selves and our families, then about various communities that we iden-tify with — our friends, our professions, our towns, our ethnic groups — then perhaps our nation. Some people go further. They think about people in other nations, animals, perhaps even trees, as having the right to moral consideration.

Many moral philosophers and religious leaders have argued that moral concern should not have arbitrary limits. I should not favor one person over another simply because the former has the same hair color as I do, or lives near me, or speaks the same language, unless these things are somehow relevant to the outcomes of my decision. (If I were hiring an assistant, I would favor someone who spoke English.)

The point is just that there isn't any good argument for making ar-bitrary distinctions. Try to think of a good reason why people with black hair deserve special consideration. Moreover, if we allow each other to make all sorts of distinctions like this, we all lose the benefits of a more general moral code. If people with each hair color care only about people of the same hair color, then we lose some of the benefits that come from mutual concern. It is thus in my interest and yours to discourage such distinctions in general (especially if we don't know what the distinctions will be).

In the last couple of centuries, people have gradually come to see that distinctions based on race and sex are arbitrary and morally irrelevant. This does not mean that these things are irrelevant when you are looking for an actor to play the part of Othello. A black man would be a good choice, and, failing that, a man is better than a woman. But race and sex are relevant here because of the nature of the role. They are not relevant for their own sake.

Likewise, we usually think it is acceptable to consider qualities that are correlated with sex or race. For example, physical strength is required for being a furniture mover, and men are generally stronger than women. We do not need to ensure that women are equally represented in such jobs, only that a strong woman is not discriminated against just because she is a woman. What is immoral is to ignore a person's concerns *just* because of race or sex, and for no other reason.

We now need to consider two other special distinctions: our neglect of people of the future — those who are not born yet — and our neglect of people of other nations. In this chapter, I concentrate on the issue of nationalism, but many of the issues are the same when we consider people not yet born. I refer to nationalism in all its forms, including loyalty to ethnic and religious groups, or social classes.

It is often argued that people evolved in small groups or tribes, that tribal loyalty is part of our nature, and that nationalism is the modern expression of tribal loyalty. Even if this claim were true, we can still discuss the morality of nationalism. Morality might require us to go against our nature. Of course, if the claim is true, it would imply that there is some cost in opposing our nature. But the cost might be worth paying.

Yet the claim might not be true. We know little about how human evolution expresses itself in our attitudes toward fellow humans. Certainly some people do care about people outside of their "tribe." Many people contribute to famine relief after responding with sympathy and concern to pictures of hungry children who are clearly from a different race and nation. We recognize these children as fellow humans. Our sympathy extends even to animals. Are these feelings in some sense unnatural? Even if they are, it does not seem all that costly for culture to have prepared us for them. After all, we have them.

Moreover, the story about tribalism seems to rest on the fact that, in small groups, people know one another and recognize each other as members of the same group. This is surely not true of the more abstract groups that define modern nations or ethnic groups. If our tribal evolution is the source of modern nationalism, then it must be modified by culture. Only from our training can we learn about what nation we are part of. We must have some flexibility here.

Modern nationalism is easy to understand as a cultural invention, as an idea that we pass on to one another through education, child rearing, and public discussion of all sorts. Nationalism is created and strengthened when national governments or religious and ethnic authorities gain control of education or communications in some organized way. For example, nations or religions set the curriculum for schools. School textbooks started using *we* to mean "we Americans" or "we Germans," and nobody was around to object. In some cases, this was not dictated by any national authority but simply by publishers' desire to reach a large market. It is natural, and unobjectionable, for groups to encourage discussion of issues peculiar to the group. National educational systems did this. Then authors and newspaper reporters started doing it. If it was okay in school, then it must be okay. The same thing then happens on a smaller scale when professional organizations, religions, and ethnic groups have their own publications, radio stations, and schools.

Of course, this is just an extension of what people have always done. Before we had nations, we had tribes and villages, which were small enough so that everyone in them had a good chance of actually meeting anyone else in them. That is not true of nations. Because I am an American, I am asked (by my fellow Americans) to care more about someone in Hawaii than about someone in Haiti, yet there is almost no chance that I will ever meet either one.

There are good reasons, sometimes, we should be more concerned about people who share some group membership with us. One is that we know more about them and can therefore do a better job of making decisions that serve their interests. A second one is that groups have set up lines of authority for making decisions. These are like contracts or agreements. National governments find it more difficult to make decisions when they are not autonomous, when they must worry about whether outsiders will approve, whether the outsiders are a colonial power or the World Bank. But the principle of national autonomy need not be absolute. The World Bank does try to influence national policies for the long-run good of the citizens of each nation. People do aid victims of famine and natural disasters, through both private charity and foreign aid, even though all these forms of aid might be seen as usurping the power of national governments.

In other cases, though, we overextend the principle of in-group concern to cases where those principles do not apply. Two examples of this are immigration and trade. These examples both involve effects of one nation's policies on other nations. Setting immigration and trade policies in ways that take into account the interests of foreign people cannot be seen as usurping the power of foreign governments.

More generally, nationalism is, like other intuitions, elevated to the status of an absolute principle.

Self-interest and Group Interest

Political action on behalf of one's group is supported by a limited kind of
reasoning. In the movement from thinking only about oneself to thinking about all of humanity, people get stuck halfway. This quagmire may
result from an intuitive confusion of self and group. People think that
by helping their group they are helping themselves. This is true, in a
way, but is just as true of actions that help all people. Many actions that
help the group do not help all people. They hurt outsiders and have bad
effects on the whole.

Suppose you are in the widget business. There is a tax on widgets,
and this cuts into your profits. You and the other widget makers take
political action to get the tax lowered. You write your representatives,
you contribute to political candidates who promise to lower the widget
tax, and you write letters to the editor to increase public support for your
plight. All of this action has a cost to you in time and effort, and let us
suppose it has some benefit to you, too. The more action you take, the
lower the tax will be for you. Moreover, lowering the tax on widgets will
require tax increases somewhere else, let us suppose. (Without these increases, interest rates would increase, which would have the same effect
on others as would the tax increase.)

You can think about your action three ways: your self-interest, the
interest of the group of widget makers, and the interest of all people.
If you think in terms of your self-interest alone, then political action is
almost never worthwhile. The amount of time and effort you spend on
your action is greater than the small benefit that will come *to you* from
that action. If you spend 10 hours and your time is worth $100 an hour,
you have spent the equivalent of $1,000. But this action will have only a
small effect on the tax rate, so you will save only $10. (Perhaps you could
be more effective than that, but you could also be less effective. What is
relevant is the expected effect — the effect you would have on average if
you did this repeatedly.) This is hypothetical, of course; yet it is similar
to real life. The moral is that the action is not worthwhile on the basis of
narrow self-interest alone.

You can enlarge your perspective and consider the 999 other people like you in the widget business. Each of the 1,000 widget makers will
save $10 in taxes from *your* action, so the total saving will be $10,000 for
an expenditure of $1,000 worth of effort. This is because lowering the tax
affects all widget makers, not just you, even if your activity is what gets
the tax lowered. From this perspective, your effort is worthwhile. The
benefits are 10 times the cost. If people think about consequences when
they engage in action, this is often the perspective that they adopt. They
think about the benefits to the group that they belong to. But they have
already gone beyond their narrow self-interest. From the perspective of
narrow self-interest, the action is not worthwhile. It becomes worthwhile

only when we consider the effect on some other people. But why stop with a certain group?

From the perspective of all people, your action has no benefit at all. Taxes go down for the widget makers, but they go up for everyone else, to make up the difference. (Note that this is about a specific tax, not taxes in general.) So, from this perspective, you should not act. Only from the middle perspective — that of your group — is your action justified by its consequences. If some intuition supports it too, such as the intuition of autonomy from government interference, then you will be more likely to adopt this group perspective.

In sum, action on behalf of a limited group, in favor of a policy that does not benefit everyone, is not justified by the consequences of the action unless you think of just the consequences for the group. If you take a totally selfish perspective, it is not justified because the expense is too great and the benefit too small. If you take the perspective of the larger group that includes everyone, the action is not justified because it helps your group at the expense of others. (I have assumed this. This is specifically the kind of action at issue — namely, actions that benefit your own group at the expense of others.) Only if you limit your consideration of consequences in a particular way is your action worthwhile.

The more typical case, perhaps, is when you have a choice between two actions, one of which helps your own group and one of which provides a greater total benefit to everyone. You can also do neither. Neither option does much harm. In this situation, many people favor the action that helps their group. They think that the action helps them more because they belong to their group. But the personal benefit to them, relative to the cost of action, really is small in either case and not enough to justify either action. If they are going to choose one of the two actions, they must care about other people. If so, they have no good reason to care just about those people who are in their group. They should choose the action that does the most good. The problem, again, is that people are partial to their own group, in part because they think they can justify this in terms of self-interest. But as in the first case, self-interest is not enough.

Typically, even the small extra benefit that people get from being part of the smaller group is not enough. (This benefit results from the overall good being spread around fewer people.) The benefit they get is so small that the effects on others would have to be very close in order to tilt the decision one way or the other, and this is highly unlikely.

Of course, those whose intuitions favor groups do not think only about consequences. They have other intuitions, some concerning group loyalty itself. But because of belief overkill, they like to believe that their action can be justified by its consequences for everyone, too. It is difficult to get over nationalistic intuitions once they start.

Moreover, the effort to think about all of humanity can sometimes go too far. When your group is under attack, you have a special obligation to defend it because you are expected to do so. Others will not defend you unless you defend yourself. Still, this does not really say that you should neglect the consequences for everyone. Presumably, when you are attacked like this, it *is* best for everyone if the attacker is repelled, if only because this deters other attackers.

Scholarships

Sometimes nationalism gives people an excuse to limit their concern, when they must limit it somehow. It is not clear that limiting it this way is the best way, however.

The University of Pennsylvania, along with most other highly selective colleges in the United States, has a policy called "need blind admissions." Students who apply for admission as undergraduates are admitted without regard to their ability to pay for tuition, fees, and room and board. Once they are admitted, students who say they cannot pay the full amount are asked for detailed financial information. On the basis of this information, the university determines the student's "need" and tries to put together a package of loans and grants that — together with some contribution from the student working — will cover the need. Students, faculty, alumni, and university officials all support this policy, even though it requires considerable sacrifice because a substantial part of the grants comes from unrestricted funds that could be used for any other purpose, from increasing faculty salaries to lowering the tuition of those who pay in full.

There is one hitch in the policy. It applies only to U.S. residents. I have asked many people why this is. One answer is that we simply could not afford to extend this policy to the whole world. If we admitted students without respect to nationality and ability to pay, we would likely fill half our entering class with cash-poor students from India. In reply, I have asked why we do not then limit the policy in some other way. One answer, which I have not received, is that nationality is truly arbitrary but that it works, both financially and politically. It does not admit too many cash-poor students, and it is not an object of protest.

The reason I do not get this answer is that most people do not regard nationality as arbitrary. They say, for example, "but this is an American university." (Yes. It is also a Philadelphia university, a Pennsylvania university, a North American university, and enough of an *international* university to accept large donations from alumni in Singapore.) This was the answer given by a former provost.

Another answer is that we are obliged to the United States because the U.S. government gives us lots of money. That is true, but all of that money is earmarked for specific purposes, such as research, and presumably the university does not make any "profit" once the research (and the overhead expenses connected with doing the research, such as maintaining laboratory buildings, computer networks, and part of the library) is paid for. Moreover, we accept funds from many other governmental and nongovernmental units (including foreign governments), and we do not feel that these funds have any strings attached. Typically, that money is for some research, and most people feel that when the research is done the obligation is discharged.

A more practical concern is that a large part of the money for financial aid itself comes from the U.S. government, which specifies that this aid cannot be used for foreigners. But this does not apply to all the aid. The university is free to use all the rest, if it wants, for those who are ineligible for government aid. It does this routinely at the graduate level, where many students are given a stipend and free tuition for some period. In some departments, almost all the students are foreign and thus ineligible for U.S. government fellowships, although many have their own fellowships from (e.g.) Canada or South Korea.

In sum, despite the fact that the University of Pennsylvania is a private institution that sometimes calls itself "international," the basic reason for the restriction on financial aid seems to be that its members think of themselves as Americans. When they use the word *we* in discussing moral questions, they mean "we Americans," not "we people." Once having accepted their intuitive attachment to their fellow citizens, they seek other reasons, such as government support, that do not apply consistently.

I am not sure what the policy should be. But I would be happier if my colleagues would admit that the present policy contains a large arbitrary element. In the great scheme of things this is a small issue, but it seems to be a good example of how intuitive nationalism influences our thinking.

Immigration

The debate about immigration policy — in the United States and Western Europe — is framed largely in terms of national interest, as if the immigrants themselves did not count. Opponents of immigration also tend to oppose efforts to help other countries. Patrick Buchanan, writing against the international effort to help Mexico in 1995, wrote, "Either America jumps ship from this doomed vessel, The New World Order, or one day, we go down with it. Let's stop the Mexican Bailout before it begins, and start building that barrier fence on our Southern border. Because, this time, we are really going to need it."[1] Even economic analyses that argue in favor of immigration do not count the effects on the immigrants themselves or on the people they leave behind.[2]

As a result, the countries that people want to get into have no coherent policies. Each wants the tired and poor to go somewhere else, just as each fisherman wants all the *other* fishermen to reduce their catch. Immigration pressure has been increasing because of growth in populations and in the disparity between rich and poor countries. Rich nations that want to restrict immigration will have to spend more and more money to keep the people out.

Of course, most of the rich countries have some provision for victims of persecution. But the question is why we distinguish these people from victims of poverty, which in extreme forms can be just as brutal. My concern here is not what the policy ought to be but, rather, how we talk about it. My main observation is that we neglect foreigners in discussions of immigration. Giving them some weight in our deliberations would not oblige us to tear down the walls, to accept a complete libertarian view of migration. It might lead to some changes in policy, however. A possible example where this factor seems to be ignored is in the move of several states in eastern Germany to increase payments to families for having children in order to stem the decline of population, while at the same time Turks and others are refused entry. If these states want to increase their populations, they could easily let in more immigrants. What is stopping this seems to be largely a national or ethnic loyalty. Perhaps they also have some desire to preserve their culture.

Of course, any rational immigration policy for rich nations requires some sort of legal distinction between those who can get in and those who cannot. Whatever the law, some sort of safety valve may be necessary in the form of tolerance for illegal immigrants, many of whom take great risks to improve their lives. But one can reasonably debate how tightly this valve should be adjusted. The status quo is not necessarily the best answer. It may be better to tighten the safety valve — reducing tolerance for illegals — while at the same time opening wider the spigot of legal immigration. (This was the spirit, at least, of the recent Simpson–Mazzoli immigration bill in the United States.)

In view of the difficulty of deciding how tightly to adjust the safety valve, we might be surprised at how strongly proposals to tighten it are resisted. In 1993, Governor Pete Wilson of California proposed several measures to discourage immigration, both legal and illegal. (Some of these were incorporated into a state referendum that passed the following year.) These included amending the U.S. Constitution "so that citizenship belongs only to the children of legal residents of the United States, not to every child whose mother can make it to an American hospital," as well as denying health benefits and public education to the children of illegal immigrants.[3] A representative of the American Civil Liberties Union (ACLU) responded by saying that the proposals were "an unconscionable effort on his behalf to target the most defenseless and voiceless segment of our society, which are children" and that the proposal to amend the Constitution "goes against the most basic right there is: citizenship." The problem here is that the definition of the right of citizenship is exactly what is under debate. For the ACLU, the status quo had already been elevated to a basic right.

The opponents of immigration engage in my-side bias — in the form of selective attention to evidence that supports their side — when they point to the increased costs of immigrants to the public treasury. They focus on limited areas and ignore the benefits.[4] For example, the following is typical of the arguments: "Does our nation need more workers competing for a limited number of jobs? Do our overburdened and overcrowded schools need more students crammed into the classrooms?"[5] Economic analyses indicate that immigrants to the United States contribute more to government coffers than they take, and other developed countries also show either the same pattern or no overall effect.[6]

Opponents such as the Federation for American Immigration Reform[7] have also formed a loose alliance with population-control groups such as Carrying Capacity Network and Zero Population Growth. These groups argue that immigration restrictions will hold down the U.S. population, thus improving the quality of life of Americans by reducing crowding and also preventing destruction of the environment. Some of their arguments take this form: "Will our scenic parks be more enjoyable when shared with additional multitudes? Does precious wildlife habitat become easier to save in the face of additional human encroachment?"[8] The environmental argument is based on the fact that Americans use much more natural resources per capita than citizens of other countries, so presumably immigrants will use more if they adopt the habits of those in the United States than if they had stayed put. This argument ignores other environmental effects, such as unsustainable use of land and water and generation of toxic pollution, which may in fact be less in the United States than elsewhere. And it ignores the fact that the reproduction rate is lower in the United States, so that immigration to the United States will help reduce world population insofar as the immigrants adopt the child-bearing habits of those around them. Finally, it fails to ask whether immigration restrictions are the most cost-effective way of reducing resource use, if that is a goal worth trying to achieve. It would appear that most of the anti-immigrant arguments are unlikely to be the original source of the attitude in question. Instead, they seem to be the sort of arguments that are uncritically recruited after an initial opinion is formed. The underlying intuition may be more purely nationalistic.

Nationalism in general, and immigration attitudes in particular, seem to result from the elevation of reasonable rules of thumb into principles that take on a life of their own. In terms of consequences, the legitimate basis of nationalism of any kind is that better decisions are made by those closer to the scene, and some decisions are truly local (national, regional) in scope. The basis of opposition to immigration is that rapid change is stressful and that excessive immigration can undermine cultural traditions worth preserving. But these principles lead to an excessively sharp distinction between the ins and the outs. We need to put them into the broader context of the purposes they serve, to see them as means rather than ends.

Foreign Aid

The greatest determinant of well-being in the world today is where you "choose" to be born. The obvious solution to this unfairness is for those in rich countries — especially the rich in rich countries — to aid the needy in poor countries. For a rich person in the United States to sacrifice an extra thousand dollars is barely noticeable, whether this is done through taxes or charity, but this same amount exceeds the annual average income of people in many countries. The benefits are thus much greater than the costs. From a utilitarian point of view, foreign aid is a no-brainer, at least if the aid is well spent. Although there is obviously a limit to how much aid could be effective, nobody claims that we are anywhere near that point.

Effective foreign aid can be indirect as well as direct. Medical research done in rich countries, for example, benefits everyone, at least potentially. But most of this research is concerned with particular diseases such as heart disease (which results in part from eating animal fat, which most people in the world cannot afford) and cancer (which occurs mostly at advanced ages that most people around the world do not reach). Meanwhile, tropical diseases that afflict 600 million people in poor countries receive almost no attention in the rich countries that have the most active research establishments.[9] A promising (but ultimately disappointing) antimalaria vaccine was developed by a Colombian, Dr. Manuel Patarroyo, who became a national hero.[10] United States pharmaceutical companies have done essentially no research on malaria in the last few years, despite the fact that the disease infects 280 million people around the world. The major exception to this neglect was the development by Merck Pharmaceuticals of an effective drug to combat river blindness and its decision to donate the drug to an African aid organization.[11] But companies responsible to their stockholders cannot do this sort of thing regularly without some additional financial incentive, such as direct research support or at least the promise that foreign aid will be used to help the poor around the world enjoy the benefits of such research.

Isolationists in rich countries oppose foreign aid because they think it is wasteful and that it may even disappear into the pockets of corrupt dictators. Indeed, much of this seems to have happened during the cold war, when leaders of some poor countries essentially sold their loyalty to one side or the other. Opposition persists, however, even though much foreign aid now goes for birth control (see chapters 8 and 9), health, and food. According to several recent reports from UNICEF (United Nations Children's Fund)[12] and the United Nations Food and Agricultural Organization (FAO), children could be saved from death, blindness, and other forms of handicaps through such inexpensive remedies as oral rehydration salts for diarrhea, vitamin A capsules, iodized salt, and vaccination against childhood diseases. The World Health Organization estimates that, in some poor countries, a person can be cured of tuberculosis for $13.[13] Nobody disputes the claim that such expenditures, even when funneled through government agencies of donor countries, are one of the most efficient ways to use money to improve the human condition. Assistance with birth control can also be effective, as I shall discuss in chapter 8.

Foreign aid for economic development is more risky, but it is clear that long-run development of poor nations requires power plants, roads, and such, and often international agencies such as the World Bank are the only source of such capital. Foreign aid can also be used as a reward (hence an incentive) to governments that reduce military expenditures, stabilize their currencies, and establish legal regimes that permit free enterprise to flourish. Perhaps the most important kind of foreign aid is the lowering of trade barriers to manufactured imports from poor countries, which still impede development.[14] This particular form of aid is complex because, while it typically helps developing countries on the whole by lowering prices, it hurts some low-paid workers in these countries. I discuss these issue in chapter 6.

Critics of foreign aid, such as Patrick Buchanan (a United States political commentator who ran unsuccessfully for the Republican presidential nomination), argue that it is costly and useless; it "creates dependency, breeds corruption, corrodes honest relations, and bloats government at the expense of the private sector."[15] Certainly some aid is wasted. But given the large benefits per dollar of other aid, it would seem that the appropriate response is to call for reduction of waste and *increases* in the more efficient kind of aid. Instead, the opponents call simply for cuts. Responses like Buchanan's seem to result from belief overkill, an unwillingness to admit that the aid might do any good at all.

Opposition to foreign aid, then, may be based on wishful thinking rather than real facts. It is convenient for opponents to believe that the aid is wasted, so they find examples of this, fail to look for counterexamples, and come to believe that waste is the general pattern, forgetting that they cooked the evidence to order. But what is its original source of the opposition, if not the evidence for waste and corruption? It is unlikely to be just selfishness. Although opposition to foreign aid is typically associated with opposition to any aid for the poor,[16] nationalism is also a strong element. As Barry Goldwater put it in 1961, "The American government does not have the right, much less the obligation, to try to promote the economic and social welfare of foreign peoples."[17] Goldwater and other opponents of aid were also opposed to internal efforts to help the poor, but the idea of shipping money out of the country was something they found particularly galling.

Some opponents take more extreme versions of this nationalistic position:

> Halloween trick or treating and greeting cards are what most Americans think about when they hear the name UNICEF. The greeting card operation alone, according to a recent Yearbook of the United Nations, brings in an annual take of $76.6 million. But behind the marketing facade that supposedly raises funds for international child welfare programs is an agenda to augment the power and influence of global government.
>
> UNICEF specifically supports, as noted in its *State of the World's Children, 1994*, "sustainable development following the guidelines of Agenda 21," the blueprint for the world's environment agreed to . . . in Rio de Janeiro in 1992. An Agenda 21 document acknowledges that it "proposes an array of actions which are intended to be implemented by every person on earth . . . ."
>
> One outgrowth of UNICEF's 1990 World Summit for children was the Convention on the Rights of the Child.[18]

In the mind of this writer, a plan promoting the idea that children deserve education, health care, food, and water has become an instrument of coercion, reducing the autonomy of individuals and states alike.

International Agreements

The problem of the fisheries is a social dilemma. It is to each fisherman's advantage to fish as much as possible, but if everyone does this, overfishing will put the fishermen out of business. The same kind of problem presents itself to nations. It is to each nation's advantage to fish as much as possible, but this too leads to overfishing. The international fishing dilemma has been solved in two ways. First, in the early 1970s, nations agreed among themselves to consider coastal waters up to 200 miles as national territory. This was formalized by the 1982 United Nations Law of the Sea Convention. Second, several international treaties and conventions have allowed limitations on fishing in waters not covered by this rule.

Notice that even the first of these methods — a sort of assignment of property rights to coastal waters — was not just a matter of freedom. It was a coercive solution, enforced cooperatively by the nations themselves. Violations were punished by military force. The conventions meant that nations would oppose any large power that tried to violate the territory of a weaker one. Rights to property or territory are not the same as "freedom" for all. The idea of national territory is a coercive solution to a social dilemma.

The other form of international treaty received a large boost in 1995, after a dispute between Canada and the European Union, in which Canada seized a Spanish trawler fishing for turbot just outside Canada's 200-mile zone. The United Nations Conference on Straddling Fish Stocks and Highly Migratory Fish Stocks succeeded in producing an agreement for the major fishing nations, which required limits on catches and "by-catches," in which undesired fish (or fish beyond the quota) are caught in a net and discarded, dead.[19]

Fishing regulation is one of many ways in which nations can benefit from cooperation and from international institutions. Others include free trade, peacekeeping by the United Nations, nonproliferation of nuclear weapons, defense against contagious diseases, and reduction of chemicals that deplete stratospheric ozone. These issues concern the whole world. Other issues are more local: the North American Free Trade Agreement, the European Union, and countless other international cooperative agreements.

All of these proposals are resisted by nationalists who fear giving up national autonomy. This is analogous to the desire for individual autonomy that weakens support for government regulation in general. Even the successful treaties are often weaker than they ought to be in order to win the support of stragglers. The 1994 agreement that produced the World Trade Organization, for example, made compromises because of French and Japanese desires to protect their (inefficient, subsidized, and protected) domestic farmers. Both countries claimed that farming was part of their "national identity."

Conclusion

It is often said that intuitions of nationalism and group loyalty arise from some kind of tribal instinct, which is beyond our power to control and therefore not worth questioning on moral grounds. Perhaps this belief is true. But it is also a convenient belief that absolves us of responsibility for the situation of those outside of our nation or group.

Nationalistic intuitions might not, in fact, be instinctual and beyond control. Instead, they might arise from a cognitive confusion between ourselves and those like us in some way. Because of this confu-

sion, we easily fall into believing that helping those who are like ourselves is the same as helping ourselves. This belief distorts our moral
motives toward helping in-groups and ignoring out-groups. We think
we are doing two things at once — helping others and helping ourselves.

But this is an illusion, perhaps a correctable one. More people
might be able to learn to spread our moral concerns more widely. Many
people do this, and it may be possible for everyone. Private aid to international relief organizations continues to flow, although there is always
too little of it. How could this be happening if in-group loyalty were an
instinct that could never be overcome? Even if such an instinct exists, it
is not in absolute control.

The dangers of nationalism are real. They become even worse
when they are exacerbated by the forces of my-side bias. Such bias allows people to ignore evidence and exaggerate the rightness of their own
side and the wrongness of their opponents.

CHAPTER 5

My-side Bias and Violent Conflict

In Central Africa, Sri Lanka, India, Ireland, the Middle East, the Balkans, and elsewhere we have seen conflicts in which people on both sides are willing to kill and die because they believe that they are morally right. Many of these conflicts are religious, so part of the problem is differing beliefs about what is natural or morally required. I shall discuss this in chapters 8 and 9. Here, I turn to the nature of the bias that preserves beliefs from challenge, even when the evidence for them is weak and the evidence against them strong.

My-side Bias and Overconfidence

I have called this my-side bias. People seek evidence in favor of their own side in a dispute, and they often ignore evidence on the other side when it is presented to them. The result is that many people tend to be excessively sure of their opinions. When people on two sides of a controversy suffer these effects, they cannot move closer. They scream at each other but do not listen. We see this all over the world: the Arabs and Israelis; pro-choice and anti-abortion groups in the United States; the Hutus and Tutsis in Rwanda. Even if one side were correct and completely open to arguments while the other side were still closed, the conflict would continue. These belief biases operate even when there is no obvious "other side." Cults, for example, are certain of their beliefs even when the rest of the world finds the beliefs so crazy as not to bother to argue against them.

The general problem is that people are so sure of their beliefs that they are willing to take extreme actions, actions that they would not take if they had doubts. When two opposing camps both behave this way, some form of war is the result, especially when the issue is moral. Moral beliefs, by their nature, do not admit the possibility that someone could disagree and be correct. In this regard they are like beliefs about matters of fact. They are not like tastes. For example, those who think that abortion is morally wrong do not think that abortion is acceptable for those who think it is acceptable. They think it is wrong for everyone, regardless of what anyone else thinks. If the two sides of an issue like this "agree to disagree," it is not the same as agreeing to disagree about whether cooked carrots are tastier than raw carrots. It is, at best, an agreement not to fight. The temptation to convert the other side remains.

The effects of overconfidence and my-side bias are not limited to angry confrontations. The behavior of ordinary people in the quiet of the psychology laboratory can enlighten us about their nature. In a classic study of overconfidence, subjects gave confidence ratings after answering objective questions such as, "Is absinthe a liqueur or a precious stone?" After each question, the subject is asked for a confidence rating in percent, "How sure are you that your answer is correct?" Subjects are told exactly what this means. If you say 100%, then you should be correct. In fact, you should be correct on *all* the cases on which you say this. If we take all the questions on which you say 75%, you should be correct on about three quarters. The main result is clear: When people express high confidence, they are overconfident. When they say they are 100% certain, they may be correct about 80% of the time, and, of course, incorrect about 20% of the time.[1]

Moreover, people take their numbers seriously. The experimenters found that they could make money by asking the subjects to bet on their own confidence judgments. Each subject was made the following offer: The subject would pay the experimenter $1 for every incorrect answer in which she was at least 98% confident. The experimenter would pay the subject $1 for every black ball that was drawn from an urn containing 98 white balls and 2 black ones. If the subject's judgments were correct, then she should come out ahead on the average because sometimes her judgments would be higher than 98%. Most subjects agreed to play, and almost all subjects lost money. The experimenter didn't keep the money, but the lesson is clear. You can make money by betting on people's being overconfident.

This kind of overconfidence is abetted by a tendency to look for reasons an initial hunch is correct and ignore reasons it is incorrect. The overconfidence effect is reduced if subjects are asked to think of reasons their answer might be wrong. Asking them to think of reasons it might be correct has no effect; they do that anyway.[2]

Another classic study shows that, even if people are given evidence against a favored view, they tend to reject the evidence. The subjects were students who had indicated in a survey that they either favored or opposed capital punishment. Each subject was then presented with mixed evidence on the effectiveness of capital punishment in deterring crime. Each subject read two reports, one purporting to show effectiveness and the other purporting to show ineffectiveness. (Although the reports appeared to be actual articles, they had been fabricated by the experimenters.) One report compared murder rates in various states in the country before and after adoption of capital punishment. The other compared murder rates in states with and without capital punishment. The first report showed effectiveness (of capital punishment in deterring crime) for half the subjects, and the second report showed effectiveness for the other half.

The effect of each report on the subject's belief was stronger when the report agreed with the belief than when it did not. Subjects rated the report that agreed with their opinion as "more convincing," and they found flaws more easily in the reports that went against their belief. (Of course, neither kind of report is conclusive evidence, but both kinds are better than no evidence at all.) In the end, subjects *polarized* — that is, they became stronger in their initial belief, regardless of whether they initially thought that capital punishment deterred crime or not. If anything, mixed evidence should have made subjects less sure of their belief.[3]

Belief biases get worse, it seems, when people are motivated to believe that something is true. People think they will live longer than average, make more money, and so on. These positive illusions are probably harmless or even beneficial in people's individual lives. They make people work harder and take beneficial risks; they prevent depression and improve our mood. But, with public issues, they can have dangerous effects. When two armies go to war, both think they will win.

These forms of my-side bias become exaggerated when fairness is involved. People disagree about the criteria for fair distribution of political power, land, access to jobs and education, and so on. People tend to favor those criteria on which their group does better. Thus, in countries with a highly educated minority group (Chinese in Malaysia, whites in Zimbabwe), the minority favors "merit" and the majority favors "equality" or "majority rule."[4]

Various efforts are being made to teach people to avoid these effects, to be "actively open-minded," to understand the need to give the benefit of the doubt to the other side on matters of fairness. Of course, when such instruction is proposed as a remedy for ongoing conflict, each side is sure that only the other side needs it. But it may be easier to agree that both should have it than to agree on all the other contentious issues.

Paranoia, Cults, and Strange Beliefs

Despite the efforts of schools and the news media to present a coherent and widely accepted view of the world, it is amazing that various organized groups adhere to such bizarre versions of the truth as the following:

- Memories of "satanic ritual abuse" are frequently repressed and recovered in psychotherapy.

- Aliens from other planets come to earth and rape people.

- The Holocaust was a hoax.

- The U.S. government is planning to bomb its own citizens in order to establish a New World Order of international government.

- Blacks are not fully human.

- H.I.V., the AIDS virus, was produced by scientists and disseminated through Black neighborhoods for the purpose of genocide.

- The end of civilization is imminent.[5]

These versions of the truth are all dangerous enough in themselves, but often these cults inspire radical and destructive acts to further their causes — the Jonestown massacre, the gassing of the Tokyo subway, and the bombing of the Oklahoma City federal building are just some that come to mind. Yet cults are not uniquely characteristic of advanced technological societies. Melanesian Islanders in the South Pacific developed "cargo cults," new religions based on that deliveries of cargo would come from ships or airplanes, as they had seen happen to colonial occupiers. They often abandoned their own traditional livelihood in anticipation. The Melanesians hurt only themselves. When bizarre beliefs combine with modern weapons, the results can be destructive to outsiders as well.

These beliefs are like those found in paranoid patients. Paranoia is a mental disturbance characterized by delusions of persecution and grandeur, typically (but not always) found in people who suffer from schizophrenia. Paranoids are the ones who think that they are Napoleon or Jesus. They often think they are persecuted because of their special gifts, just as others were persecuted in the past. Paranoids without other symptoms of thought disorder typically have highly systematic and internally consistent delusions. Like scientists who defend theories in the face of mounting counterevidence, they develop elaborate explanations of why others reject their beliefs. Often they view those who question them as allied with their persecutors.

The lines between paranoid delusions, cults, and fringe political ideologies are difficult to draw. Consider, for example, the following statements by John Salvi III, accused of murdering several workers in an abortion clinic in Brookline, Massachusetts, in 1994.

> This is not an admission of guilt. However it is a statement about the persecution which the catholic people face. The catholic people are being persecuted in the workplace as well as in a whole. There are leaders in Government both Local, state and Federal which are well aware of the abuse taking place.
>   There is a movement in society which seeks the destruction of the church. One method these individuals use is to buy up companies, corporations and businesses after which putting themselves out of business and or laying off catholic employees. This layoff procedure for Catholics occurs to a great extent in the U.S. school systems, police departments, fire depts. etc. The catholic church is being floored financially.
>   Why do the free masons persecute the catholic people? Because their good at it. The catholic church is dealing with a group of people who are intelligent, mean, nasty and judicious. These individuals run society and have a good system for themselves but seek to keep the catholic church from printing a currency and having the same system.[6]

Experts interviewed argued that some of Salvi's ideas — of which these excerpts are a part — were taken from political literature and others were his own embellishments and additions. The belief in a conspiracy of Freemasons, for example, has been around for centuries. The idea that Freemasons were preventing Catholics from printing their own currency is, very likely, Salvi's own. But delusions may range from beliefs of a single individual to the beliefs of great masses of people.

What makes a delusion a delusion? What is the problem? It is not just the fact that delusions are not shared. Some of them *are* shared by everyone in a person's immediate circle. Social consensus, if only within a small group, makes beliefs more reasonable. In general, true beliefs are more likely to be widely held than are false beliefs. People who share in delusions may thus be less seriously disturbed than those who hold them idiosyncratically. They are at least sensitive to social consensus, which is a legitimate (if somewhat fallible) kind of evidence. But the group as a whole still holds the delusion, and we still need to characterize it.

One answer to the question of the nature of delusions is that they are beliefs whose strength wildly exceeds the evidence for them. They seem to result from biases in the search for evidence and in the way in which that evidence is used. People look for evidence that their initial belief is true, and they tend to give too little weight to counterevidence.

It is easy to see how such delusions develop in people who think in this way. All of us suffer setbacks. Sometimes we would deserve these in a just world, but the world is not completely just, and we often do not know all the facts. Thus it is easy to find explanations in terms of anti-Semitism if you are Jewish, or racism if you are black, or reverse discrimination if you are a white male. If we look for further evidence, we can usually find it.

Most delusions are not completely impossible. Prejudice exists. Conspiracies exist. People are persecuted for all sorts of things. Where normal nonparanoid people might think, "Perhaps I have been the victim of discrimination, but I really can't be sure," paranoids will become certain. They will do this by looking for evidence only on one side and then taking it at face value as if there *were* no evidence on the other side and as if there were no other explanation of the few facts at hand. The problem is *not* that paranoid beliefs are impossible. It is just that they are held with excessive strength, the kind of strength that can come only from cooking the evidence to order.

It is even difficult to draw the line between delusional beliefs and those that are considered completely sane only because they are commonly held, like the belief in a God capable of intervening in human affairs and overriding the laws of physics. Those who hold this belief — probably the majority of people — are often quite sure it is true, but their evidence is often secondhand and easily explained by alternative accounts. The evidence for this kind of God, after all, is similar to the evidence for flying saucers: personal testimony, unanswered questions that can be answered through the belief, consistent theories, and so on. Of course, those who believe in God (and not in flying saucers) will think their evidence is stronger than the evidence for flying saucers, but the opposite holds, too.

My point here is not to tear down the belief in God. It is rather to point out that delusional beliefs are not that different in character from beliefs held by many people. *Everyone* has some beliefs that are held much more confidently than the evidence warrants. (People differ, however, in their tendency to hold such beliefs.)

Moreover, these beliefs sometimes turn out to be correct, confirmed by new evidence. Such is often the case with revolutionary scientific theories when they are first proposed, such as Copernicus's theory of the solar system, with the sun at the center. Copernicus himself did not believe his own theory with enough confidence to want to publish it, although he finally did so. He felt — correctly — that he could not clearly demonstrate its superiority to the main alternative theory of Ptolomy, which placed the earth at the center of the solar system. A few scientists accepted the theory right away, despite the lack of evidence and despite their occasional persecution. Only with Newton's theory of gravitation was the evidence for Copernicus so strong that it could not be denied. (Even then, technically, the center of the sun is not really at the center of the solar system. Rather, the sun and the earth, for example, rotate around a common center of gravity, which is much closer to the sun than to the earth.) Thus, what is irrationally held at first may turn out to be true, and the irrational strength of the original belief may turn out to speed up the search for evidence leading to its ultimate acceptance.

This type of situation reinforces my suggestion — which I may have myself elevated to an irrational belief — that paranoia, cults, and fringe ideologies are not discrete phenomenon, completely outside the experience of ordinary people. Rather, they are part of a common pattern of thinking: my-side bias.

This pattern of thinking can sometimes turn out to be useful, by chance, when our initial belief is correct and when we would give up on it too quickly without such thinking. History is full of examples of people who stuck by some idea that everyone else thought was crazy but turned out to be correct. But such cases invite judgment in hindsight. When we focus on them, we are unaware of cases in which people felt just as strongly that they were correct despite all the odds and turned out to be incorrect. We cannot predict when such thinking will be useful and when it will not be. We would do better to be on guard against it. Perhaps we can do even without it. Perhaps we do not need to deceive ourselves in order to motivate the search for creative ideas. We can, instead, tell ourselves about the tremendous benefits that will result if our unlikely idea turns out to be correct, even while believing that this *is* unlikely.

Violent Conflict: Hindus versus Muslims

In a battle of any sort, one side can inflict serious damage on the other. This includes legal battles, personal feuds, and especially war of the usual military sort. A battle is a risk. People often take these risks irrationally, in ways that go against even their own self-interest. Such irrationality can arise when people are fighting for sharply conflicting values. A common contributing factor is overconfidence, not only in the beliefs about the rightness of their cause but also about their chance of winning.

Overconfidence in winning can result from wishful thinking. Happily, there is a countervailing force here, which is people's general aversion to risk. Risk aversion exists for many reasons — some rational, others less rational. In this case, reason is usually on the side of restraint. However, when people see themselves as threatened by losses unless they fight, they tend to lose this protective aversion to risk.

Moral conflicts have special difficulties beyond those concerning mere material resources. Each side cannot see the other side's winning as a gain for anyone. Each side's moral claim may mean nothing to the other. Negotiation becomes difficult. In some cases, the moral claim is seen has having enough value so that any risk on its behalf is justified. Because religious principles are often of this sort, some of the most serious disputes throughout history have been religious.

The moral principles involved can also be those of fairness and justice. If one side feels unjustly treated, then it is fighting for justice as well as a material outcome. If both sides choose conceptions of justice that put them in the right, then negotiation will be more difficult and fighting more likely. Typically, each side does feel unjustly treated, whatever the original cause of the dispute.

A recent example is the conflict between the Hindus and Muslims in India over Babri Masjid, a mosque in Ayodhya, a small town in the northern state of Uttar Pradesh. According to Hindu nationalists, the mosque was built in 1528, when a Muslim king who conquered parts of India destroyed a Hindu temple at the same site. The Hindus claimed that this site was also the birthplace of the god Ram, one of the major Hindu deities, about 5,000 years ago. In recent years, the mosque was surrounded with a number of smaller temples and monuments associated with Ram and used for Hindu worship. Hindus have made many attempts to "liberate" the mosque, including one in 1948 in which some of them placed an image of Ram in the middle of it, at which time a court ordered the mosque to be padlocked. In 1984, a Hindu nationalist organization (the Vishwa Hindu Parishad [VHP], or World Hindu Council) called for another movement to liberate the mosque and rebuild the original temple, and they opened discussions with a Muslim group.[7]

Meanwhile, India was occupied with the divorce case of Shah Bano. In 1975, after 43 years of marriage, she and her husband, a lawyer, separated as a result of a dispute between their families over a piece of land. She continued the battle by going to court. Among other requests, she asked for support from her husband. The main issue in this claim was whether the Indian courts should honor Islamic law, which held that no payment was required (since divorced women were supposed to be cared for by their families and the community). The case was in the courts for 10 years. In 1985, the Indian Supreme Court ordered the husband to pay about $18 per month.

The decision was front-page news around all of India. It was noteworthy because the Indian constitution required a certain respect for Islamic law in disputes of this sort. The Chief Justice's opinion not only had attempted to interpret Islamic law — to the chagrin of the Muslim clergy, who thought that this was not the business of a secular court — but had also suggested that India should have a uniform civil code (as specified in the constitution, a provision that conflicted with the provision that required respect for Islamic law). n Reactions were strong on both sides. A prominent Muslim cleric said, "We don't recognize this decision. We will not accept such a direct interference with Moslem personal law."[8] A feminist writer said, "It is a dangerous trend when a minority community says it should be exempted from a Supreme Court judgment because of religion. A woman's right to claim redress before a court of law should not be compromised."[9] This decision, following after another court decision to remove the padlock from the Ayodhya mosque, led to Muslim riots throughout India.

Prime Minister Rajiv Gandhi was caught in a bind, both political and moral. Politically, he was worried about his Muslim support because of some earlier decisions he had made to send some Muslim refugees in Assam back to Bangladesh. Morally, he was caught between, on the one hand, the promotion of rights for women and the equal treatment that would result from a uniform civil law and, on the other hand, the protection of rights of minorities (i.e., Muslims) and the real fear of continued violence. Since the founding of modern India, the government had tried to maintain a secular law, with separation of state and religion, and also to recognize the rights of minorities, particularly Muslims, to follow their own traditions, especially in matters concerning families. At first, Gandhi sided with the court. Later, he changed his mind and supported a law to overturn the court's verdict. The law was passed, to the dismay of many of Gandhi's feminist supporters (and of some Muslims who favored a strong secular government).

One could imagine telling this story in the United States in a class on moral dilemmas. What should Gandhi have done? It is not the sort of decision that one could make confidently after a few seconds of thought, and an objective observer might sympathize with either choice. Yet it tore the nation apart, each side fully confident of its moral rightness. Of course, this was indeed a fundamental moral question concerning not just minority rights but also the rights of women and the role of the state in regulating family affairs. This is typical of modern violent conflict, as is the my-side bias that characterizes the arguments of those on opposing sides.

On December 6, 1992, a group of young men, part of a Hindu mob of about 100,000, defied police and destroyed the mosque with sledge hammers, crow bars, and their bare hands. The situation was ambiguous. Permission had been given for a demonstration, but the leaders said they lost control. Others said that they did too little to exert control. After the incident, Muslims retaliated against Hindu temples not only in India but also in Malaysia, Pakistan, Bangladesh, and England. Hindus retaliated against the Muslims with violent attacks. The incident has been central to recent Indian politics, with the Hindu nationalist party, the Bharatiya Janta Party (BJP), taking the side of the Hindu mob.

Much of the public debate, for years, had concerned the actual history of the site. The Muslims pointed to the existence of a mosque for hundreds of years (even though it had not been used since 1947). They, and secular moderates, disputed the Hindu claim that a Hindu temple there had been razed about 1528 by Muslims, and the claim that the god Ram had actually existed as a person. These claims were debated in court cases, mostly unresolved, and in academic literature, which defended alternative theories about almost everything: the original mosque was built in the 1400s, and not by the Muslim invaders; or Ram was born somewhere else in the town. But, to quote one commentator, "None of these appeals to fact seems to alter the minds of those who say it is the spot and hold that a temple once stood there."[10]

Except for their legal implications, the facts would seem to have little bearing on the moral dispute from a consequentialist point of view. It was clear that both sides had some claim to the land and that the facts were not clear enough to resolve the dispute in terms of any simple idea of property rights. In terms of people's feelings, the conflict was real, no matter what the scholars found. Intuitions about property and the status quo colluded with my-side bias and nationalism to produce conflict that was, for a while, irreconcilable. Each side thought that it was being treated unfairly.

Surprisingly, even the majority Hindus perceived unfairness: "What is this frustration that rankles in the minds of a considerable section of the Hindus? It is nothing but the growing conviction that the Government, the secular parties, the Press, and the elite are all the time pampering the Muslim . . . in the garb of secularism."[11] While Muslims think of themselves as a minority in India, whose rights are not fully respected, Hindu nationalists see Muslims as invaders, with India almost surrounded by Islamic countries, and with India one of the few countries in the world to resist an Islamic invasion.

The debate about fairness turned in part on questions of balance. Who did what to whom, and who is justified in attacking in order to restore balance? The answer to this question depends, of course, on how we count harms and on how far we look into the past. And the history of Hindu-Muslim conflict is bloody and long. Yvette C. Rosser, a graduate student at the University of Texas, interviewed Hindu Indians. She says,

> One tack taken by the secularist school and the central gov-
> ernment was to say that in ancient times Hindu kings had
> plundered Jain and Buddhist temples and built Hindu tem-
> ples on the ruins. Hindu Nationalists have commented at
> length about this accusation. In regards to this, Bhima [an
> informant] refers to the "ridiculous arguments brought for-
> ward by secularists that Hindus have destroyed temples (Bud-
> dhist), too. Turns out that in total there are 6 such cases and

all of them contentious." Bhima went on with his story saying that while "in Berkeley, I heard Shabana Azmi, a well
known Indian actress, using the argument, 'Well, Hindus have
destroyed some temples and Muslims have destroyed some.'
The idea being that the roles are the same. I pointed out to
her that comparing six contentious destructions and that too
for plundering, versus thousands, if not hundreds of thousands of destructions of Hindu temples by Muslims, is a bit
of a stretch. Guess what her response was? 'Well, I said some.
Some can be six or some can be ten thousand!' "[12]

Other arguments on both sides presented evidence of persecution
by the other side. It has a whole history. Here in this country, the majority
people are so much harassed. The policies of the Government are to
appease the Muslims for petty political gain."[13] Muslims compared the
mobs to modern German skinheads attacking foreigners and to Nazis
attacking Jews.

My-side bias is often accompanied by considerable emotion, as is
evident from the following BJP argument concerning the destruction of
the mosque in Ayodhya:

It is . . . outrageous that unscrupulous politicians who are responsible to bring India on the moral disaster and economic
bankruptcy, and armchair intellectuals who take pride in de-
nouncing everything Hindu, and mercenary scribes who continue to shout National shame . . . but close their eyes to
the worst kind of muslim [sic] communalism, and pontificate
Hindus to ignore and endure this in the name of tolerance,
completely overlook the sense of hurt of the Hindus, and
even justify the triggering of the riots after Dec. 6 by Muslims
all over India because they were angry at the destruction of
their "shrine." As though Hindus who have been feeling hu-
miliated, insulted, cheated, being treated as second class citizens, made refugees, made to flee from neighboring lands,
abused unjustly day in day out, termed communal for es-
pousing for national unity, and so on . . . DO NOT HAVE ANY
RIGHT TO BE ANGRY! WHAT HAPPENED ON DEC. 6 WAS THE
EXPRESSION OF THIS SUPPRESSED OUTRAGE OF CENTURIES.
IT WAS NOT A DESTRUCTION OF A "MOSQUE," IT WAS A SIG-
NAL THAT HINDU HAS AWOKEN FROM ITS CENTURIES OLD
SLUMBER AND WILL NOT TOLERATE ANY MORE INJUSTICE.
ENOUGH IS ENOUGH. PEOPLE HAVE TO LEARN TO LIVE IN
HARMONY WITH EACH OTHER, THIS CANNOT BE A ONE-
WAY STREET.[14]

Conclusion

The errors of my-side bias — selection and excessive weighting of favorable evidence and rejection of unfavorable evidence — are found in paranoid delusions, cults, fringe political ideologies, and warring nations and ethnic groups. These errors in thinking are typically obvious to everyone except those who engage in them. Yet we are all at risk for such thinking when the circumstances are ripe for it. Thousands of other examples illustrate my-side bias, overconfidence, and when moral issues are involved, violent conflict. Even in 1841, Charles Mackay described a number of "popular delusions," such as the Tulip mania in Holland in the seventeenth century, the persecution of witches, and various speculative financial frenzies. He attributed these to group influence. People, he said, "go mad in herds, while they only recover their senses slowly, and one by one."[15] Modern psychological research has found that such delusions do not require herd behavior. However, when many people convince themselves of the same overconfident belief, they reinforce each other, and when the belief inspires hatred and violence, they protect each other from their opponents and are thus emboldened to act.

If everyone thought in a way that was actively open-minded — a way that tries hard to see the other side's point of view, to look for counterarguments, for reasons to doubt — it seems likely that most violent conflicts would disappear. In questions of morality and politics, such thinking is particularly necessary because people do not experience the consequences of their intuitive judgments as quickly and surely as they do when these intuitions concern matters in which they have personal control.

A hopeful sign is that people differ in their tendency toward my-side bias.[16] Some people value looking at the other side, and they follow their own values when they evaluate arguments, so that they do not overvalue arguments that happen to agree with conclusions that they favor. Because people's values are involved — rather than some sort of biological limit on their abilities — education and culture may affect these values.

The world's great conflicts are a result of several forces, including conflicting interests, justified mistrust, and moral differences, as well as my-side bias. But these other factors may be harder to control. Rather than asking about the greatest cause of the problem, we might ask instead where we have our greatest leverage, and that may be in explaining to each other the value of actively open-minded thinking.

CHAPTER 6

Do No Harm

When one nation attacks another, plunders its resources, and kills its people, we think of that as an unmitigated harm. There is no excuse for it, and nations that engage in this are international outcasts at best. But when people in one nation merely let those in other nations suffer from poverty, disease, war, and hunger, little scorn or reprobation is forthcoming. This distinction between acts and omissions is understandable, but it is overdone.

Why do I say it is understandable? After all, national distinctions are just as arbitrary as those based on race and sex. Here is why. If acts and omissions do not differ in their effects, then we have no reason to distinguish them. But often they do differ because of the way in which institutions are set up, because of the lines of authority that people have drawn. Social custom, convention, and law dictate that certain decisions are to be made by certain people. We say that these people are "responsible" for the decision. At one extreme, national governments are responsible for certain decisions about their citizens. At the other extreme, individuals are responsible for certain decisions about their own lives. In the middle, decision-making authority is allocated in complex ways within institutions like corporations. Social groups differ in how they assign responsibilities.

If someone violates these lines of authority by doing something in someone else's domain, then the whole system of responsibility allocation is thereby weakened. Other people will be tempted to step across the same line. For example, the United Nations' invasion of Somalia created a precedent that was seen as weakening somewhat the power of national governments. Of course, Somalia had no such government, but

95

many other nations could be described in the same terms without too much exaggeration. At the other extreme, health professionals sometimes override the expressed desires of a patient on the grounds that anyone who expresses such desires (e.g., against treatment for an easily treatable condition) is incompetent to decide for himself. This weakens the "autonomy" of individuals, the authority that they are granted for making health decisions for themselves. In the middle, if one member of a company reports a problem occurring in another division to her own boss, that weakens the lines of authority for dealing with similar problems, even if the report helps to solve the problem.

Notice that these good acts — helping the people of a desperate nation, treating a sick patient, helping another division — have bad side effects. The harm from the side effects may be even greater than the benefit from the acts. Thus, these otherwise harmful omissions become excusable or even desirable because of their side effects. Harmful acts, by contrast, typically have no such compensating benefits. We are thus led to a distinction between acts and omissions. The distinction results from the conflicts that would arise if two people were responsible for the same decision.

Notice also that, in all of these examples, the bad effects of going outside of the line of authority are just bad effects to be weighed against other effects, not absolute prohibitions. Thus, intervention into the affairs of other nations, violations of individual autonomy, and reporting problems in another division are sometimes justified. Moreover, in some cases, the bad effects are not so bad. Arguably, some lines of authority *should* be weakened. Laws against child abuse may weaken the authority of parents over their children, but this kind of authority we do not need. If such laws weaken parental authority more generally, that may well be a price worth paying.

Against such arguments, people often raise the slippery-slope argument. Yes, it may be best in this case to violate the lines of authority, but that will set a precedent toward other such decisions, which will go too far. One answer to this slippery-slope argument is that the slope slips both ways. Allowing parents to beat their children, allowing people to starve because they have no government, and allowing people to die because they refuse helpful treatment, all in the name of preserving the lines of authority, can lead to further callousness, indifference, and suffering. Perhaps the best precedent is to make the best decision.

In sum, we have feelings about not being responsible for harm caused by our omissions, our failures to act. We have some reason for these feelings. Often we fail to act because our action would violate a line of authority. In other cases, though, we have no reason except our feeling, which — like all the feelings that distort decisions — takes on a life of its own. This intuition affects many of our attitudes, such as our reluctance to cause harm through vaccination, which I discussed at the beginning of this book. That example and others will come up again in later chapters. The rest of this chapter discusses opposition to reforms that have costs as well as benefits, such as the making of trade agreements.

Trade

Trade agreements such as the North American Free Trade Agreement (NAFTA) and the General Agreement on Tariffs and Trade (GATT) are complex, and their effects are complex. Expansion of free trade has costs and benefits. On the benefit side, first, are the basic economic arguments. Free trade increases consumer choice, allowing consumers the chance to buy what they prefer most; trade restrictions limit this choice. Thus, if a producer in country A can make something that will have a market in country B — because of either its uniqueness, its quality, or its price — the producer can do so and reap the rewards. Second, free trade is thought to prevent war among nations by creating a constituency against it. This may be the single most important argument. Any particular trade agreement may be unlikely to prevent some war, but a general regime of free trade may reduce the risk of war in general and thus reduce the enormous costs of preparing for war. Third, trade limits based on national borders seem morally arbitrary. Most of the arguments against expanded free trade among nations are just as relevant to contraction of free trade among states or provinces, but they are not applied in this way, possibly because of the status-quo bias.

On the cost side, expansion of trade (or failure to contract it) reduces local autonomy. In particular, it reduces the ability of local or national governments to regulate business. For example, if a country passes a law to make producers protect the rights of workers or the environment, producers in that country will lose sales to those in countries without such laws, so long as conforming to these laws raises the price of production. This would not happen if trade were restricted enough so that these producers did not compete with such foreign producers in any markets. Free trade thus forces governments to choose between local regulation and local prosperity, even more than would otherwise be the case. The laws that are involved include such things as minimum wage laws, which essentially require businesses to help in the redistribution of income. In principle, many of these effects could be overcome by different kinds of laws (e.g., use of the tax system to redistribute income, as opposed to minimum-wage laws) or by ceding more power to international governmental agencies, but these alternatives are just as controversial as the trade agreements themselves.

The imposition of *new* free-trade agreements also creates lots of short-term harm. As competition increases, jobs are lost. In theory, the net effect of free trade on jobs is not very great, but the short-term effects involve real pain, and a regimem of constantly expanding trade over a long period causes repeated jolts to specific groups.

I do not intend to settle here the question of whether the benefits exceed the costs. Rather, my concern is with the way that trade questions are framed in national debate. As in the case of immigration, very little attention is given to the effects on noncitizens. Again, there are exceptions. In the NAFTA debate, the issue was the encouragement of bad environmental practices in Mexico. In the GATT debate, it was the question of whether the United States could ban the products of child labor. These considerations were not, however, weighed against potential benefits of free trade for the poor in other countries.

Trade agreements help some people and hurt others. People think that this is wrong even when they judge the harm to be less than the benefit. My own results find that people who oppose trade agreements think this way. They worry more about the harm from acting than that from not acting. This is a particular problem when the harm from not acting affects people of other nations. People think of them as outside of their zone of responsibility.

Reduction of trade barriers against poor countries is one way to promote their development. If the reduction is reciprocal, then it becomes politically feasible. Reduction of trade barriers does not interfere with the national lines of authority of those who are helped. One country can reduce its barriers even without reciprocal reductions from other countries. If it refuses to do so unless others also reduce their barriers too, that still does not violate the autonomy of the others. This is how negotiations work. Of course, this is a complex issue. Even if a given trade agreement is a net improvement over the status quo, we might do more good by holding out for another agreement that is better still. (But we'd better watch out for the utopian fallacy.)

It appears, however, that some of the U.S. opponents of the recent North American Free Trade Agreement (NAFTA) were opposed to it primarily because they made an intuitive distinction between acts and omissions. Accepting the agreement was an act that would harm some people, especially Americans. They did not want to be a party to such harm. Of course, once this view was adopted, the usual wishful thinking set in, and people accepted arguments that they would not otherwise have accepted. For example, many believed that the agreement would really do more harm than good, despite the fact that practically all expert opinion said otherwise. Or they thought that rejecting the agreement could lead to a better agreement, again going against expert opinion.

To examine opinions about NAFTA, I carried out two questionnaire studies. One questionnaire was given to 44 university students in the weeks just before the U.S. Congress voted on the NAFTA in late 1993, and one was given to 53 students in the weeks just after the vote. These questionnaires examined both the act-omission distinction and the question of responsibility to foreigners.[1] Although slightly more subjects favored NAFTA than opposed it, most subjects had no strong opinion. On whether it would help or hurt employment in the United States and in Mexico, a majority thought that it would help on the whole, in the long run.

One of the items dealing with acts vs. omissions asked: "Suppose that a trade agreement would cause 10,000 job losses in the U.S. but prevent 11,000 job losses in the U.S. over the same time period. (The jobs would be of the same type.) The agreement would have no other economic effects. Would you favor such an agreement? Why or why not? (In this case and all other cases, imagine that there is no doubt about these predictions. . . .)"

Although less than a third of the subjects opposed this hypothetical agreement, these subjects also tended to be NAFTA opponents. This result suggests that some of the opposition to NAFTA was based on the do-no-harm heuristic, the intuitive distinction between acts and omissions. Even those who may have otherwise admitted that NAFTA would increase employment in the United States were reluctant to hurt some people in order to benefit others.

Most justifications for "oppose" responses showed clear evidence of the do-no-harm heuristic: "No, because you would be giving someone else a job at your expense. Everyone has a fair share to their jobs." "No, because 10,000 jobs would be lost even though 11,000 would be saved." "No, because you still lose 10,000 jobs!" A few answers showed a simpler form of the bias toward omission, in which the default was favored in the absence of a very strong reason to change: "No. It basically cancels itself out, so what's the point?" "You would only save 100 jobs."

Several subjects tried to rationalize their response by adding information not stated in the question, such as the possibility of better agreements or the possibility that the prevention of 11,000 job losses was uncertain (although the loss of 10,000 was certain). "[No] because of the job losses . . . . There are other ways of dealing with the problem." "I don't support job losses for any reason. I would much sooner find another way to prevent the 11,000 jobs from being lost." "No, because 10,000 job losses is no comparison to 11,000 *prevented* job losses. There is no guarantee that that 11,000 would lose their jobs [without the agreement]." Of course, the subjects were instructed to take things at face value. The last subject quoted did this only when the given information supported his conclusion. He questioned the job gains, but not the job losses, although both were presented as equally certain. When people want their conclusion to be right, they will make things up to support their view.

A question about nationalism asked: "Suppose that a trade agreement would cause job gains in Mexico and job losses in the U.S., and no other effects. The gains in Mexico would be 10 times the losses in the U.S.

The jobs in question would mean just as much to the Mexican workers as to the U.S. workers. Would you favor such an agreement?"

Over three quarters of the subject opposed this agreement. Subjects who opposed this hypothetical agreement also tended to oppose NAFTA itself. Most of the opposition came from outright, admitted, nationalistic bias: "No, because U.S. jobs are being taken away from the U.S. workers and more people will be unemployed in the U.S." "No, because we should not enter an agreement where we lose jobs." "Absolutely not. The purpose of American government is to provide protection . . . for its citizens. While the reasoning may sound selfish and isolationist, American economic policy should protect American workers . . . . Any sacrifice of American workers, no matter what the benefit in Mexico, cannot be accepted. We must still protect ourselves and not always try to be the world's policemen and guardian." "No, because, for me, Americans are far more than 10 times more important than Mexicans." This response, and a couple of others like it, remind me of Rabbi Yaacov Perrin's statement in his eulogy for Dr. Baruch Goldstein, who was beaten to death after killing 40 Palestinian worshipers: "One million Arabs is not worth a Jewish fingernail."[2] Of course, that is an extreme view on the continuum of nationalistic sentiment.

A few subjects raised more general questions of fairness: "No — there should be an equal gain by both countries involved in the agreement or some gain by both countries." "No, because one country would benefit while another suffers." "No. I don't think it is just to offer so many jobs to one country's people at the expense of another."

A few other subjects raised questions of responsibility: "No, . . . because they should be responsible for their own jobs." "No, it's not the U.S.'s responsibility to provide jobs for Mexico." "No, because the U.S. can't afford to lose no more jobs. They need to help themselves." Such arguments are more easily understood as applications of a simple heuristic of limited responsibility than as an application of the utilitarian argument for national lines of authority.

Subjects who favored the agreement usually did so on grounds of best overall consequences: "Thinking globally, or about the *whole* picture, yes, the agreement would be better. This is because more people would have jobs." "Yes. Here I see the larger continent or world as a general welfare unit." A few of these subjects, however, favored the agreement because of side effects such as reduced immigration from Mexico to the United States.

An additional series of questions followed up the question about nationalism. The questions were roughly ordered so as to increase the level of challenge to the opponents of the hypothetical agreement. First, subjects were asked: "Do you think that such an agreement would be better on the whole?" Many subjects who had opposed the agreement favoring Mexico thought that it *would* be better on the whole, so that opinion was about equally divided as to whether the agreement was better on the whole or not. Many of the nationalistic subjects were therefore admittedly ignoring their own views of the best consequences.

Most subjects who said that the agreement was not better took "better on the whole" to mean "better for both nations"– for example, "I think it would be better for the Mexicans, who would have a major increase in the employment rate and probably a boom in their economy. However, I don't think it would benefit the U.S. at all. So I don't think it would be better on the whole." Those who thought the agreement was better on the whole were about equally divided between those who simply referred to the greater number of jobs and those who referred to beneficial side effects. Some subjects (counted as neither agreeing nor disagreeing) were unwilling to make a holistic judgment based on a loss to some and a gain to others — for example, "Would be better for who[m]? It would be better for the families with the additional income, but what about the families where the job was lost?" "Maybe for the Mexicans it would benefit but for us we would be at a loss." If we are going to make decisions on the basis of consequences, then we will have to be willing to balance consequences against each other.

The next follow-up question asked about morality: "Do you think that it would be morally better to accept such an agreement or reject it?" Again, subjects were about equally divided on this point, and again, many subjects who had originally opposed the agreement thought that it was more moral, so their initial opposition went against their own moral judgment as well as against their judgments of overall consequences.

Most subjects who thought morality favored the agreement based their responses on the total number of jobs in both countries — for example, "Morality demands that we accept such a deal. Any other course of action would suggest that an American's desires are up to 10 times more important than a Mexican's." Many people do reason in terms of consequences.

Subjects had a great variety of reasons for thinking that the agreement was immoral, however, for example, "Accepting it would be insensitive to the suffering of those who would lose their jobs." "For me, it wouldn't be morally better because I would feel responsible for the loss of jobs to hardworking Americans." "Reject it because, although you may be helping others with the creating of more jobs, you would hurt the ones who have lost jobs, which is wrong." "Of course it would be morally better to help ten Mexicans at the expense of one American, but I think that this country has a duty to look out for the interests of its citizens first." "Reject. We must look out for the U.S.A. first." "We should look out for ourselves." "Mexicans are losing nothing but gaining jobs. Americans are losing jobs but gaining nothing. Fair, right? WRONG!" "Reject it because, by accepting it, problems would be created in the U.S. (more unemployment)." "Absolutely not . . . . The U.S. was created by U.S. citizens. They have a moral right to exist for themselves and not be an altruistic sacrifice for any and all people with wants." Notice that some of these reasons referred to obligations of a presumed decision maker rather than overall consequences. The subjects were therefore not answering the question as given. Instead, they were answering the earlier question about whether they, as Americans, would support the agreement.

No justifications simply asserted that U.S. citizens counted more than Mexicans. (Nor did any justification clearly say this in response to the previous question.) It appears, then, that nationalistic bias is morally based on specific obligations of citizens and political leaders rather than on inherent moral worth. Some subjects gave answers for both roles — for example, "In terms of the constituents you represent, no. In terms of the world . . . , accept it." Political leaders may well have a line of authority that requires them to look out for their constituents first, but it is more difficult to see why citizens, as individuals, should also have this commitment. If they do, who looks out for effects on people in other nations? People may confuse themselves with the leaders they elect in terms of their responsibilities.

The next follow-up asked: "If you were living in a third country, neither Mexico nor the U.S., would you favor the agreement or oppose it?" More than three quarters now favored the agreement, thus admitting that opposition to it was not based on an impartial perspective of the sort that morality requires. The strong approval of the agreement here supports the view that most opposition is role-specific (or what philosophers call agent-relative).

The next follow-up presented subjects with an analogy: "Suppose that all the jobs created were in one state of the U.S. and all the jobs lost were in another state of the U.S. There would be ten times as many jobs created as lost, and no other effects." Most subjects rejected the analogy — for example, "The boundaries between states are very different than borders between countries." One subject accepted the analogy: "This agreement would hurt Pennsylvania, but it would greatly help the economy of the whole country, so I would support it. I realize the implications of this last question, and it makes a valid point: If different countries could work together and look out for the benefits of the whole world, as the states of America are united, then everyone would benefit."

The opposition that existed was based on the do-no-harm principle and on fairness: "I would oppose it. . . . I don't think one should gain from the loss of others." "Oppose it. The job employment should be dispersed." "Things have to be kept *even*." "It wouldn't be fair for the state with the job losses while the state with the job gains flourished." "It doesn't seem fair to put one state in jeopardy for the benefit of another."

A final question asked, "Suppose that all the jobs created and all the jobs lost were in the same state of the U.S. There would be ten times as many jobs created as lost, and no other effects. Would you favor such an agreement or oppose it?" Eighty-one percent of the subjects now supported the agreement. The remaining opposition was based mostly on the do-no-harm principle — "Oppose it because it would hinder some people."

In sum, some of the opposition to free-trade agreements seems to come from two intuitions: that we ought to favor our own nation in making decisions, and that we ought to weigh the harm from action more heavily than the harm from omission. Both of these intuitions lead to departures from the results of thinking in terms of consequences alone. Notice that subjects had opinions about consequences. It might have been even simpler for them to form their attitudes solely on the basis of these opinions, without having to add their intuitions into the balance. The role of intuitions in this case is not an obvious way to simplify thinking; quite the opposite.

The situation just described illustrates an advantage of thinking in terms of consequences from the outset. Such thinking can sometimes direct our attention toward facts that can be used as a basis for such decisions, such as predictions of total employment. Such predictions can, of course, be incorrect, but they are typically just as likely to be incorrect one way as the other. Our intuitive principles will, in such cases, lead us in the correct direction only if we are lucky. Moreover, when we find intuitive principles on both sides, we have no way of weighing them. Predictions of consequences sometimes give us simpler criteria, each of which combines several concerns into a single number.

Opposition to Reform

Trade agreements, if they are beneficial on the whole, are reforms. Reforms are social rules that improve matters on the whole. Other examples of reforms are the institution of motor-vehicle laws, the regulation of drugs, the granting of rights to women and repressed minorities, the recent deregulation of markets in Communist countries, and on a smaller scale, countless minor changes in rules and traditions within smaller institutions such as schools and businesses.

Reforms hurt some people and help others. If they are truly reforms, then the benefits outweigh the harms. These reforms run afoul of the do-no-harm principle. Most reforms are not just actions, as opposed to omissions. They also change the status quo. Thus, two intuitions work together: one that opposes harms from action (as compared to harms from omission) and one that opposes harms that result from changes in the status quo (as compared to harms that result from failing to change). In principle, action might be required to keep the status quo, so that the status-quo bias and the bias toward omissions would pull for different choices, but this rarely happens, especially in the case of reforms.

Some reforms also decrease the options available to some people, and these are coercive. These reforms also run afoul of intuitions concerning autonomy. People often express their support for autonomy in terms of "rights." Most rights are options that cannot be taken away by someone else. Thus, support of a right is an expression of support for autonomy in some domain.

Reforms may also be opposed because they are unfair, because the benefits are not distributed according to whatever principle of fair distribution is favored. We have seen this in the case of opposition to fishing regulations and, to some extent, in opposition to trade agreements, although the unfairness was also seen as harm relative to the status quo.

To look for these intuitions, James Jurney and I presented subjects with six hypothetical reforms, and we asked the subjects whether they would vote for or against each reform.[3] The reforms were:

1. A ban on campaign advertising on TV (to reduce the influence of big money)

2. A law requiring everyone to be vaccinated (in order to end a serious flu epidemic)

3. A college rule requiring all students to be tested for a bacterial infection and, if they are positive, use mouthwash five times per day (in order to stop an epidemic)

4. A no-fault automobile insurance law (limit lawsuits in order to lower rates)

5. A ban on suing obstetricians (to reduce the decline in their numbers)

6. A 100% tax on carbon-based fuels (oil, gasoline, coal, and natural gas; to reduce global warming that results from burning them)

We also asked whether each reform would improve matters on the whole. That is, we asked subjects to judge the situation from a utilitarian perspective. For each reform we asked about, many subjects said that they would vote against it and that it did no good on the whole, and others said that they would vote for it and that it would improve matters on the whole. Some subjects also said that they thought it would improve matters on the whole, but they would still not vote for it. For example, in one study, 39% of subjects said they would vote for a 100% tax on gasoline (item 6), but 48% of those who would vote *against* the tax thought that it would do more good than harm on the whole. Why did they still vote against such proposals?

When we asked subjects this, they almost always referred to one or more of the intuitions just mentioned: do-no-harm, autonomy and rights, and fairness. Here are some examples of responses from subjects who said that they would oppose a proposal even though the proposal would do more good than harm (with the number in parentheses indicating the proposal).

Harm Arguments

- Though it has overall good effects, this law would leave many people helplessly stranded if suddenly they could not afford to buy gas, or buses were forced to stop running because of this new tax. (6)

- Although the vaccine will reduce the chance of getting the flu . . . and possible death, by passing the law we accept the possibility that a few will die . . . for the good of the rest. That is not a power of passing a law — control over the welfare of a person's life. Welfare yes, but not at the expense of others. It would do more good than harm but why [not] let the flu choose who will die. (2)

- If this particular law is passed, costs *would* go down, which would make many patients happy, but not those whose child was delivered with some type of birth injury. (5)

- On the whole our environment will be helped and industries, businesses, etc. will be forced to change their energy sources. On the other hand, new energy sources can be expensive and less efficient. Limiting the availability of petroleum, natural gas, and coal could also diminish the progress of modern production and development. (6)

- Ideally, this would be better for the earth and its inhabitants for the future. But this is too drastic. Some people cannot afford the alternative energy sources. (6)

Rights Arguments

- I would not vote for the rule because it is not simply a case of harm or good but there is also a moral question, and a question of constitutionality in relation to privacy. Is it right to make someone take a test in which they will then be told that they have a disease if they don't want to know? The person might feel that they will suffer some ridicule if they are known to be infected, or he or she might somehow feel less of himself. It is one thing to have everyone be vaccinated against something, but in this case you are singling out certain individuals. I'm not sure I agree with this. If this example was in reference to a harsher disease such as something that was fatal like AIDS or cancer, I might be willing to overlook this issue of singling out and treating certain people differently. (3)

- It should . . . be the candidates' individual choices whether they want to spend the money for TV ads regardless of the success rate. (1)

- Those who are deserving of a larger settlement would not even have the opportunity to get it. We can't compromise the rights of the minority. (4)

- People cannot be compelled to do things they don't want to in order to prevent sickness in others. (3)

- It is not the right of the government to impose laws which could cause bodily damage for the sake of the whole. (2)

- While it would prevent the mudslinging campaigns, I don't believe in limiting the freedoms of the candidates. (1)

- The reason is because you can't infringe on others' rights and force them to do something. If they were smart, or conscientious, they would follow the rule. (3 — with wishful thinking?)

Fairness Arguments

- I wouldn't vote for it because it favors the affluent, who would not mind the tax increase as much as the penurious. (6)

- Totally unfair to such countries whose livelihood depends upon oil and natural fuels. (6)

- The right to sue should not be eliminated, as a case the truly merited suing would not be able to go through [if the right were eliminated]. (4)

- If I was in a very bad accident my hospital and doctor bills and various other bills may be more than what the limit will allow for settlements. Therefore I would not get what I truly deserve for my pain and suffering. My settlement might end up being the same as a person who had a less serious accident. (4)

- The injured victim of an accident should get what he or she deserves and not have to "settle" for the law's settlement rates. (4)

Conclusion

This study illustrates how intuitions can lead to worse outcomes. The cases in question were those in which subjects would oppose reforms that they themselves thought would produce better outcomes on the whole. In real-life cases like these the same thing may happen, and people may be correct in thinking that the proposals are beneficial on the whole. In other cases, the effect observed here may be only the tip of an iceberg, the rest submerged by my-side bias and belief overkill. When people have a moral objection to some proposal — such as the fact that it causes harm, that it is unfair, or that it violates autonomy — they may then convince themselves that, in fact, it is not beneficial on the whole. Thus, without the intuitions in question, even more people may think that some proposals are better on the whole.

This may have happened with trade agreements. People who initially opposed these agreements on moral grounds, such as unfairness or harm, may have looked for evidence that the proposals were in fact harmful on the whole. The economics of trade is complex, so it is possible to construct such arguments. Whether these arguments are correct is not the point. Rather, the way in which people reached their conclusions would have led them to the same conclusions regardless of the evidence about the effect of trade agreements on overall consequences. When people think like this, they are likely to produce outcomes that do not lead to the greatest overall good.

The study thus illustrates that people sometimes admit what many, more often, will not admit: that their intuitions, played out in the public domain, cause harm, perhaps even to others who do not share those intuitions. In some abstract sense, these intuitions may be "correct." Certainly they have their defenders, even among philosophers. But we still pay a price for honoring them. Their defenders do not argue that these intuitions are justified by the consequences of following them. The price for them is admitted. My point is that we should demand the reasons that we should pay this price, and we should not simply try to convince ourselves that it does not exist.

Note, again, that these intuitions are not there because they simplify decision making. In the cases discussed in this chapter, people who think only in terms of consequences have an easier time than those who try to balance consequences against other intuitions. Nobody ignores consequences completely.

An interesting variant of the "harm" response to the proposal to ban suits against obstetricians is this: "From a utilitarian point of view — that is, 'on the whole' — it must be said that, generally, more obstetrician availability is both good and necessary under the given conditions and, therefore, the law would do more good than harm. As a prospective parent, however, greed (for safety) and love in anticipation for my child would require me to [oppose the law] just in case there was malpractice to my particular child (money needed, in this event, for health care, special upbringing, etc.)." The increased availability of obstetricians is something that also benefits prospective parents. Prospective parents face both the benefit and the harm of the proposed law. This subject seems to think that the benefit outweighs the harm from a social perspective, but not from an individual perspective, when thinking about risk. In the next chapter, we will focus on what risk entails and how we think about it.

CHAPTER 7

Risk

Risk makes decisions difficult just because, by the nature of risk, the outcome is uncertain. When patients decide whether to have risky surgery, for example, they like to think that there is a right answer to whether they should have it or not. But, in a sense, the real answer will come after the surgery is performed and we know whether it succeeded or failed. The same with investments, or, more to the point here, governmental decisions about permitting new technologies or regulating old ones. When a spaceship blows up or a new wonder drug turns out to have awful side effects, it is easy to say that someone made a mistake. If, however, we knew what the decision maker knew, we might agree with the decision.

Such difficulties as these make decisions under risk particularly prone to intuitive thinking. But if we can think about risks in a quantitative way, as if we made the decision by weighing the positive and negative effects of each possible outcome in proportion to its probability, we can balance the possible outcomes and decide accordingly. This quantitative way of thinking about risk has the advantage of producing the best outcomes over the long run. Occasionally, we will experience bad outcomes, but quantitative thinking can minimize their frequency and severity or, at least, make sure that they are compensated by good outcomes. Quantitative thinking about risk is difficult, however. It is more difficult than weighing cost and benefits when risk is absent, and it is more difficult than relying on intuition. So when risk is present, we tend to rely more on intuitions. Take, for example, our strong intuition that we should avoid doing harm. The less quantitative our thinking, and the more we are induced to focus on bad events, the more we try to

109

avoid harm at all costs — even when the probability that such harm will occur is slim.

Decisions about risks are made by individuals and governments. They involve avoiding risk by taking (or mandating) safety precautions, taking (or imposing) risks in order to get some benefit, and mitigating the effects of risks — after harm has occurred — through insurance or lawsuits. This chapter will look at some of these decisions, but the topic is immense, so it, like other chapters, will look at a few snapshots rather than a complete map of the terrain.

A Case of Risk: Drugs and Vaccines

The approval of new drugs in the United States is the responsibility of the Food and Drug Administration (FDA). Many other governments, such as India's, base their own approval decisions in part or entirely on those of this agency. Thus, advocates of birth control in poor countries were elated when the FDA approved Depo-Provera as an injectable contraceptive for American women. Although very few Americans were expected to use it, it suddenly became available in India, where it could have had considerable use.[1]

The powers of the FDA to assess efficacy as well as safety were increased substantially in 1962, after the discovery that the tranquilizer thalidomide caused birth defects when taken during pregnancy, typically in the form of limbs that were absent or incomplete. Thalidomide had been approved in Europe, but the FDA never approved it in the United States, because of questions having nothing to do with potential birth defects. It was never tested for its effect on birth defects, the FDA did not request such tests, and if it had been tested on animals, no effect would have been found. The effects occurred in humans but not in guinea pigs or mice. But the disturbing picture of "thalidomide babies" increased public support for the FDA, and Congress increased the powers of FDA to efficacy as well as safety. Usually the safety tests are done first, but the entire process is now quite long and expensive. The effective anticancer drug Taxol required nine years of human tests for approval, which began only after six years of tests in the laboratory. The FDA's review process alone typically can take more than a year, after all the research results are submitted. The difficulty of getting approval discourages the development of new drugs in the United States and increases the cost of drugs because companies must pay for the necessary research.

The American public has generally supported such a policy because, in part, it regards harmful acts as worse than harmful omissions, especially when the harm in the latter case can be blamed on "nature." Steven B. Harris, an internist interested in drug issues, put it well:

Politically, the FDA comes under severe pressure for passing a drug which is later shown to be unsafe, but (in an unbalanced way) comes in for much less political pressure as regards the equally dangerous failure to swiftly pass a drug which proves to be efficacious. This lack of balance results from the fact that patients who die as the result of a drug-reaction are seen to die because of the drug, but patients who die as the result of lack of a drug (especially one which the local docs are not familiar with) are seen to die of the *disease*. Even if the local doctor understands the FDA's role in preventing the patient from being properly treated, "Stenosis of the Government" is not a medical diagnosis, and cannot be written on a Death Certificate.[2]

In recent years, the FDA has become more sensitive to the concerns of dying patients, particularly AIDS patients, who are — quite reasonably — not very concerned with small safety risks if a drug might prolong their lives. The FDA will allow an unsafe drug to be marketed if the disease it cures is much worse than the harm it causes. But it would bring about more total good if the balance between causing and preventing harm were considered from the outset. Such a policy is prevented by people's feelings that causing harm is worse than failing to prevent it — the omission bias.

Another classic case of omission bias — the do-no-harm intuition at work — is vaccination. One example is the vaccine for pertussis, a bacterial infection that causes whooping cough and that can cause infants and toddlers. Pertussis is the "P" in "DPT," a commonly used combination vaccine that immunizes babies against diphtheria and tetanus as well. Some governments have not required pertussis vaccination in any form because it causes serious side effects and perhaps even death in a tiny fraction of a percent of children vaccinated. The officials responsible feel that the harm from requiring the vaccine is worse than the harm from doing nothing, even if the latter leads to more disease and death.

Before the DPT vaccine, about 7,000 children died each year from whooping cough caused by pertussis infection.[3] The death rate from whooping cough is now less than 100 per year. (Many children are still not fully vaccinated.) Despite this record of success, people do not like the idea of causing a disease with a vaccine. When a few cases of brain damage apparently caused by DPT vaccine were reported in England and Japan in the mid 1970s, requirements for vaccination lapsed and many children were not vaccinated.[4] In Great Britain, rates of vaccination fell from 79% in 1971 to 37% in 1974. A two-year epidemic that followed killed 36 people. The epidemic ended when vaccination rates increased. Similar epidemics occurred in Japan, also involving 30 to 40 deaths per year.[5]

Another example is polio. In the United States, people who contracted polio from the polio vaccine or who developed disabilities around the time of DPT vaccination began to sue the manufacturers. As a result of lawsuits, research on new vaccines declined, even while millions throughout the world still suffer and die from infectious diseases that may be preventable.[6] Companies stopped making vaccines that were targets of lawsuits. By 1986, only one company was left making DPT vaccine, Lederle, and the price had gone from less than a dollar per shot to more than 10 dollars in a few years, with most of the increase put aside to pay liability claims.[7] In that year, the U.S. Congress passed the National Childhood Vaccine Injury Compensation Act, which has stabilized the situation by providing a fund for limited compensation.

Two polio vaccines are available. The original Salk vaccine uses a killed virus. It is much less effective than the Sabin oral vaccine, which uses a live virus. The Sabin vaccine, the one generally used, is the one that sometimes causes polio. Nobody ever sued the makers of the Salk vaccine for failing to prevent polio, but many people have sued the makers of the Sabin vaccine for causing polio. Both results — causing and failing to prevent — are inherent properties of the vaccine. They cannot be avoided by more care in manufacturing or in any other way. It is clear that a suit against the Salk vaccine would be a waste of time. No judge or jury would take it seriously. But people have won suits against the Sabin vaccine. Some people still advocate going back to the Salk vaccine even though it is less effective.[8]

Many people think this is a mistake. They think — along with most pediatricians — that the Sabin vaccine should be used because the number of cases of polio is less. If you are one of those, imagine that you are a child and that you will get one of two vaccines. You know that, with one vaccine, you face a 4% chance of getting polio. (Suppose there is an epidemic.) With another vaccine, your risk is 1%. Which would be better for you? Clearly the 1% risk. Now you find that the 1% risk is from the vaccine itself and the 4% is because the vaccine fails. Would this change your answer to the question of which is best for you? It is difficult to see how it could. Your good depends on your ability to make use of your life, and this depends on the length of your life and the state of your health.

The distinction between harm caused by action and harm caused by inaction is built into various laws that affect pharmaceuticals. For example, California has a law requiring warning labels on anything that causes cancer — at least anything that is made by people. Tamoxifen is a drug that seems to reduce the risk of breast cancer, and research to test this preventive effect has begun. The drug seems also to increase the risk of cancer of the endometrium of the uterus. The beneficial effect on breast cancer is apparently many times greater than the harmful effect on endometrial cancer, so we can think of Tamoxifen as something that decreases the risk of cancer overall. However, the scientific panel that decides what is to be listed as a carcinogen in California felt that it had to include Tamoxifen. The result may be that a large experiment to measure the overall effects will not get done. The experiment's sponsors fear that the warning — which will emphasize the risk beyond the usual information about risks that all participants must get — will scare women away from participating.[9]

As a final example of the do-no-harm heuristic applied to pharmaceuticals, consider estrogen replacement therapy for menopause. Estrogen is a hormone with many effects, one of which is to regulate the menstrual cycle. When women reach the age of about 50, they produce less estrogen. Along with the gradual cessation of menstruation come many other symptoms, such as hot flashes and reduced sexual function. These symptoms can be reduced by giving estrogen supplements, essentially the same chemical as the active ingredient in birth-control pills. Estrogen also affects the risk of other conditions. When taken over a long period, it reduces the loss of bone tissue — osteoporosis — that often leads to fractures in older women; the complications of such fractures, especially hip fractures, are a frequent cause of death. It reduces heart disease and hardening of the arteries, which also cause death. And it reduces colon cancer and colon-cancer deaths. However, it seems to increase the risk of breast cancer and cancer of the endometrium (lining) of the uterus.[10]

Some of the benefits, particularly those on heart and arterial disease and on colon cancer, are fairly recent discoveries. In the 1970s, the main issue seemed to be the tradeoff between osteoporosis and endometrial cancer. Even though the increase in endometrial cancer was on the order of 400%, this risk was tiny because this kind of cancer is extremely rare. (400% of very little is still very little.) Osteoporosis is common, however, so that on the basis of these two factors alone, estrogen replacement would still be expected to reduce the death rate of older women and thus to prolong their lives. Still, even though most gynecologists were familiar with these results, they did not routinely recommend estrogen replacement to their patients, and major organizations did not recommend that they do so. This may have been because of the fear of harm through action. The increase in endometrial cancer was caused by recommending the therapy, but continued high risk of fractures was caused only by doing nothing.[11]

Bias toward the natural might be involved here. "For many women there is something fundamentally disturbing about turning a natural event like menopause into a disease that demands decades of medication. . . 'Why fight vainly to remain in a stage of life you can't be in anymore, instead of enjoying the stage you are in?' asks Dr. Nada Stotland, 51, a hormone-replacement-therapy dropout."[12] And ordinarily it is indeed better to let nature take its course, when all else is equal. In matters of health or biology, evolution has created a complex system that works fairly well; nature has had a lot of time to get the bugs out. However, that argument cannot apply to this case. Evolution has essentially no influence at all over what happens to women after menopause, exactly because they do not reproduce. If some women live longer than others at this point, they have no chance at all of passing on their desirable traits selectively to their offspring.

As it turns out, the effect of estrogen on endometrial cancer can be eliminated by adding progesterone in a monthly cycle (thus maintaining menstrual periods). This may reduce some of the other benefits, but it is now standard practice. Moreover, with the discovery of other benefits — despite the discovery that the benefits for osteoporosis were not as great as once thought — most gynecologists now favor recommending estrogen replacement to most or all of their patients. Still, though, many women do not take estrogen. One of the major concerns they cite is the increased risk of breast cancer. Even if this risk is as high as the highest estimates suggest, estrogen is still beneficial on the whole. It slightly increases life expectancy, and the diseases that it prevents are just as unpleasant as breast cancer. (The latest evidence suggests that while estrogen makes breast cancer more likely, the type of cancer involved does not cause death as often, so estrogen has almost no effect on mortality.[13]

Critics of estrogen typically point to the risks without attempting to weigh them against the benefits. A simple number that combines many of the effects is life expectancy, which is apparently increased by estrogen. Here is an example of how thinking about consequences can lead to simplicity, although the simplicity is only partial here. Effects on quality of life are relevant, too.

Sometimes the critics engage in belief overkill and wishful thinking. Dr. Susan Love, a prominent breast surgeon who opposes estrogen replacement (perhaps because her profession has put her in a position to see the most negative effect), has even distorted the facts, apparently through misreading. Love argued that breast cancer was three times more common than heart disease in women under 75, so (by implication) these women would be more affected by the increased risk of breast cancer than by the reduction in heart disease. Apparently Love read the statistics almost exactly backward; the risk of heart disease is three times as great as that of breast cancer for this group.[14]

Love also argues that the risks of heart disease and osteoporosis can be reduced through other means, such as exercise. This is true, but the benefits of estrogen are at least as great in those who exercise as in those who do not. This may illustrate another sort of intuition: if you do something to solve a problem, then the need for another solution is reduced. Although this is often true, it is not true here.

Estrogen replacement is yet another case where the do-no-harm principle and perhaps the bias toward nature — abetted by wishful thinking, my-side bias, and belief overkill — have slowed the adoption of a beneficial new technology.

The Public versus the Experts

In the early 1980s — before the massive explosion of the Chernobyl nuclear power plant in the Soviet Union — college students and members of the League of Women Voters in the United States were asked about the risks of various activities and technologies.[15] They rated nuclear power as the most risky, but experts rated it as 20th out of 30 items, behind railroads and commercial aviation. The Chernobyl disaster undoubtedly did nothing to reduce public fears of nuclear power plants around the world, despite expert assurances that such an explosion was extremely unlikely in any other countries (because other nuclear power plants are better constructed and have many safety features lacking in Chernobyl).

This difference between public and expert views has been ascribed to differences in the way in which the two groups think about risk. Experts tend to think of risk as what you get when you multiply the probability of a bad outcome times some measure of its badness, such as the number of people who die. Although hundreds of people, perhaps thousands, were killed by the Chernobyl explosion, the annual probability of such a disaster elsewhere is — according to the experts — very small. Commercial aviation is more dangerous in the United States because it is nearly certain that many people, perhaps hundreds, will die in plane crashes each year.

The public, on the other hand, tends to define risk in terms of other qualities aside from the expected or average number of fatalities per year. These other qualities include "dread," the potential for catastrophe, lack of control, and the feeling that we don't really know what the risk is. Airplane passengers know they are taking a risk, and if they are scared enough they can avoid flying. People have little control, however, over radiation produced by a power plant. And estimates of the risks must be based on subjective judgment rather than on years of experience and actual statistics. The same feelings apply to new technologies such as genetic engineering of foods. These feelings of uncertainty make it more difficult to think quantitatively about risk, so people fall back more on their do-no-harm intuition.

It seems that these feelings work themselves through the political process. Nuclear power plants are heavily regulated. When the first ones were designed, many people thought that electricity from them would be so inexpensive that the power companies would not need to charge for it. But conforming to safety regulations has now made them more expensive than alternative sources of electricity. The level of regulation is so stringent that most extra expenditures on safety would save additional lives only at a cost of hundreds of millions of dollars for each life saved.[16] This estimate may be slightly biased, but it was made at a time when a life could be saved for a couple of hundred thousand dollars through improved highway safety in the United States or for less than $200 through childhood vaccination in poor countries.

Concerns about nuclear power are ongoing, but other risks seem to have their 15 minutes of fame. For example, articles about teenage suicide appeared suddenly in United States newspapers in 1984. Although the suicide rate had been steady before that, it increased slightly the following year, perhaps because of the articles themselves. Meanwhile, news coverage fell off.[17]

Often these spurts of public concern last long enough to lead to legislation. The discovery of a buried chemical waste dump in a residential development called Love Canal led to the Superfund law in the U.S., a massive piece of legislation designed to reduce hazardous waste and clean up what was already there. Although the reduction of waste has been successful, the cleanup effort has been accused of spending what may amount to hundreds of billions of dollars to clean up insignificant amounts of waste or, worse, to pay lawyers to argue in court about whether and how the waste should be cleaned up.[18]

Such efforts always create losers. For example, the Superfund law was crafted (or interpreted by the courts) to minimize the burden on the taxpayers, so a number of methods were created to make companies pay for cleanups. Among these were strict, retroactive, and joint-and-several liability. Strict liability means that a company must pay even if it broke no rules and tried to be careful; negligence need not be shown. Retroactive liability requires companies to pay for cleanups even if the waste in question was not known to be hazardous (and was not illegal) when it was initially deposited. Joint-and-several liability concerns a situation in which several companies use the same site, such as a landfill. In such a case, any one of the companies can be held responsible for cleaning up all the waste, even if the company deposited only a small fraction of it. In theory, that company can then sue the others. But the reason for this provision was in case most of the companies that deposited the waste were out of business. Intuitively, people regard such provisions as unfair, and economists consider them to be inefficient.[19] In some cases, intuitions and analysis of consequences agree.

Horror stories soon emerged about dry cleaners, small chemical companies with only a few dozen employees, small battery makers, and fruit growers required to pay millions for the waste deposited by extinct behemoths — or else fight the charges in court at their own considerable expense.[20] Such horror stories, in turn, created political pressure to overturn the law and to reduce regulation in general. Ideally, the law could be reformed to deal with these problems, but much of the political discussion has concerned regulatory issues in general rather than specific reforms. In particular, it has concerned the overall conflict between protection of nature and autonomy of individuals — for example, property owners.

Some have suggested that democratic political processes need to be tempered by an expert and highly qualified bureaucracy.[21] France has such an elite corps, and it seems to help. No system will work unless it ultimately inspires public trust, or at least public tolerance. Ultimately, we must cope with the gap between public and expert perceptions. But this gap might not be so wide as it appears. In particular, the experts have information that the public does not have, mostly about numbers. It might be easier than we think to create the kind of trust that is needed by simply providing the numbers.

In other cases, experts and everyone else might be subject to the same biases. Training in toxicology, immunology, or epidemiology is about the basic sciences, not about decision making under conditions of uncertainty.

The Delaney Clause

If we can reduce risks to zero, then we do not have to worry about causing harm. Reducing a risk from one in a million to zero seems much better than reducing it from two in a million to one. This has been found in questionnaires and surveys,[22] and it is embodied in the infamous Delaney clause, part of a U.S. law, which outlaws any food additive that increases the risk of cancer by any amount. The clause was inserted by Congressman James Delaney into the 1958 Food Additive Amendment bill, in response to concerns about the use of diethylstilbestrol (DES), a potent carcinogen, in cattle feed to promote growth. It still is not clear whether DES fed to cattle has any effect on human cancer risk, although minute traces of it were occasionally found in beef.[23] Fortunately, the Delaney clause has now been repealed, but it took almost 30 years.

Complete elimination of risk is so popular that companies advertise their interest in it. In their 1994 Annual Report, DuPont Corporation said: "During 1994, we adopted a new Safety, Health and Environment Commitment. Historically, we have maintained that the only acceptable standard for injuries and illness is zero, and this has served us well. Our new commitment extends that same philosophy to environmental incidents, wastes and emissions" (p. 3).

Laws like the Delaney clause have more effect when they are coupled with the widespread use of "conservative" methods of risk assessment. For example, to determine whether chemicals cause cancer, scientists feed the chemicals to test animals, such as rats, in high enough doses to kill some of the animals. If the animals die of cancer, then this is considered relevant evidence, along with other evidence. By this test, many inexpensive pesticides have been banned, despite the absence of any evidence that these chemicals or similar ones cause cancer in humans. As a result, production of fruits and vegetables has become more expensive, prices are higher than they would otherwise be, and consumers buy less than they would otherwise buy. Statistical studies of humans indicate that consuming fruits and vegetables reduce the incidence of cancer. Thus, the effort to reduce pesticide risk to zero might actually be increasing the number of cancer cases, albeit by a very small amount.[24]

The bias for things natural led the public and legislators to focus entirely on synthetic chemicals. Harm from people is the issue, not harm in general. California's law that requires labeling of food with cancer-causing chemicals does not require labeling if the chemical is naturally part of the food, even if it is more dangerous. Even the Delaney clause itself applies only to processed foods, not foods that are eaten raw.

When farmers stop using artificial pesticides, many plants produce their own pesticides. Unlike the artificial pesticides, most of these natural pesticides have not been tested for cancer potential, even in rats. When natural chemicals are tested, their rate of causing cancer, according to animal tests, is about the same as that of artificial chemicals that are tested.[25] Even the components of broccoli, a healthful vegetable that seems to help in cancer prevention, can cause cancer when tested in this way. Yet artificial chemicals are withdrawn after positive tests, but natural chemicals are not. Thus, according to rat tests, removing artificial pesticides will very likely increase people's exposure to cancer-causing pesticides, as well as increasing costs. Despite the higher cost, we should still keep eating broccoli; it helps to protect us against cancer.

Nuclear Power and Nuclear Waste

I have already mentioned how fears of nuclear catastrophe have led to heavy regulation of nuclear power. Yet nuclear power could still be a good way to reduce global warming, since it produces less CO_2 than other ways of producing energy. (It would produce none at all, but much energy is used to construct the power plants themselves.) And other forms of nuclear energy are useful in medicine, medical research, and elsewhere. But wastes from nuclear power generation and research remain a problem and must be put somewhere.

Why is the fear of nuclear energy and waste so great? Part of the answer is that explosions of nuclear power plants are large catastrophes, like major earthquakes. But we seem less frightened of earthquakes. Perhaps part of the difference is that earthquakes are natural, and we think of nature as relatively benign, as I have argued, or at least beyond our control. (The effects of earthquakes, however, are within our control, through building codes and insurance policies, for example.)

Nuclear power and waste go against our intuition of naturalism in other ways. These feelings emerged in interviews with residents of Nevada and others about the burial of nuclear waste in an underground repository.[26] One of the problems of nuclear power plants is that the rods used to power them run down and must be replaced. But the rods will remain dangerous to people for thousands of years, gradually losing their radioactivity. Now the rods are kept near the power plants themselves in almost all countries. The United States and a couple of other countries have begun to consider the long-term problem. Perhaps if the rods could be buried deep underground, they would be less dangerous than they are now. In fact, they are not very dangerous now, and most experts think that the present situation can easily continue for decades or even centuries with essentially no risk. Still, the U.S. government went so far as to select a possible site for burial, at Yucca Mountain in southwestern Nevada, near the place where testing of atomic bombs was done. The plan became a political issue in Nevada. Most residents opposed it, and the plan is now on hold.

Again, it seems the bias toward the natural is at work. Interfering with the structure of atoms seems to some people to go further than even modern science gives us the right to go. It seems to be excessive tampering with the most basic building blocks of nature itself. The health effects of nuclear accidents seem to be especially insidious, unlike "natural" diseases, because they are unnatural. Viruses, bacteria, and even cancer have been around for a long time, but radiation sickness is the result of human intervention. As one California resident put it in a dispute over disposal of nuclear waste from medical research, "I don't want to worry about my children glowing in the dark."[27] The thought of radiation-induced birth defects is especially agonizing, much more, perhaps than birth defects resulting from "natural processes."

Some members of the Western Shoshone tribe also feel that burying waste in the earth is an interference with the earth itself. They believe that the earth is a living being, sustained by the underground rivers that run through it, which could be contaminated by the waste. Opposing another site in California, one Native American said, "For us to have this unnatural project in a natural land that is sacred to us just doesn't go. I'd rather have a nice drink of clean water than a pocket full of gold."[28] Moreover, "It is likely that persons living outside Native American cultures also reject the repository on the grounds that it 'injures' the earth, even if they don't anchor this belief with a theory as elaborate as that held by the Western Shoshone."[29]

Intuitions about unfairness also contribute to opposition to nuclear power plants and waste repositories. Plants and repositories must go somewhere. This means that someone will be nearby wherever they are built, and others farther away will benefit from their existence. Typically, those who live nearby receive special compensation in the form of growth in employment or some sort of monetary compensation to their community. But opponents rarely see the offered compensation as sufficient, especially if their opposition to the facility is based on an intuition that has become absolute. They also choose a concept of fairness that tells them they are being treated unfairly, whether they are or not.

Another problem here is that the compensation offered is not of the same kind as the supposed risk. People favor in-kind compensation, and they think that those who do harm should undo it as well.[30] Thus, opponents of the Nevada repository argued, "Why should Nevadans take the risks (no matter how small) of having nuclear waste transported on our streets and highways and stored in our state? We haven't any nuclear power plants! Let the states that allowed nuclear power plants to be built store their own waste."[31] Of course, the answer is that Nevada is a better place for the waste, so the harm is lower overall.

Note that the opponents are, according to experts, probably correct that the Nevada repository is not needed now. The trouble is that, if it were needed, they would still be able to stop it by bringing their intuitions to bear.

But the opposition to nuclear facilities has many sources. Opponents not only feel that nuclear energy is unnatural and that they are being asked to bear an unfair burden but also that the risks are high, that the authorities who downplay the risks are not to be trusted, and that the procedures for giving them a say were unfair.[32] It is difficult to tell whether any one of these beliefs is the root cause of the others. Once one of them enters the scene, the others rush in to join it, through the processes that I have called my-side bias and belief overkill. Indeed, my suggestion that naturalness is the primary intuition may be wrong. It does, however, account for the special way that people seem to feel about nuclear energy and waste.

Lawsuits

In the siting of facilities, people exposed to risk are often compensated in advance. In other cases involving risk, the compensation occurs after the fact. In general, when one person (or group) puts someone at risk, and when the risk comes to pass, people think that the injurer should compensate the victim. Tort law can compel compensation when the victims sue the injurers. Such a transaction not only compensates the victim but also punishes the injurer.

Compensation and punishment are different functions. Compensation, in the form of money, provides resources to those who can put them to good use to recover their way of life — for example, to rebuild a house that burned down or to replace a car that was destroyed in an accident. Punishment sends a message to those in the position of the injurer (including the injurer) to take care because they will be held responsible for the consequences of their recklessness.

When the injurer compensates the victim, as when a child is induced to give back something he has taken or when a victim sues an injurer in court, punishment and compensation are linked. But sometimes these functions are separated. Criminals are punished whether or not their victims are compensated. Insurance — both private insurance and government insurance such as disability programs — can provide compensation for misfortunes regardless of whether they are caused by people or nature, and regardless of whether the insurer collects from the injurer. We can, then, and we sometimes do, think separately about the functions of compensation and punishment.

When many people think about tort law, however, they tend to treat all cases as if they were a single standard type, in which punishment and compensation are linked and in which the beneficial consequences of punishment are irrelevant. As a result, tort law does not always produce the best consequences. Tort penalties have caused highly beneficial products — such as vaccines and birth-control products — to be withdrawn and have led to a reduction in research and development expenditures for similar products. For example, pertussis vaccine might cause brain damage or death in small numbers of children, although whooping cough, the disease it prevents, is far more dangerous. Production of this vaccine in the United States declined drastically as a result of lawsuits and the price increased.[33] Likewise, research on new birth-control methods seems to have decreased for the same reason.[34] Although it is likely that *some* products *should* be withdrawn from the market, or not developed, because their harm exceeds their benefit, these examples suggest that many successful lawsuits do not involve such harmful products.

Why does the tort system sometimes discourage products that are, on the whole, beneficial? Part of the problem may be the intuitions of those involved in the system — judges, lawyers, plaintiffs, defendants, and juries — about what penalties ought to be assessed and what compensation ought to be paid. In particular, two basic intuitive principles may be involved: the desire for retribution against an injurer, whatever the consequences; and the feeling that harms caused by people are more deserving of compensation than those caused by nature. The latter intuition may result from the standard linking of punishment and compensation: compensation is considered most appropriate when it is connected with punishment. These intuitions are not based on expected consequences, so it is not surprising that they sometimes lead to consequences that we find objectionable.

If we think in terms of consequences, we will penalize people or companies when we need to provide them with an incentive to be more careful. If they are already being as careful as they can be — given the need to make a profit — the penalty is futile. Even the safest vaccines made under the safest conditions, for example, sometimes cause harmful side effects. Punishing the company for such effects will not cause it to be more careful because it can do nothing more than it is already doing. A penalty with no such beneficial incentive effect is simply a wrong against the injurer, and "two wrongs don't make a right."

Providing compensation to victims is a different matter. Compensation from lawsuits fills much the same function for victims as compensation from insurance. Victims, because of their injuries, typically need money more than they did before their injury. This is why people rationally pay money to buy insurance, even though the insurance company makes a profit. Ideally, we might think that compensation should be provided as a function of the injury. In general, the more serious the injury, the greater the compensation. If there isn't enough money to go around, it might be best to follow a principle like this and give everyone less money, rather than compensate some people fully and others not at all. New Zealand (and, to some extent, Japan) have systems designed along these lines. People who become ill or disabled can be compensated according to a schedule — so much money for being blind, so much for losing a leg, and so on — regardless of the cause of their injury. When someone injures someone else through negligence, the injurer may still be forced to pay, but the injurer pays a fine to the state rather than providing additional compensation to the victim.

Critics of the U.S. legal system maintain that those who sue successfully are well compensated while others who suffer the same injury — at the hands of nature, through unavoidable accidents, or from an injurer without wealth or insurance — are left to fend for themselves. In other words, we would do better to divide the compensation among all the victims, even if we could not increase the total amount of it, to help those who would have to do without any.

In a study done with Ilana Ritov, I gave a questionnaire to retired judges, law students, other students and other groups.[35] The questionnaire asked respondents to imagine that the United States had a legal system much like New Zealand's, in which separate decisions were made about penalties against injurers and compensation for victims. But all decisions were made on a case-by-case basis by a panel, not according to a schedule. We asked the respondents to suppose that they were on these panels.

We presented two cases. In the first, a woman becomes sterile as a result of taking a new (but well-tested) birth-control pill. In the second, a child dies from a vaccine against a disease. The disease is far more likely than the vaccine to kill the child. Each case was followed by questions about two different situations, one in which the penalty would bring about improved behavior (making a safer product) and one in which the penalty would bring about a less desirable state (no product). For example, the vaccine case in which the penalty would improve future behavior said, "The company knew how to make an even safer pill but had decided against producing it because the company was not sure that the safer pill would be profitable. If the company were to stop making the pill that the woman took, it would make the safer pill." The question in which the deterrent effect was reversed was, "If the company were to stop making the pill that the woman took, it would cease making pills altogether." Most of the respondents, including judges, did not think that this made any difference. They thought that the penalty should depend on the harm done, not on its effect on anyone's future behavior.

In two other experiments, we gave student subjects the argument for incentive and asked what they thought of it. About half of the subjects rejected the argument. These subjects generally felt that fines should be based on the facts of the case, what happened in the past, or the need for compensation, not on effects in the future. For example, "We are dealing with solely what happened to the woman." "The damage was already done to that woman." "It should have to pay damages if it was at fault." "[The company] should pay for its previous actions on account of those actions." And another response was, "Either the company is to blame or it isn't."

Some subjects explicitly rejected future consequences as a basis for legal decisions, for example, "The liability issue should be decided based *only* on the facts of the particular case. The possible consequences of the company losing the suit *should not* in any way have a bearing on the particular woman's case." "The legal consequences of a past action on decision should not be judged based on its ramifications for future actions/decisions." "The question is whether the company did any wrongdoing against the woman. The decision on whether they pay has nothing to do with their future actions." "The amount and the decision to pay damages depends on the company's *past* performance, not on what it may or may not do in the future." "The court's decision may cause an increase in research, but that doesn't make a difference now."

We also found that compensation for the victim depended on whether the injury was caused by a product (pill or vaccine) or a natural disease. Remember that compensation could be provided even for natural injuries. Differences in the need for penalties could not provide a reason for differences in compensation because these two decisions were independent. Most subjects still thought that compensation should be greater when the injury was caused by a product.

We also asked subjects to compare compensation — not penalties — in two cases regarding action versus inaction by a company, one in which the injury resulted from a company making a pill and one in which the company decided not to make a safer pill, so that the victim had to take one (made by another company) that was less safe. About a third of the subjects thought that the victim should receive less compensation when the injury was caused by omission. (Almost none showed the reverse pattern.)

In sum, these results suggest that intuitions about punishment and compensation in the context of tort law are not typically based on a desire to bring about the best consequences. Many subjects regard penalties as an automatic consequence of causing injury, regardless of the incentive effects of assessing the penalties. Many subjects have not even learned the deterrent rationale to the point where they can recall it and bring it to bear on cases. Others have learned it but still reject it. Some who are presented with the rationale for what seems to them to be the first time accept it, but others reject it because it conflicts with their intuition.

Likewise, many people assign compensation not in terms of the injury but, rather, in terms of setting the balance right between the injurer, if any, and the victim. Victims thus can receive less compensation for injuries caused by omissions or by nature than for injuries caused by acts.

These attitudes, together, constitute a kind of support for a system in which people are compensated for injuries caused by acts but not for other injuries. Compensation is provided even when the incentive effects of providing it are harmful in the long run, as in the case of vaccines (clearly) or (only a little less clearly) medical specialties such as obstetrics, which are losing practitioners because of frequent lawsuits.

As in the case of other intuitions, these intuitive attitudes have their defenders — mostly the judges who write the opinions when cases are appealed. These defenses typically appeal to our social concepts of fairness — that is, to other people's intuitions. Perhaps there is a way in which these attitudes are correct, so that they should be followed whatever the consequences. I do not think there is, but that is not my main point. As usual, my point is that we cannot have our cake and eat it, too. If we follow intuitions that are not based on consequences, then we cannot be surprised if they yield consequences that are sometimes not so good.

How to Think about Risk

We can avoid the deleterious effects of intuitive thinking if we learn to think quantitatively. This does not mean that we must have numbers. It does mean that we realize that a well-made decision requires comparisons of quantities. If we have a feeling for the quantities, we can make a good guess at what the decision would be even if we do not know the numbers themselves. This is what we do all the time in other domains. Tennis players, for example, realize that the intended placement of a shot is based on a tradeoff of the probability of its going out and the probability of its winning the point if it does not go out. They do not know these probabilities as a function of where they aim, although some tennis statistician could, in principle, compile them. They do, however, think in this quantitative way even without the numbers.

When we think this way, we will be able to make everyday decisions in a sensible way, and we will also know when some public decision, such as whether to build more nuclear power plants, requires a more detailed quantitative analysis by experts. We will also understand that it does not matter whether risks arise through action or omission, or whether the cause of a risk is human or natural. And we will understand why we should not pay more to reduce risk to zero, if we can use the money better in other ways by reducing some other risk imperfectly.

Quantitative thinking of this sort is not widespread. People do not even notice its absence. Many people, for example, say that decisions such as whether to recommend estrogen replacement are "difficult" because there are costs as well as benefits. Many of these people do not seem to consider the possibility of looking at some overall measure, such as death rates or life expectancy. Or one can even get a more precise measure by weighing each condition (various cancers, heart disease, strokes, hip fractures) by some measure of their seriousness and their duration. It is clear from looking at the evidence now available that this sort of analysis would strongly favor estrogen for most women.

The same goes for government regulation, such as regulation of clean air. If, for example, we ask people how much money they are willing to pay to prevent one person from getting asthma or emphysema, the answer is a fair amount. The same for the time they are willing to spend. They may be telling the truth. Yet when the U.S. Congress passed the recent revisions of the Clean Air Act and the Environmental Protection Administration (EPA) proposed new regulations requiring extra inspections of motor vehicles, people rose up in anger at intrusive government regulation. Exasperated EPA officials think that the public is inconsistent: their representatives, after all, voted overwhelmingly for this act. But *none* of the public statements of these officials, or news articles about these issues, told us how many cases of which disease would be prevented by how many extra car inspections. It is easy for public opinion to swing wildly from side to side under these conditions.

Another necessary part of quantitative thinking about risk is the need for evidence that risks are worth considering at all. We face too many real risks for us to waste time worrying about ones that don't exist or freak accidents that have happened once. Should we stop going to the dentist after reading that a few patients contracted AIDS from their dentist? At minimum, we need some evidence of a statistical association between a cause and an effect. The mere fact that a cause was associated with the effect in a few people is not enough. We need to know whether the number of people is more than would be expected by chance.

The drug Bendectin, for example, was an effective treatment for morning sickness, which is often a serious threat to mother and infant, but it was removed from the market after a series of lawsuits claiming that it caused birth defects. The defects were never established, but the maker got tired of the cost of defending itself. Even if Bendectin had caused such defects, it might have been better to have it available for severe cases. These court cases should have been thrown out, but because of them, the public lost a beneficial drug.[36]

Risks can also be established by an understanding of their causal mechanism. Often maverick scientists present theories of such mechanisms that, in connection with the most tenuous bit of evidence, cause panics over essentially nonexistent risks.

An example is the near panic that occurred in Memphis, Tennessee, on December 3, 1990, after Iben Browning's prediction of an earthquake at that date on the New Madrid fault, which runs through the town of New Madrid, Missouri. Browning — an author, inventor, but not a seismologist — believed that earthquakes were caused in part by the gravitational force of the moon — the same forces that cause the tides. He claimed to have predicted the San Francisco earthquake of 1989, although he actually said that there would be an earthquake somewhere in the world roughly at that time, so he might well have been correct by coincidence even if there was any other reason to believe his theory. More important, essentially all geologists thought that, although the idea was not crazy on its face, in fact the tidal forces were much too weak. There were no earthquakes in 1746, 1807, 1862, and 1929, when the forces were just as strong as on December 3, 1990. Yet, body bags were bought for victims. TV camera crews filled the local inns. The story was big news for weeks. The earthquake never came.

After the San Francisco earthquake of 1989, payments for earthquake insurance in California went up by 49%, but in the New Madrid region, where the earthquake did not occur, payments went up by 119%.[37] Perhaps it is a good thing that people realized they were in an earthquake region — Californians already knew that — but it shouldn't have taken a baseless prediction to convince them. What they gained in protection, they lost in respect for science.

Conclusion

Our thinking about risk is governed by intuitive fear of doing harm. Of course, it is perfectly reasonable to want to avoid harm. But our intuitive fear of it is governed by factors that are only imperfectly related to the probability and magnitude of the harm in question. The solution here, as in some other areas, is to think quantitatively. This does not necessarily mean doing calculations. Rather, it means thinking about things in terms of the balance of arguments, the force of each of which depends on some magnitude.

CHAPTER 8

Too Many People

The world now has close to 6 billion people. Within the lifetime of today's children, the number will double or perhaps triple, depending on how quickly birth rates decline, and then it will level off. Most of the new people will be in countries that are now poor. Many people are concerned about whether the world can handle this increase. They worry about many things, which I enumerate here.

- *Food.* Food production has so far kept up with population growth.[1] We have some cause for concern, though. The amount of fish available per person has been declining for years. The growth of cities and industrial parks is using up farmland throughout the world. Even if the raw amount of protein and calories per person is maintained, it is likely that changes in diet will continue to result from population growth and stress on resources, just as various fish species once cheap and plentiful have now become delicacies. The fact that the price of the substitutes will be comparable to what is replaced — which to some implies that value is maintained — does not mean that the substitutes are just as good. This is a recurring theme. Many of the effects of population growth will not be disastrous. We will just see that many things that we now take for granted will be increasingly expensive, and we will learn to make do with other things.

- *Water.* More serious, perhaps, is the problem of water. People now use more than half of the available fresh water,[2] so a doubling of the population will require either use of less water per person or else increased expenditures on energy for making fresh water from

129

ocean water. Water is used for irrigation as well as for cleaning and drinking, so the water problem is related to the food problem. In many areas of the world, particularly the Middle East, water shortages are already combining with population growth to create serious conflicts among nations, which could ultimately lead to war.[3] Often water is used for irrigation of food for export, so that the problem affects other economic concerns as well.

- *Pollution.* More than half of the world's population now lives in cities. (If they did not, there would be even less land for agriculture.) Most of these cities have increasing pollution, which leads to disease, low intelligence (when lead is involved), and early death. Pollution, of course, can be controlled, but at a cost that poor countries cannot easily afford.

- *Social disorganization.* The rapid growth of cities often leads to social disorganization, such as that in Brazil, where large gangs of children roam the streets without adult supervision of any kind.

- *Disease.* Reliance on marginal sources of water, crowding, pollution, and social disorganization all lead to the spread of infectious diseases such as cholera, tuberculosis, and AIDS.

- *Refugees.* Population growth leads to greater use of migration to escape famine, disease, or political upheaval.

- *Resources.* Population growth puts a strain on all other resources, such as fuel, wood, minerals, and space for recreation. It does not seem that we are going to run out of energy for cars. Substitutes for gasoline will clearly be available in time. But the situation would be easier if growth were slower. Again, this is something we can handle, but it would be easier to handle if the change were slower. For example, if we had more time to develop new, inexpensive, energy sources, we could solve the water problem through desalinization.

- *Amenities.* Those who can appreciate both the quiet beauty of the Rocky Mountains or the Adirondacks and the wonderful diversity of Greenwich Village in New York City have mixed feelings about the effect of population growth on the quality of human life. It is clearly not all bad. But we do make choices about this by allowing population to grow. It would be nice to give ourselves time to reflect on these changes. Perhaps we have enough big cities.

- *Adaptation.* Population growth increases the difficulty of adapting to other problems, such as the possible disruptions caused by global warming.

On the other side, I have seen no arguments that population is growing too slowly. The main issue is to take action to slow the rate of growth or whether to do nothing. Many say that we ought to do nothing special. Perhaps we should even reduce the efforts we now make, which include international aid for birth control and women's health, government subsidies for birth control, government campaigns to reduce birth rates, and (in China and a few other countries) legal penalties for large families or rewards for small families.

The critics, those against action to slow population growth, point out that this issue has been on the table since at least 1798, when Thomas Malthus published the first edition of *An Essay on the Principle of Population as it Affects the Future Improvement of Society*. Malthus suggested that the world might soon run out of food because of population growth. It didn't. In 1968, Paul Ehrlich wrote *The Population Bomb*,[4] in which he said that "the battle to feed humanity is already lost, in the sense that we will not be able to prevent large-scale famines in the next decade." But over the next 25 years, the world rate of chronic malnutrition declined.[5] New technology — such as new varieties of crops, new methods of storage and distribution, fish farms, and increased use of land — kept ahead of population.

Some critics, particularly Julian Simon, also argue for the benefits of population.[6] The more people, the greater the total creativity of humanity and the greater the chance to solve our problems, including, presumably, those that result from excessive population growth. Gregg Easterbrook — not himself a population alarmist — replies, "Simon is right about the inherent worth of the mind, but if you have walked the streets of Delhi, Jakarta, Lagos, Mexico City, and a dozen other places, you cannot believe that each new postnatal cry is a cause for celebration. Thoughts are what human existence is about: and the thoughts of millions of annual new arrivals in poor nations are ordained to be confined to misery and deprivation."[7] One might also add that, just as the chance of great creativity increases with more people, so does the chance of great malice, including terrorism by one person against millions. We must consider costs as well as benefits.[8]

This chapter examines people's thinking about population issues. Such thinking would be of little interest if the problem were not real, or if it didn't much matter what we did. So I want to say at the outset why it might matter. I am not sure it matters, but all judgments of this sort are uncertain, and we must sometimes act despite our uncertainty.

First, projections of the effect of population growth are indeed uncertain. Even though we have managed to adapt in the past through new technology — beginning with the invention of agriculture — we cannot be *certain* that such adaptation will continue indefinitely.[9] Thus, population control reduces the *risk* of major catastrophe, such as new plagues or outbreaks of war and revolution. Moreover, population control *is* a new technology. Why should we use and promote other technologies but not this one?

Second, some parts of the world are already seeing population pressure. In India, China, Bangladesh, most of Africa, and parts of Latin America, life would be better for people if populations were lower. It is often said that population control is not the only solution to the problems of these countries. More efficient production and fairer distribution of income would help. But population control might help too, with or without the other solutions.

Third, even if the earth can sustain indefinite growth in human population, too high a *rate* of growth puts stress on human societies. This is part of the problem in sub-Saharan Africa, where population pressures exacerbate the stresses that have led to repeated ethnic wars and famines in the last few years. Africa has the natural resources to support many more people than it has — in comparison to Europe it is vastly under-populated — but its rate of growth is too fast.

Fourth, an expanding population means that the poor countries can never attain the standard of living of the rich ones — at least not in the same way. There is just not enough oil, water, or meat for everyone in the world to use it half as much as the average citizen of the United States or Western Europe. We must choose among population growth, worldwide reduction in inequality, and substitution of new things for old — such as soybean products for meat and fish, or public transportation in place of automobiles. Slowing population growth will increase our choices concerning inequality reduction and substitution of goods.

Fifth, adaptation to increased population can conceal a declining quality of life that results from excessive population. An increasing part of the world economy is concerned with the production of goods and services that would not be needed as much except for increasing population, such as antipollution devices, fish farming, irrigation, and fertilizers. In Bangkok, concern about water pollution, itself a product of high population density, has created a large industry in bottled water, and the discarded plastic water bottles are now creating a new environmental problem of their own, requiring more workers to deal with the bottles, engage in public relations campaigns to encourage drinking of tap water (now heavily chlorinated by yet other workers), and so on. People who do these things are part of the "economy." Because they do provide valued goods and services, the prices of what they produce are included in economic measures of well-being. But their labor could be put to other uses if population were lower, uses that would truly improve our well-being rather than fixing the problems we have created and getting us back to where we would be without them. With increasing population, more of the world's labor and talent goes to removing the obstacles that we have placed in our own path, as a result of population expansion, leaving less labor and talent for other things we could use — education, better television programs, safer buildings, and so on.

Part of the declining quality of life involves changes in the natural world. I do not think that nature has value unless people value it, but people *do* value nature. And we value it all the more as it becomes harder to avoid seeing the imprint of people. Even if we can feed ourselves and maintain our societies with substantial further growth, it is difficult to see how we can maintain the natural world as we know it today. Because of human activity, species of animals and plants are disappearing today at a rate that is comparable to geologic catastrophes of the past, such as those that led to the extinction of the dinosaurs. Perhaps, as Glenn Easterbrook argues, this is not so bad, in the great scheme of things.[10] But we are rushing into this without stopping to think. It might be something we can mitigate at reasonable cost, just to allow ourselves time to open our eyes.

The good news is that birth rates have declined in all countries over the last few decades. Sometimes this is partly the result of government policies. Sometimes it has happened despite government policies. Some countries and states still encourage births (and discourage immigration). But it appears that governments *can* help reduce population growth by providing modern birth-control methods and by systematically encouraging couples to use them; and as side effects of policies adopted mainly for other purposes, we may also see increased education of women and increased openness to television programs and movies from other countries. (I point to some evidence about this later.)

Some of these things cost money. A cheaper method for reducing population is to apply heavy economic and social pressure on parents who have more than one or two children, as China has done in the last two decades. If China had not done these things, the world would be inundated with Chinese seeking refuge, and those remaining in China would either be rich enough to buy food — putting the price out of reach of others — or else the rest of us would see them starving on TV. So we have all benefited from China's very strict policies. Yet many people feel that China's policy is a violation of fundamental rights. Few people defend the right to fish, whatever the consequences, but the right to reproduce freely has acquired a kind of sacredness. People fleeing China's one-child policy are often seen as victims of human-rights abuses.

Perhaps we will be lucky, and the more humane methods of population control will work magnificently well. To fund them, the poor countries will dismantle their armies, and the rich nations will provide generous aid. If not, many countries are going to go where China has gone. The rest of us will have to decide whether to aid them, trade with them, and accept their emigrants.

Even the more humane methods of population control run into deep feelings about human rights, autonomy, and nationalism. The issue of abortion is also necessarily relevant. Most methods of birth control are fallible, even under ideal conditions.[11] If abortion were unavailable, serious efforts to reduce population growth would force couples to use only the most effective methods, since no backup would be available in case of failure. These include sterilization and chemical methods (birth-control pills, Norplant, Depo-Provera). Sterilization is often resisted, and the chemical methods are relatively expensive — especially for people in poor countries or for their governments — and are often resisted because of their side effects. If birth-control methods were limited to the most effective ones, then fewer couples would choose to use them at all.

More than half of the countries in the world, mostly those with high rates of population growth, do not allow abortion for economic and social purposes. Yet increased access to abortion can be an important step toward controlling world population.[12] The need for access to abortion is denied even by many of those who generally favor access to contraception, as if adequate use of contraception could eliminate the need for abortion. Again, this is true only if the most effective birth-control methods are used, and these often have other costs (e.g., sterilization is often irreversible). The next chapter discusses the intuitions that affect public policy about abortion.

Although abortion opponents are usually on the political Right, left-wingers are also opposed to direct efforts to reduce the birth rate. They tend to think of them as an unnecessary distraction from the more important issues of redistributing wealth and protecting the environment from unbridled capitalism. They thus see birth reduction as at best a temporary relief that masks the underlying symptoms of the world's true illness and, at worst, an attempt by the rich and powerful to hold back the masses.

Both sides may be engaging in wishful thinking about the tradeoff between individual freedom and economic well-being. The Left would prefer to see birth control included as part of a general improvement of health and educational services, thus increasing well-being without any intentional effort to reduce births and with every intention of increasing choices. The right also thinks that free markets, without government subsidies or controls, will lead to the best outcomes, so that government birth-control programs are just wasteful. It may be that we are really faced with a choice, though, in that we could increase well-being by encouraging people both to desire fewer children and to have fewer children.

The point, then, is that the idiosyncrasies of intuitive judgment may be preventing one of the easiest things we could now do to ensure a better future — or prevent a worse one — for humanity. We do not know this. But we cannot *assume* that population control is a worthless enterprise. To ignore this avenue is to take a big risk.

Recent History of the Debate

Concern about population growth goes back at least to Malthus, who published six editions of his influential *Essay on Population* between 1798 and 1826. Malthus saw no way out of the conflict between exponential population growth and (at best) linear growth in resources. The population would ultimately be controlled by war and famine. In the last half of the 19th century, effective methods of birth control became more widespread, including condoms made of rubber and sterilization of both sexes. Around this time, various individuals and organizations, such as the Malthusian League, began to campaign for tolerance of birth control and more widespread use, and to provide services. Serious campaigning on behalf of birth control began in the early twentieth century, with the writing and speaking of Margaret Sanger in the United States and Marie Stopes in England. Sanger was concerned with the alleviation of poverty and what she saw as the excessive breeding of the poor (which worsened their condition). Stopes was more concerned with alleviating the stress that successive pregnancies and births placed on women.

Over the years, the main opposition to birth control has been primarily religious. Yet specific religious doctrines concerning birth control are hard to discover and require a bit of imagination to understand. One could easily read the entire Bible carefully without concluding clearly that it expressed any condemnation of birth control or even abortion. Most of the passages cited by opponents are ambiguous at best. For example, censure of coitus interruptus is inferred from the fact that God killed Onan, son of Judah, for letting his seed "be lost on the ground." But Onan was also disobeying his father's order to sleep with his recently widowed sister-in-law, and the punishment could have been for disobedience. Those who have inferred that the Bible presented a clear message about these issues were probably searching for evidence for a conclusion they had already accepted.

Birth control, like abortion, is seen as unnatural, and this may be the source of the opposition to it. Another source of opposition to both birth control and abortion is the desire to strengthen the traditional family. The Comstock Act passed by the U.S. government in 1873, for example, prohibited the distribution of birth control devices or information about them through the mail. The impetus for this act seemed to be largely the association between birth control and prostitution. A sympathetic reading of this concern is that prostitution and free love could weaken the family. Increasing the link between sex and childbearing increases the cost of out-of-wedlock sex.[13]

Nationalism, including tribal loyalty, is another source of modern resistance to population control. In Africa, until very recently, for a politician to speak firmly in favor of population control "would be to challenge the growth of an individual's tribe" (as well as "to deprive parents of the hands needed to till the fields today and care for the elderly tomorrow" and "to denounce religious and traditional beliefs that have belonged to Africans for generations").[14] Likewise, as late as 1977, South Korea's minister of health and social affairs, Shin Hyon Hwack, "worried that the success of his country's population control program might lessen South Korea's chances for victory in a war with the North."[15] In Brazil, some opponents of family planning were concerned about the population of Portuguese speakers relative to Spanish speakers. Indonesia tried to increase population of its outer islands as a defense against Chinese "infiltration."[16] Jordanians, despite a high level of female education, continue to have many children in part because of national security concerns.[17] Tibetan nationalists, despite Tibetans being allowed higher birth rates than other Chinese under China's birth-control policy, claim that any limitation amounts to an attempt at genocide.[18]

Even China had a pronatalist policy until the 1970s. In 1949, Mao Zedong (who was later to embrace population control for China) said, "Even if China's population multiplies many times, she is fully capable of finding a solution: the solution is production. The absurd argument of Western bourgeois economists, like Malthus, that increase in production cannot keep pace with increase in population was not only thoroughly refuted in theory by Marxists long ago, but has also been completely exploded by the realities in the Soviet Union and the Liberated areas of China after their revolutions. . . . Under the leadership of the Communist Party, as long as there are people, every kind of miracle can be performed."[19] Wishful thinking of this sort undoubtedly delayed China's turn toward population control and required the resulting policy to be more coercive than it would otherwise have been.

Until fairly recently, many poor countries looked at the rich countries' emphasis on family-planning assistance as a way of keeping their numbers down in order to maintain the economic and military upper hand. In the United States, the same kind of concern is raised about attempts to reduce the high birth rate of unwed black adolescents: "Putting off parenthood may be better for black women, but its effect will be to reduce black Americans to an even smaller minority."[20] The concern extends even to AIDS prevention. In 1992, a "master healer" in Swaziland said: "Swazis including traditional healers believe that AIDS is fictitious. It is a European plot to trick Swazis into using family-planning devices in order to reduce the size of their families."[21]

More recently, with the Cairo conference of 1994, opposition to population control has decreased substantially, although funding of population-control efforts is still far from enough to insure that those who want contraceptives are using them. Currently, people have different reasons for concern about population growth. One reason is that rapid population growth in poor countries leads to hunger, because food production does not increase as fast as population, and to disease, because people move into areas (such as urban slums) without adequate sanitation. A second political source of concern is with the environment. Higher populations lead to deforestation, soil erosion, pollution, and increasing carbon dioxide concentrations. These things affect all people in the long run, but some environmentalists seem to care about them for their own sake. Finally, another strand of opposition to population growth is concerned with the quality of life in rich countries. This theme merges with the environmentalist concerns in pointing out that people in rich countries use resources, such as oil, more than those in poor countries. This view also takes an anti-immigration stance because (it is argued) immigrants can increase the population of rich countries and in so doing cause more environmental damage than if the immigrants had stayed put.

The Current Debate

The current debate about population has more than two sides, and I enumerate these several positions in the following pages.

Free-market Neutrality

According to this view, population growth is a "neutral phenomenon," not a matter for government regulation. Advocates of this view think that we have not yet reached — and perhaps never will reach — the point at which more children do more harm than good. Any child can become a future Einstein. Reducing population growth is cutting off future opportunities.

Support for this view comes largely from the difficulty of finding any effects attributable to current or past population growth.[22] If population is increasing faster than economic growth, then prices should rise for goods with a fixed supply, such as minerals. This has not happened.

Each time, in the past, the world seems to have reached some inherent limit on population, some new invention has overcome the difficulty. First, perhaps, was agriculture, which permitted human populations to grow far beyond what could be supported by hunting, fishing, and gathering. Nothing quite so dramatic has happened since the first plow broke the soil, but a series of minor improvements have increased the amount of food available essentially as fast as the population has grown. Among these are breeding of crops, mechanized agriculture, transportation and distribution of food products, and refrigeration. Other more local limitations have often been similarly overcome. Firewood has been replaced with other fuels. Rivers have been dammed for water. Desalinization plants have been built to get fresh water from sea water. Cities have been built for the excess population that would otherwise crowd farmers off of their land.

Yet recently, more of our resources and labor have been spent on antipollution devices, recycling systems, and enforcement of rules that would not have been needed if population growth had been lower. If all of our "economic growth" were the result of such activities, our lives would be no better even though the gross national product would increase. As population grows, more of our work is devoted to removing obstacles that we have placed in our own path.

Technological change has a hidden cost. With each adaptation, something is lost, which does not always show up in economic statistics. The losses could take the form of destruction of natural beauty or of diversion of talent and labor from useful activities. The chain of events is complex. The growing population of southern California required pipelines to be built to bring in water from the Colorado River, which now no longer flows into the sea because all the water is removed first. This required labor and ingenuity that could be used for other projects, and it reduced natural beauty. Dams on rivers of the northern Pacific coast of North America have reduced the salmon catch, leading to greater use of fish farming, which in turn has ruined the ecology and beauty of the coast in some areas of the world. Growing populations of cities lead to traffic jams, which cause pollution, which leads more rich people to buy air conditioners for their cars not only increasing the pollution but also leaking chlorofluorocarbons into the atmosphere, depleting the ozone layer, which causes other people to buy more sunscreen to protect themselves from ultraviolet rays. The companies that make sunscreen could be making vaccines. The extra air conditioners and sunscreen are, of course, counted as beneficial products in any economic statistics. But we can also see them as defensive adaptations made necessary by our own behavior, a medical treatment for a self-inflicted illness. Such things do not truly increase our standard of living. We could have used the same resources to improve our situation beyond its original level, instead of using them to restore the original level after we have reduced it.

The free-market view puts great faith in new technology. Why limit the technology to new methods of food production, desalinization of ocean water, and energy production? Why do these same arguments not include contraceptives as a technology? We will see that the free market underproduces contraceptives both because of political opposition and because the people who need them most are too poor to pay for them. (The U.S. legal system doesn't help, either.)

More to the point, the free market alone might be insufficient to produce the socially optimal amount of contraceptives. If we recall the example of overfishing, we can compare the results of overfishing to the results of overpopulation. We must consider overpopulation as a social dilemma, since parents have more children than is best for others. One couple's children do affect other families. The size of this effect is, of course, uncertain, but we cannot be sure it is absent or small, just as fishermen cannot be sure that pessimistic scientists are always wrong. The effects of past and current birth rates may be hard to observe just because there are so many other factors that affect economic growth. Again, we have seen this problem before with fisheries. There, too, it was difficult to detect the effects of overfishing against the background of other effects, but there was always reason to worry about overfishing, and in some cases the worriers turned out to be right.

Economic Growth

According to this view, population growth *is* a problem, but the solution is again to promote economic growth. "Development is the best contraceptive." With economic growth of the usual sort, population will stabilize on its own. Rather than spending money on subsidized birth control, poor countries should increase trade, reduce government waste, and strengthen protection of property. In the past, countries that have done this have adopted a new way of living in which large families were less desired and contraceptives were easily provided by the market itself.

     The Catholic Church supports this view, although without the usual emphasis on the free market as the solution.

> It is . . . morally unacceptable to encourage, let alone impose, the use of methods such as contraception, sterilization and abortion in order to regulate births. The ways of solving the population problem are quite different. Governments and the various international agencies must above all strive to create economic, social, public health and cultural conditions which will enable married couples to make their choices about procreation in full freedom and with genuine responsibility. They must then make efforts to ensure "greater opportunities and a fairer distribution of wealth so that everyone can share equitably in the goods of creation. Solutions must be sought on the global level by establishing a true *economy of communion and sharing of goods*, in both the national and international order." This is the only way to respect the dignity of persons and families, as well as the authentic cultural patrimony of peoples.[23]

     Over the course of history, most developed countries have gone through a period of declining death rates with continued high birth rates, followed by a period of industrialization, followed by declining birth rates. Moreover, certain kinds of economic development seem empirically to reduce the birth rate, particularly those that involve the education of girls and employment of women.

Although there is substantial evidence for these mechanisms, there is also now considerable evidence that, for poor countries, such development may be very slow or impossible without additional support for birth control, and many countries have found that they can reduce their birth rates in a variety of ways without developing first.[24] Indonesia has been successful in reducing rural population growth with birth-control programs that emphasize contraceptives.[25] Some writers have answered the emphasis on development with "contraceptives are the best contraceptive."[26]

There is, of course, some debate about what works — other than economic development. Lant Pritchett argued that providing contraceptives has little effect and that the main determinant of family size is desired family size (even when desired family size is measured *before* all the children are born, so that respondents are not put in the position of saying that they wish their children had not been born).[27] If family-planning programs are mainly providers of contraceptives, then they don't do much good. In reply John Bongaarts pointed out that even small differences in the rate of using contraceptives can have significant effects on the rate of population growth.[28] Note that 2 children per woman will keep population constant in the long run. If the current number is 2.5 children, population will continue to grow, but a 20% reduction in the birth rate will eventually cut the growth rate by 100% — that is, to zero growth. ("Eventually" because increases in births from year to year cause increases in women entering their childbearing years two decades years later.) And small effects may be cost-effective.

Other steps can change the desire for children. China achieved massive declines in birth rates as a result of government policy, and these began well before the current increase in economic production. These policies were effective in part because they put people under strong economic pressure. People with one child or none got benefits that others did not get. But the policies also had the effect of changing people's real desires for children. Public attitudes changed from those favoring large families to those favoring the one-child limit. "Villagers' worries about the erosion of their land base are reflected in a new form of gossip: neighbors are grumbling about young couples who, despite the one-child policy, give birth to two sons. Such couples, they believe, are making unfair claims on village resources, for their sons will require twice the average family's allocation of housing and agricultural land when they grow up."[29]

The state of Kerala in India experienced birth-rate reductions as a result of increases in education and health services, even while most of the population remains quite poor. These were not the result of any sort of direct economic pressure not to have children. Other countries have found that birth rates decrease when attitudes toward large families change as a result of such influences as television soap operas in which glamorous women have small families, advertising campaigns that associate large families with poverty, or increased education for girls and women. Education is surely an expensive and indirect way to reduce fertility, but it has other benefits.

If members of rich countries are concerned and want to do something to help, it is difficult to know what will get the most benefit for a given cost. Some things, such as reducing tariff barriers to goods made in poor countries, may promote development at very little cost. Whether foreign aid is more effectively spent on health in general, education in general, women's education, or birth control may depend on the details. It seems that all of these things help some of the time. Development is a good contraceptive, but so are other things, including contraceptives.

Human Rights

By this view, people should have the right to control their reproduction. Where they do not have access to birth control, they should get it. Giving people other rights, such as the right to health care and education, may well reduce population growth where it is a problem. But rights are the main thing. As U Thant put it in 1968, when he was secretary general of the United Nations, "The Universal Declaration of Human Rights describes the family as the natural and fundamental unit of society. It follows that any choice and decision with regard to the size of the family must irrevocably rest with the family itself and cannot be made by anybody else."[30] This view largely prevailed at the International Conference on Population and Development held in Cairo in 1994.[31]

Advocates of this view are often particularly concerned with birth control as a means by which women can avoid domination by their husbands, work outside the home while remaining married, and avoid the deleterious health effects of repeated pregnancies.[32] These are worthwhile goals. Achieving them might help with population control, but it might not be sufficient, and it is expensive.

Unlike the free-market proponents, many human-rights advocates believe that population growth is a problem. These people deny implicitly that the problem is a social dilemma, however. They think that all that is needed is for the free market to work — that is, for the market to provide goods and services that people want. They acknowledge that the market may take some outside prodding or help to get to this point, in the form of government services or subsidies. They also think that legal, cultural, and religious barriers to birth control violate rights, although they also recognize the conflicting rights of people to practice their religion.[33]

The fundamental principle behind the human rights view is autonomy. As one article put it, "a woman-centered approach to reproductive health is fundamentally about trusting women. For when all the rhetoric is stripped away, the key to improving reproductive health is women's autonomy — enabling women to take control over their reproductive lives by trusting to them both the authority to make decisions about reproduction and the ability to make those decisions based on access to adequate information and appropriate services."[34]

Autonomy is also an argument against any kind of family-planning programs that try to change the desire of people for children (as opposed to programs that simply provide contraceptives, thus "increasing choices"). For example, "who should decide whether citizens of other countries should have more income or more children? Parents everywhere know that they could have a higher per capita income, and more material assets, if they had fewer children. It is then the right or duty of government to make this choice on parents' behalf?"[35]

Opponents of family planning have applied the autonomy principle to nations and cultures as well as to individuals, causing resistance to international family-planning assistance. This was the major source of resistance to international family-planning assistance from the United States during the early 1960s, when it first began to increase: "it was one thing for Kennedy's international activism to express itself in the Peace Corps, or the advisors in Vietnam, and quite another for the United States government to tell people they were having too many children."[36] Similarly, Robert G. Marshall of the American Life League argued, "We don't think the Government should fund these things — artificial means of birth control. They lend themselves to coercion and centralized control over family life."[37]

In sum, the free-market view has much to teach us, but we can acknowledge that free markets are important without denying that other approaches have merit as well. Yet all of the views presented up to this point may require wishful thinking. They start with some sort of antagonism to more active interventions. Two sources of antagonism seem basic. One is the principle of autonomy. This is the principle that stands in the way of solving any social dilemma. If population is in part a social dilemma, then the principle of autonomy will likewise stand in the way here too. The other, which I will develop in more detail shortly, is the principle of naturalness. Birth control seems to go against nature.

The principle of autonomy is a good rule of thumb, and in general, so is respect for nature. But, as often happens, these rules of thumb are elevated into absolute principles, and wishful thinking is used to conclude that nothing else is needed.

Population Control and the Rights of Women

A strong element of the 1994 Cairo conference, also generally accepted, was an emphasis on the association of population policy with women's rights. Advocates of this view noted a happy convergence between declining population and increased status for women, including especially medical care and education. Population aid should thus be devoted more to women's education and health.

Critics see two related problems with this proposal.[38] First, although girls' schooling and women's health are laudable goals, and although these factors have played important roles in reduced birth rates in some regions, they have had small effects at best in other regions. Some countries have reduced their birth rates without substantial changes in women's health and education. If we want to reduce the birth rate, it is more efficient to spend money on promotion of birth control than on these indirect measures. Second, the funds requires for birth control are relatively small compared to those required for significant improvements in women's health and education. Reducing the funding for birth control in order to increase funding for health and education could have large negative effects on the former and only small positive effects on the latter. Although the delegates to the Cairo conference hoped that funding for women's education and health would increase without any reduction for other programs, this is unlikely to happen.

Wishful thinking may lie behind this approach. Women's health, education, and access to modern methods of birth control are all desirable goals in the eyes of the Cairo delegates. Ideally, trade-offs among these goals should not be required. But thinking it does not make it so.

Incentives and Coercion

The alternative to the idea of rights and autonomy is that some sort of intervention may be needed to change people's desires. Those in charge of family planning programs have been constantly pulled between this view and the human-rights view.[39] Advocates of the human-rights view have held that satisfying the unmet need for contraceptives was sufficient. This may be an example of wishful thinking, not because this position is clearly wrong but, rather, because it might be held with a certainty not justified by the evidence.

Several kinds of intervention are possible. The easiest is public education. The birth rate in Brazil has recently declined in part because of government-sponsored family-planning programs, which have a "demonstration effect" that goes beyond the provision of services to particular women. Advertising and even TV stories that emphasize birth control, small families, and consumption of new consumer goods have also played a role. These change people's desires, possibly against their own will. If they had been asked before exposure to the advertising and TV whether they would want their desires for children to change, they might have honestly and rationally said no. We are used to this sort of manipulation because TV is part of modern capitalism, but it is still a matter of doing something to people that changes their behaviors in ways they did not choose in advance. Perhaps it is not so manipulative if it is simply a matter of providing information, but effective interventions and cultural changes usually do much more than that. (Although government and population organizations can play a large role in such changes, in Brazil many of the changes may have been unplanned: "The director of [a] population control NGO . . . has often claimed to have a long-standing agreement with Roberto Marinho, the owner of the most influential television network in Brazil [TV Globo], to disseminate messages favoring the small-family norm in the Brazilian media. However, [program] directors convened to discuss this issue . . . had never been given such a message; indeed, they had not the slightest idea that their product could be having any influence on fertility."[40])

At the other extreme, China has reduced its birth rate by strong incentives. Provincial governments provide extra welfare and nutrition allowances to families with only one child; priority in housing, education, and medical care; and extra maternity benefits. Those who have more children are often given fines, salary reductions, and cuts in maternity leave and health coverage. In addition, local officials and peers apply heavy social pressure to obey the policy. Some local officials go beyond what government policy dictates, using physical threats and other powers to force women to have abortions, for example. China's "coercive" policies have been roundly condemned. They are considered to be human-rights violations, and they have been a major argument against funding of international family planning by the U.S. government. The opponents of such funding, such as Senator Jesse Helms and Representative Christopher Smith, rail against coercion, typically without distinguishing the incentive system (which is consistent with government policy) and the threats (which are not, although the government could surely do more to prevent such abuses, and it may well have tried harder in recent years).

In between are the kinds of policies being debated in the United States as I write, such as limits on the number of children that can be supported by welfare payments. Such limits would, presumably, discourage excessive births among the poor. Many other countries, such as India, have tried some incentives for population control, but these policies have not been consistently implemented and the results have been unclear.

At issue here is what coercion is and why it is wrong, and what rights people should have to construct their own values. A utilitarian answer considers both the value of autonomy and the nature of social dilemmas. Autonomy is valuable because people do know their own values best and because respect for the principle helps people learn to make decisions. Social dilemmas, on the other hand, pit the rational self-interested decisions of each person against the goals and values of others. Families may achieve their own goals best if they have three children on the average, but this rate of births may make life worse for everyone. At some point, the effects on others justify interference with autonomy. We are so used to this in many cases that we do not notice it: property rights are a government-enforced constraint on freedom.

So, in principle, the need for population control can justify some sort of intervention, but what sort? (The same kind of problem arises in management of fisheries.) Should we impose a limit on families, as China has done? try to persuade people to have fewer children? or provide incentives? One problem with persuasion is that it has differential effects. Appeals to the common good may discourage the most civic-minded families from having children, while the least civic-minded continue to reproduce freely. Incentives in the form of benefits for restraint, as used in China, may affect mostly the poor. Such policies are beneficial because they encourage childbearing among those most able to care for children, but they may breed envy among the poor, as well as children among the rich. Absolute limits, enforced with heavy incentives and disincentives, hit especially hard at those with a very strong desire to have children. In this respect, the regulation of childbearing is unlike the regulation of fishing. The question of which policies are best has no obvious general answer. In such a case, toleration of different approaches may be the best approach.

Some would argue that positive rewards for few births are morally acceptable but disincentives for too many births are not. Thus, the Chinese policy of giving extra salary to those with one child is acceptable, but reducing the salaries of those with two children is wrong. However, what we take as a reward or a disincentive depends on our reference point. If the reference point is the salary of those with no children, those with one child gain and those with two children lose. If we take the reference point as the status of those with two children, then everyone else gains. If we use families who obey the policy, the majority, everyone else loses, including those without children. In all cases, the total amount of salary available to everyone remains fixed, and the issue is simply how it is distributed. If some of these goods are removed from some people, then other people necessarily get more. (This is not always true. Pure punishments like prison have no compensating benefits to anyone. But Chinese policy does not provide such punishments.) The question of what we take as the reference point does not seem morally relevant. The real question is whether it is acceptable to make distinctions between the salaries of those who follow the policy and those who do not.

The Mexico City Policy

The U.S. government, for better or worse, was a major donor to international population-control programs from about 1965 to 1985. Its efforts focused on direct provision of birth control — condoms, pills, sterilization, intra-uterine devices (IUDs) — to women of underdeveloped countries.[41] Some of these efforts were more effective than others, of course, but some did help to reduce the birth rate.

Meanwhile, in the United States, after the Supreme Court decision that legalized abortion in 1973, Senator Jesse Helms, an abortion opponent, proposed an amendment to a foreign aid bill that would cut off money for abortions as part of birth-control assistance abroad. A 1970 law (Title X) provided funding for all family-planning services except abortion, and some abortions were funded by a program of medical assistance for the poor (Medicaid). In 1976, the Hyde amendment prohibited the use of any U.S. government funds of abortion except in cases of rape, incest, and when the woman's health was threatened.

President Jimmy Carter, before his defeat by Ronald Reagan in 1980, commissioned a report on the future of world environmental issues, called the Global 2000 Report. It predicted serious overpopulation and resource depletion, and it urged increased efforts to control population. Conservative social scientists, led by Julian Simon,[42] objected to the doom-and-gloom tone of the report, and they argued that it underestimated the power of the free market.

At the Mexico City world conference on population in 1984, the Reagan administration, represented by former Senator James Buckley, argued that population growth was "a neutral phenomenon." Moreover, the United States, while continuing to support international family planning, would tighten its restrictions on abortion: "The United States does not consider abortion an acceptable element of family planning programs and will no longer contribute to those of which it is a part. Accordingly, when dealing with nations which support abortion with funds not provided by the United States government, the United States will contribute to such nations through segregated accounts which cannot be used for abortion. Moreover, the United States will no longer contribute to separate nongovernmental organizations which perform or actively promote abortion as a method of family planning in other nations." This is the essence of what came to be called the "Mexico City Policy." As a result of the last condition, money for the International Planned Parenthood Federation — an umbrella group of local agencies — was cut off immediately ($17 million per year), as was funding for the United Nations Fund for Population Activities ($40 million).

Funding for a third group, Family Planning International Assistance (FPIA), was threatened in 1987, when its contract with the U.S. Agency for International Development (AID) came up for renewal. A study directed by Charles R. Hammerslough of the University of Michigan School of Public Health attempted to estimate the effects of this third cutoff. Many women were depending on FPIA affiliates for birth control. Even when Hammerslough made generous assumptions about other means of obtaining birth control, he estimated that the number of births would increase by about 300,000 in the next three years, and over 60,000 additional abortions. A policy inspired by opposition to abortion was going to increase the number of abortions performed. It seems difficult to deny that this would happen without arguing that the birth control aid was having no benefit, and that was not argued.

Instead, supporters of the policy simply denied the conclusion. The National Right to Life Committee (NLRC) said simply, "This manufactured 'study' was commissioned and funded by PPFA [Planned Parenthood Federation of America] itself." It also argued that a previous cutoff of government funding for abortions (under Medicaid) had no detectable effect on maternal mortality, despite predictions that pregnancy-related deaths would increase. In fact, the number of births went up, as predicted, so the number of maternal deaths very likely increased as well, although perhaps not enough to detect statistically.[43] NLRC also argued that the cutoff would in the end reduce the number of abortions because the agencies that lost funding would be unable to lobby foreign governments to ease restrictions on abortion. So the NLRC believed its own predictions of reduced abortions, based on no actual data, while disbelieving a study that at least tried to get the numbers right and that was based on a mechanism at least as plausible as that envisaged by the NLRC. Likewise, when Secretary of State James Baker was asked about the study and its bearing on the policy that he said was "hammered out around the table in my office," he responded, "don't agree with it."[44] Wishful thinking, again, appears at work.

Why didn't supporters of the Mexico City Policy change their mind on the basis of this study? First, they had committed themselves already to a course of action. This commitment became more important than their commitment to the goals of that action. Second, their concern may have had little to do with consequences to begin with. It was not so much that they wanted to minimize the number of abortions but, rather, that they "just didn't want to pay for them."[45] It was the direct causal link between taxes paid and abortions performed that mattered, not the amount of taxes per se or the number of abortions per se. This is an intuition similar to the do-no-harm principle discussed earlier. People want to avoid going against their values *through their actions.*

The issue is still alive, as some Republican members of Congress continue to oppose funding of international family planning, with some success. A recent statement by the Christian Coalition made yet another argument against the claim that abortions will increase: "[Senator Mark] Hatfield . . . asserted that abortions will increase if international family planning funding decreases. However, his claim ignores the fact that Norplant, Depo-Provera, the Pill and other contraceptives often cause chemical abortions." Again, no statistics are available to support this claim.

Conclusion

Both sides in the population debate seem to ignore the possibility of a real tradeoff between current desires for children and current reproduction, on the one hand, and the quality of life of people, on the other. One side holds that, just by chance, reproduction is optimal, that it has no negative externalities. The other side holds that, while there is a problem, it will be solved if only people are allowed to increase their reproductive choices through greater access to contraceptives and to alternative lifestyles that do not depend on childbearing as the only means by which women can fulfill themselves. It is possible that these views are right, but it is also possible that some changes would be helpful.

Opposition to population control is partly the result of an intuition favoring autonomy. It is surely harmful to go against people's desires, other things being equal. Desires for children, however, have already been shaped by a host of subtle and not-so-subtle pressures from families, religions, and other social institutions. Autonomy has already been compromised. The state and other institutions have reason to be concerned about excessive population growth. These institutions can also influence people's values in a way that promotes greater use of birth control. Failure to exert this influence is to assent, by omission, to the values imposed by others. The honoring of autonomy seems to rest on a distinction between acts and omissions.

In a way, preferences for different numbers of children are like preferences for different kinds of automobiles. In countries where gasoline is inexpensive, such as the United States, people prefer larger cars. In Europe and Japan, where gasoline is heavily taxed, most people prefer smaller cars. This is not just a matter of grudging acceptance of an imposed policy. In time, it has become a matter of aesthetics and even perhaps morality. Europeans surely appreciate the styling of the smaller cars they drive. They have traditionally regarded American cars as gross, out of proportion, overdone, tasteless. Doubtless many people who at first bought a small car because they simply could not afford the gasoline for a larger one have now become convinced of the moral superiority of driving a car that has less effect on the environment. In the same way, attitudes toward large families may change. Once they were extolled as patriotic. In most developed countries now, they are considered lower class, foolish at best.

The imposition of values is distinct from the coercion of behavior. Coercion has greater cost because it requires going against the values that people have rather than changing these values so that people do not regret their choices. Family-planning programs typically try to change values rather than coerce behavior, although China and a few other countries have applied external incentives because they feel they must. But even China relies primarily on persuasion.

So there can be true costs of violating autonomy. The question is whether the costs are justified or whether changing people's desires is also a violation.

The principle of autonomy works together with a second principle, the principle of naturalism, to create opposition to birth control and abortion. The next chapter will focus on this intuition.

CHAPTER 9

Naturalism and the Sanctity of Life

Societies all try to maintain some kind of moral code or set of principles. One common way for people to convince each other of the importance of the code is to encourage the belief that the code is not a mere human invention but that it comes from outside, from nature in the broad sense that includes everything other than humanity. This belief in naturalism makes the code less subject to questioning. But codes invented by people can be questioned by people, and such questioning is the common fate of nonreligious moral ideas — specifically, the work of moral philosophers.

This idea of naturalism was common in ancient Greece, particularly among the Stoic philosophers such as Zeno. Aristotle adopted it as an essential part of his ethical theory. Largely through Aristotle, the idea of a natural moral law was developed by Catholic writers such as St. Augustine and St. Thomas Aquinas. It was taken seriously by writers of the Enlightenment, such as Hugo Grotius and Thomas Hobbes, and it continues up to modern times as a major philosophical tradition, outside of religion as well as within in.[1] My concern here is with our everyday intuitions, not with philosophical criticism. However, the writings of popes and bishops are still relevant because they are written for public consumption, not for philosophers.

Catholics think that it is wrong to go against nature in decisions about life and death, including euthanasia and birth control. Pope Paul VI drew heavily on this idea in condemning abortion and artificial birth control: "The Church . . . , in urging men to the observance of the precepts of the natural law, which it interprets by its constant doctrine, teaches that each and every marital act must of necessity retain its intrinsic relationship to the procreation of human life. . . . The reason is that the fundamental nature of the marriage act, while uniting husband and wife in the closest intimacy, also renders them capable of generating new life — and this is a result of laws written into the actual nature of man and of woman."[2] Catholics, of course, are not alone in thinking that human intervention in these decisions amounts to taking over the role of God.

Naturalism expresses itself in other ways. We have already seen, for example, how people are less worried about, and less willing to compensate, harms caused by nature as opposed to those caused by people. Opposition to human intervention in nature — from genetic engineering to artificial pesticides — is widespread. A more subtle form of naturalism is the belief that we can know what is right through our intuition. Presumably our intuition has been given to us by some natural force, such as evolution. This is a major strand not only in religious thinking but also in modern philosophy and jurisprudence. One problem with this belief is that intuitions disagree, both between people and within them. Another is that it is unclear just how our intuition came to reflect what is right. What is the causal connection between something being morally right and our intuition that it is right? It is easier to understand our intuitions as arising from overgeneralizations of learned principles, or from the emotions that evolution gave us, such as anger, which may be better suited for individual survival and reproduction in the wild than for moral conduct in society.

The idea of naturalism has been criticized on logical grounds. Moral statements are recommendations, but statements about nature — including statements about God — are presented as facts. Recommendations cannot be derived from statements about facts without some additional premise. If God said "Do not commit adultery," then it does not follow that we should not commit adultery unless we add the premise, "We should do what God said." Of course, religious people are happy to accept this added premise, but nonreligious people need not accept it. They might well ask why they should do what God said. Even religious people may wonder why they should do what someone else's god said when it conflicts with the dictates of their own. The added premise is itself a moral recommendation, not a matter of fact. To someone who thinks that a particular act of adultery is not wrong, this logic would not be convincing because the added premise can easily be rejected.

Of course, if we tried to follow the rules of strict logic, we would question everything. But the issue is not just a point of logic. The skeptic demands some reason that we should outlaw abortion or certain forms of genetic engineering. Appeals to God or nature are just unconvincing to those who feel that nature isn't always good, for those who question the existence of God, or for those who believe in some other god who says something quite different. And the strict logic is on the side of those who remain unconvinced.

One problem is this: the general idea that we should do what is natural is difficult to state in a way that includes only what its proponents want. Even the most primitive people use tools that were not given to them by nature alone. Today, the most antitechnological groups, such as the Amish, use a great variety of technology (including, for some, refrigerators driven by propane), although they do not have telephones or electricity. The rejection of technology is almost more a matter of preserving independence from the outside human world than it is a preference for what is natural. Catholics who maintain that the rhythm method of birth control is acceptable because it is natural — despite the use of thermometers, graphs, and mathematical calculations — have similar difficulty explaining where to draw the line.

Application of the natural-law idea often relies on a false distinction between acts and omissions. People confuse not acting with not deciding. When we decide to let a painful and degenerative disease take its natural course — rather than taking steps to hasten the patient's death and end her misery — we are, in fact, deciding to do this. We could have prevented this, so we are just as much responsible for the outcome as if we had "directly caused" it. We cannot walk away from the fact that we have control, that we have the power to change things. Refusing to exercise that power is a decision.

Pope Paul VI drew on the act-omission distinction in explaining why artificial birth control goes against nature while the use of the rhythm method does not: "Neither the Church nor her doctrine is inconsistent when she considers it lawful to take advantage of the infertile period but condemns as always unlawful the use of means which directly prevent conception, even when the reasons given for the latter practice may appear to be upright and serious. In reality, these two cases are completely different. In the former the married couple rightly use a faculty provided them by nature. In the latter they obstruct the natural development of the generative process."[3]

As in other cases we examined, people often buttress their belief in naturalism by wishful thinking. A good example of this is the reaction of many residents of Oklahoma City to the bombing of the Federal Building by an antigovernment terrorist (Timothy McVeigh), in which dozens of children and adults were killed. As one resident put it, a man who acquired the name of Angel Man for his heroic kindness in helping victims' families, "Even if [the bomber] meant to do evil, he managed to accomplish some good. All he did was cause the genuineness of Oklahoma to come alive." When asked why God allowed the death of children, he said, "What's so amazing is that God can take bad situations and make wonderful things out of them . . . in a way it overshadows — it may not look like it overshadows, but in the long run, He's made a miracle out of it. Sometimes He allows things to happen to bring people together."[4] In this sort of thinking, people do not perform the overall cost-benefit calculation. If they weighed the good against the bad, objectively, they would find the bad to be heavier. Failing to do this allows them to maintain their belief in the goodness of God and get on with their lives. Of course, this in itself may be a good thing, perhaps even enough to outweigh the bad effects on their beliefs. My point is simply that wishful thinking helps to maintain a belief in the goodness of nature or God.

This chapter will discuss the role of naturalism in debates about abortion, birth control, euthanasia, life-sustaining therapy (in both infants and adults), fetal testing, and bio-engineering. These issues are important for two reasons. First, they are of some importance in their own right. For example, medical costs are increased because of people's unwillingness to prevent the births of severely impaired fetuses, and population may be increasing too quickly because of opposition to artificial birth control and abortion. Second, issues of this sort often set people at each others' throats, preventing political systems from dealing with more pressing problems.

Abortion and Nature

At the beginning of his book *After Virtue*, the philosopher Alasdair MacIntyre asks us to imagine a world in which science has been destroyed in a cultural revolution. Laboratories are wrecked. Books are burned. After the revolution subsides, people try to re-create science, but all they have are fragments. "Adults argue with each other about the respective merits of relativity theory, evolutionary theory, and phlogiston theory, although they possess only a very partial knowledge of each. Children learn by heart the surviving portions of the periodic table and recite as incantations some of the theorems of Euclid." Although this has not happened to science, MacIntyre suggests that it has happened to morality. Or, more precisely, it might as well have happened. Our moral discourse is in disarray. We posture, make arguments, but we talk past each other. We are as unable to think about morality as MacIntyre's postrevolution people are to think about science.

The abortion debate, particularly in the United States, encourages such despair. We do not need to accept (or deny) MacIntyre's solutions — a return to an ethical system based on personal virtues — in order to be concerned about the situation. Total confusion reigns.

We can see this by examining some arguments commonly made about abortion. My interest here is in the intuitions that people use to support their positions. Of course, the debate is conducted in many other ways aside from verbal expressions of intuitions. The opponents of abortion, in particular, rely on powerful images of fetuses, which arouse our sympathy because they look so much like the babies they would soon become. But these images are effective just because they play into intuitions that we already have. In particular, the anti-abortion argument gains part of its power from its reliance on the intuition of naturalism. It seems natural to let the fetus develop. When people argue against abortion, they bring many other intuitions to bear. But most of them seem unable to stand on their own without something more basic serving as the underlying motive. Once this underlying motive is present, people seize on arguments to buttress their position — arguments that they might not otherwise accept.

To examine moral intuitions about abortion, in a study carried out at the University of Pennsylvania in 1988, I asked subjects to imagine that they were going to participate in a class discussion on the topic, "Are abortions carried out on the first day of pregnancy [e.g., by the "morning after" pill] morally wrong?" I asked them to prepare for this discussion by making a list of the arguments that occur to them concerning the topic. I chose the "first day" question in order to avoid issues of disputable scientific fact, such as when the fetus first feels pain, when it is conscious, and so on.

Many of the arguments were weak in the sense that they ignored an obvious rebuttal. I begin with some pro-choice arguments, just to show that bad arguments are found on both sides. But I want to concentrate on the anti-abortion ones.

A common pro-choice argument is that "Women should have power over their own bodies." One rebuttal is that the fetus may be considered as a separate body. (At least one must explain why not.) Another rebuttal is: "Why should I accept this rule if I think that the fetus is being harmed by a woman's decision? Perhaps this should be an exception to the general rule that people should be allowed to control their bodies." Another form of this argument is: "The child is not yet an independent, thinking human. It's still being carried by the mother. Therefore, it's her choice whether or not to continue carrying it." Again, this argument neglects the other side: the fetus also may have rights. Again, a critical objection is ignored.

Another weak pro-choice argument is that abortion is a personal decision, of no concern to others. "A couple should be able to decide what decisions are best for them without the coercion (governmental or moral) of any other person." "It's a personal decision, and people must decide if they themselves feel it is morally wrong or not." "It is not for anyone else to label as moral or immoral, since it is the pregnant woman who can make that judgment based on her own measures of morality and the conditions surrounding the situation." "People have no right to force their morals on someone else. Who is to decide what is morally right or wrong?" "No living animal is born (or conceived) with an intrinsic 'right to life.' Any 'right to life' to anything exists because we humans posit it, not because of any a priori circumstance or condition. Positing this right is arbitrary; therefore, the existence of a 'right to life' is arbitrary." Again, a critical counterargument is ignored. The opponents of abortion think it is akin to murder. Imagine saying these things about, for example, killing your spouse's lover. Is this not a topic for moral judgment and legal constraint? If something is very bad, very immoral, then perhaps we *should* interfere with those who do it, both by expressing our judgments and perhaps by legal sanctions, too.

A final weak pro-choice argument — relevant only to the morning-after pill rather than abortion in general — is based on uncertainty. "*Morality* involves consciously recognizing right and wrong. In the case of the morning-after pill, the woman does not *know if she is pregnant*. Therefore, the moral argument does not apply." In other words, if you don't know you're pregnant, then what you are doing does not amount to killing a fetus. Clearly, this argument would not be applied to other cases in which people put others at risk of harm — for example, serving food to your guests without washing it. "Since you don't know that it is contaminated with salmonella, then you cannot be blamed if someone gets food poisoning." Very likely, this argument is not a primary reason for accepting the morality of the morning-after pill. It is more likely to be a post-hoc rationalization, the result of wanting the proposition to be true and then searching for arguments that would make it true.

Turning to the anti-abortion side, the most common argument is a form of a fallacy first pointed out by Aristotle, "begging the question." This amounts to simply asserting the conclusion, or asserting it in a slightly disguised way: "Killing a fetus is murder." "Abortion is the murdering of an innocent child." Such an argument cannot persuade anyone who does not accept the conclusion. Nor does it even provide a reason for the speaker to oppose abortion. It is simply the conclusion that he has reached.

The problem is that most of us find it acceptable to kill some beings but not others. Most of us tolerate the killing of mosquitoes, the "harvesting" of fish (thus causing them to asphyxiate on the deck of a fishing boat), the "slaughter" of chickens, pigs, and cows, and the killing of adult humans in self-defense. Many of us also tolerate predictable deaths of noncombatants in war, capital punishment, passive euthanasia, and even active euthanasia. So the question is not whether killing is wrong but, rather, who or what can be killed morally. (Surely there are some abortion opponents who do not eat meat or swat mosquitoes, but probably not very many.) This is exactly what the question-begging argument does not address, and exactly what the major dispute is about.

It is surprising that people make such question-begging assertions in public discourse, if we think they are trying to persuade by reasons, for they give no reasons. They act as if they think they can wear down their opponents through repetition. When both sides do this, we have the kind of exchange that MacIntyre finds so depressing — arguments flying past one another. Deanna Kuhn has documented this attitude in interviews.[5] For example, one respondent said that the only way to affect others is to "repeat yourself parrot-like. . . . there's no way you can convince the other person . . . [but] you reduce their resistance to a point." Many respondents seemed to think that opinions were never formed on the basis of reasons, so reasons were useless in public discourse. Such a belief allows people to ignore reasons in forming their own view. It is a kind of fatalism about the irrationality of belief. Although it is doubtless often a correct belief, it cannot *always* be correct. Some people form their beliefs on the basis of reasons some of the time. When everyone else is divided, these people may make a critical difference in the determination of public outcomes.

Another anti-abortion argument is that abortion is not ideal; it is a second-best solution. "Abstinence is the best method." "One wouldn't have to decide about an abortion if they didn't get impregnated in the first place." This is the same sort of argument made by fishermen who opposed some regulation on the grounds that some other (unattainable) regulation would be better; and by some left-wing opponents of population control, who argued that redistribution of wealth would be better. In all these cases, the rebuttal is that the ideal is in fact unattainable. Abortions are sometimes needed because abstinence has not occurred. Of course, abortions may be needed in other circumstances, such as the discovery that the fetus has a serious genetic disorder. More generally, abortion is sometimes the best of the options available, not the second best.

Perhaps this kind of argument is really a shorthand for an argument about sex. A traditional view of sex holds that it is wrong outside of marriage. A tradition of self-denial associated with many religions fosters the view that sex for pleasure is suspect, even within marriage. Thus Catholic doctrine opposed "artificial" birth control because it goes against the natural and legitimate purpose of sex, which is procreation. Sexual pleasure is not wrong so long as it is, in some sense, a by-product. Religious or legal prohibition of abortion may thus be part of an overall plan to channel sex into marriage and into procreation. The availability of abortion outside of marriage makes sex less risky. It is this connection that makes some Freudian liberals claim that abortion opponents are "sexually repressed." In fact, they simply want to place limits on sex. I shall return to this argument later on.

Another common type of argument seems to get more at the heart of what bothers people about abortion, rather than being a post-hoc rationalization recruited after an opinion is formed. This is that people should not decide the fate of the fetus. "How can you decide its fate?" This argument assumes that not to abort is not to decide, and therefore not to have the "arrogance" that comes with taking a decision upon oneself. The counterargument is that not acting is also a decision, once the option of acting is known. This is another example of the distinction between omission and commission. Abortion is wrong because it is a commission. Preventing life by abstaining from sexual intercourse, an omission, would not be considered blameworthy even though it, too, can be seen as deciding the fate of a future person.

A clear example of the use of this distinction by opponents of abortion is in the case of Mandy Allwood, a British woman who became pregnant with octuplets after fertility treatments. Doctors thought that it was practically certain that none of the children would survive, and they advised Allwood to abort most of them, in order to allow some to survive rather than none. Abortion opponents, however, were happy with her decision to do nothing. "I want nature to take its course," she said. Professor Jack Scarisbrick, head of the anti-abortion organization Life, said, "There are all these surgeons sharpening their scalpels when all that needs to be done is let nature take its course. . . . She will undoubtedly lose some of these embryos without resorting to the knife. If eight survived it would be unparalleled, but life is life. If she has many children she will be a celebrity and they will be taken care of. . . . I am delighted by her pro-life response to this challenge. It's wonderful news."[6] The fetuses all died.

Interestingly, the same confusion of omitting and not deciding is found among environmentalists who oppose tinkering with the natural environment. In explaining why killing species was immoral, one person said, "I don't see why we should be able to decide what species live and which die."[7] Again, the problem here is that we *can* decide, and nothing can undo that fact. It may well be that we should decide to preserve all species (at a great cost, because we would have to forgo many human activities), but that is our decision.

A related argument is this: "I believe that the fetus is a person because once it 'starts,' nothing can naturally stop it except for abortion; thus it is equivalent to murder." The problem is that the reason it is wrong to kill may not apply until the change from fetus to person has taken place. A stone may turn into a statue, and it would be a crime to destroy the statue but no crime to destroy the stone. The same argument is found in religious texts: "It is anticipated murder to prevent someone from being born; it makes little difference whether one kills a soul already born or puts it to death at birth. He who will one day be a man is a man already."[8]

Other arguments aside from these appear in public writings on abortion. One that is common in Catholic writing is that "direct killing of the innocent is always wrong."[9] The emphasis here on innocence is the result of a good heuristic rule for distinguishing morally justified from unjustified killing. Killing in self-defense, for example, is not killing the innocent. But this is a rough rule at best. Wild animals that we hunt are also innocent, as are some civilians who die from bombs in war. To take the innocence of the fetus seriously, we must already think of it as having the kind of right to life that people have after they are born, so this argument is a more subtle way of begging the question.

Some of the arguments I have presented, on both sides, are so weak that they seem like rationalizations, believable only because they support a conclusion that someone wants to be true. Other arguments seem to be of a sort that played some role in forming the opinion.

On the pro-choice side, perhaps the most basic argument comes from a desire for personal autonomy. For example, in opposing a reduction in welfare payments to teenage mothers, Kate Michelman, head of the Abortion Rights Action League, argued, "It's just as wrong to force a woman into an abortion she may not want as to prevent her from getting an abortion she may need."[10] What rankles many pro-choice people most of all is the idea of being told that abortion is wrong, and perhaps prohibited, when they have decided otherwise in good conscience. This is much the same feeling that leads fishermen and others to oppose government regulation. It also leads to opposition to population control, which may involve changing people's values for having children. All of these positions may be right, but this intuition by itself is not enough to establish their rightness.

On the anti-abortion side, the fundamental issue seems to be that abortion goes against nature. This assumption would make sense of the last two anti-abortion arguments that I presented. We should not "decide" the fate of the fetus when our decision leads to an unnatural outcome, abortion. Likewise, in the anticipated-murder argument, it seems critical that nothing can *naturally* stop the fetus from developing.

The importance of naturalism is more obvious in religious writing on abortion. The Catholic Church, in particular, has opposed abortion as part of a larger opposition to "unnatural" methods of birth control and procreation. For example, it condemned a surrogate pregnancy of a baby whose genetic mother was killed in a car crash on the grounds that such a pregnancy was tantamount to "trampling the right to be born in a human way."[11] Other religions use similar arguments.

The same appeal to naturalism may support the opposition to sex for pleasure. There is just no evidence that abortion opponents are particularly "repressed" sexually. More likely, they see sex for pleasure alone as an attempt to cheat on nature's rules by taking the benefits without "paying the price" — that is, bearing a child. The same argument leads to opposition to birth control, and indeed, abortion opponents tend to be less enthusiastic about birth control as well, although many of them tolerate it.

It is easy to make fun of this sort of reasoning. The basic premise is that what is natural is morally good, and what goes against nature is wrong. Thus, we should not fly in airplanes because (as someone once told me), "If God had meant for us to fly, He would have given us wings." Technology itself would be immoral. Possibly some groups, such as the Amish, manage to hold a view like this consistently, adopting only the minimum technology needed for survival. But many people who take this line are somewhere between inconsistent and hypocritical.

And yet it seems quite reasonable to limit the doctrine of natural law to special events, like those connected with the creation of life. There is a mystery in such events. If one is going to be religious at all, one must think that the coming into existence of a sentient being is a miracle of the first order, however often it happens. If one is going to apply a doctrine of natural law anywhere, this would seem to be the place. If we are going to criticize the natural-law opponents of abortion, it will not be for flying in airplanes or using telephones.

The argument is still subject to criticism, however. The problem can be stated many ways. One is this: Suppose I respect the miracle of creation, but I think that this is within the human power to control and that there is nothing wrong with our controlling it. What reason can abortion opponents give me to change my view? We are back to question begging. They would state that not exercising this control is natural, so therefore it is good and exercising control is wrong. But this is precisely what I just disputed. Humans — with our culture, power, and technology — are arguably part of nature.

The argument about nature may be understood as a useful heuristic that is overextended and to which people have become overcommitted in some areas. We have good reason to respect natural processes, to see them as quasi-intelligent designs that are meant to serve purposes that we consider good, such as our own survival and our survival as a species. Thus, when we read an article claiming that people recover from flu more quickly if they do not take aspirin, that is reasonable (whether true or not) because we can imagine that the mechanism of fever evolved exactly because it helps us get rid of infections.

We need not, however, adopt this principle blindly. It might turn out that fever is the result of the evolution of viruses and bacteria, not mammals, and that its evolutionary purpose is to provide a better host for their reproduction. And it might turn out that changes have occurred since we evolved. In the early days of human beings, the problem was to get the rate of reproduction high enough so that we did not die out (as many closely related species apparently did). Now, it seems that the risk of underpopulation is not very great. If anything, we are more likely to face extinction from some catastrophe associated with overpopulation. So what was once natural and good about human reproduction is now natural and not so good. We can understand this. We do not need to fall back blindly on the rule that natural is good. We can see when that rule is a good guide and when it is not.

Likewise, the idea that reproduction is "God's domain" (and therefore not to be trespassed by people) is based on the useful heuristic of property rights. Property is a human invention that has served us well. When we allow people to buy and sell property, they have more of an incentive to maintain it than they would have if anyone could use it. Property may be related biologically to territorial possession in animals, which has also served to reduce conflict among members of the same species and to distribute food more efficiently. It is reasonable to ask whether we ought to apply the same rule here, but it is difficult to see how we might arrive at any reason one way or the other (unless we are already committed to an answer). The idea that reproduction is God's property is an extension of this concept beyond the domain where its purpose can be understood.

Part of the problem with the abortion debate is that people do not expect much from their arguments. They tend to see moral argumentation as an extension of politics. The idea is not so much to convince anyone as to exercise force or power. This attitude justifies my-side bias by making reasons irrelevant.

At a deeper level, this problem applies to religious arguments, too. Ambiguous arguments are taken as supportive of a preexisting position based on something else. As in the case of birth control, the Bible provides many ink blots for the reader to interpret. Some passages (e.g., Psalms 139:13–16) can be interpreted as extolling the wonders of the creation of human life, but in a way that is fully consistent with the belief that creation is a gradual process. Other passages (e.g., Hosea 13:16) refer to the extreme horror of "ripping open" a pregnant woman as an act of war. But the horror is easily understood as injury to the woman, both physical and because of the fact that the child is *wanted*. The penalties recommended for injuries that cause a miscarriage depend on the injury to the woman; this is the famous "eye for an eye" passage in Exodus (21:22–25). Other passages cited by abortion opponents simply recognize the undisputed fact that a person is formed in the womb, without moral comment (Isaiah 44:2; Psalm 51:5; Jeremiah 1:5; Genesis 25:24; Luke 1:15; Job 31:15) or proscribe the taking of innocent life without giving the fetus as an example (e.g., Deuteronomy 27:25). One passage (Numbers 5:11–31) even suggests abortion as a remedy for adulterous pregnancies. (For what it is worth, the Bible can also be interpreted to justify slavery: "You may acquire male and female slaves from the pagan nations that are around you" [Leviticus 25:44, see also Timothy 6:1]. These passages were recently cited by an Alabama state senator running for congress.[12])

Even Pope John Paul II admits that the Bible does not directly condemn abortion, although he is quick to argue that such condemnation is implicit: "The texts of *Sacred Scripture* never address the question of deliberate abortion and so do not directly and specifically condemn it. But they show such great respect for the human being in the mother's

womb that they require as a logical consequence that God's command-
ment 'You shall not kill' be extended to the unborn child as well."[13] And
"Although there are no direct and explicit calls to protect human life at its
very beginning, specifically life not yet born, and life nearing its end, this
can easily be explained by the fact that the mere possibility of harming,
attacking, or actually denying life in these circumstances is completely
foreign to the religious and cultural way of thinking of the People of
God."[14]

Even if the Bible condemned abortion clearly, additional arguments would be required to justify its moral authority as a sufficient basis
for law. The Bible provides little basis for reasoned argument, although
much basis for posturing.

A Pro-choice Argument

Opponents of abortion — and even some advocates of choice — often
fail to recognize the moral argument for abortion. They tend to think of
themselves as occupying the high ground, and they consider the other
side to be making excuses for what they know is basically wrong rather
than making a positive case. The proponents of abortion, however, have
cogent arguments that abortion is sometimes a good thing.

Can we reason at all about abortion, or about any moral issue? If
we remove all the bad arguments, is anything left? The purpose of this
section is simply to show that good arguments can be made. A complete presentation of these arguments, including rebuttals of counterarguments, would take another book. These arguments are, in one sense,
moral. That is, they concern questions about what we endorse for (and
enforce on) each other, not just what we do individually to achieve our
own goals. But in another sense, they are about consequences. I have advocated that all decisions should be made on the basis of their expected
consequences, and decisions with moral implications are no exceptions.
I have thus been advocating what, in moral philosophy, is called consequentialism or utilitarianism. By these views, there is no conflict between
what is morally right and what brings about the best consequences for
everyone. The only relevant distinction between moral decisions and
other decisions is the "for everyone." Consequentialist views or morality are truly in conflict with the idea that we should each bring about the
best consequences for our self-interest. This was the problem of social
dilemmas, the problem of the fishermen. Consequentialist arguments
have been made for abortion.[15]

The first argument is simple. When births are limited within nations or families, abortion of child A may permit child B to be born — or,
putting it differently — stopping the abortion of A prevents the birth of
B. (This is true even if the limits are flexible. If limits have any bite, then,

eventually, this tradeoff is made, if only through separate and apparently unrelated decisions.) If A would be very handicapped or if B came into a family more ready to care for it (or the same family at a better time), then at least something can be said for abortions. Abortion is a way of making the choice between A and B, when the choice must be made. If A is not aborted, this prevents the birth of B, yet we have assumed that the birth of B is the better result. The question is whether abortions are so wrong on other grounds that this kind of benefit is not enough. The consequences alone argue for abortion in cases like these.

Another moral argument for abortion puts it in a broader context that includes, on the one hand, the rights of animals, and, on the other, the morality of any attempt to limit births, including not only artificial birth control but also abstinence. Viewed in this context, the opposition to abortion appears to be a clear example of the use of intuition rather than reason in moral debate. Most of the intuitions I have discussed in this book apply as well to moral decisions as to any other decisions. Indeed, I have made no distinction between moral decisions and other decisions.

Why should we think about moral decisions this way? Here is a sketch of how this approach might be justified. This is just a sketch, and this is just one kind of moral argument that leads to the conclusion that abortion is sometimes a good thing (or at least less bad than the alternatives).

Imagine we live in a society without any morality. Obviously, it is relatively new or else it would have done itself in. Praise, blame, punishment, and gossip are unknown. Then someone gets the idea of having a moral system. The idea is that certain things will be counted as right and others as wrong. We will teach our children to do the right things and abjure the wrong things. We will say nice things about people who do the right things and nasty things about people who do the wrong things. We will try to stop people from doing the wrong things by "punishing" them publicly, so that others see what will happen to them if they do these things. And so on. We agree to do this. Now all we need to do is to draw up the lists for what we count as right and wrong.

So each of us has the chance to say that X is right or Y is wrong. This is what happens in the abortion debate. Some people say that abortion is wrong and others say it is not always wrong and may even be right sometimes. But in the imaginary world, we have no prior views. This is nice because it gets us out of the problem we have now. If I say "X is wrong" because I have always thought it was wrong without knowing why, you have very little reason to pay attention to me unless you already agree. I have given you no reasons. I have just asserted my view. But in the imaginary world this cannot happen because we have no prior views. We have just gotten the idea of having a morality. Thus, I must give you a reason, and I must even have one myself, or else there is no reason for me to say anything.

One reason that we all have is that we care about each other; we suffer when others suffer. We even desire that suffering be avoided whether we know of it or not, so it is not just our own personal discomfort that is at issue. If I say that "infliction of suffering is wrong" out of this kind of motivation, you have reason to agree with me. You share the same concern. A moral rule against suffering is likely to decrease everyone's suffering (including yours), and suffering is something you too would like to reduce. We can thus agree on moral rules because we already have certain desires for each others' good. The rules that we agree on in this way will be those that, in general, advance our good — that is, those that bring about good consequences and prevent bad consequences. And our judgment of consequences does not require any preexisting morality. We will thus endorse moral rules that bring about good consequences and prevent bad consequences. It is difficult to see any other reasons we would have for endorsing moral rules, since we have no prior moral beliefs. Our concern with consequences can thus justify a moral system.

Let us apply this kind of argument to questions about killing. To do this, we need to look at the reasons that people — or, more generally, beings — might not want to be killed. When we understand these reasons, we can ask how they apply to difficult cases such as abortion.

Some killing involves the infliction of pain. It is reasonable for each of us to disparage the infliction of pain. If we sympathize with each other's pain, then we do not want each other to suffer it. When someone inflicts pain on another, we speak badly of that person, and when it is bad enough we punish the person through the law. Our moral rules thus condemn the infliction of pain, other things being equal.

Late abortion may cause the fetus pain. Use of anesthetics may prevent this. Probably they are not used because everyone involved wants to believe that there is no harm being done. This is surely a mistake. But the infliction of a few moments of pain may be a necessary cost for some other good, even if it cannot be avoided. Early abortion, before the nervous system develops, can involve no pain. One might suppose that certain reflex reactions indicate pain, but one might also say the same of a Venus fly trap. We understand pain well enough to have a well-founded belief that a fairly mature nervous system is required for it. The moral rule against inflicting pain is irrelevant to early abortion.

A second set of reasons not to kill involve going against the desire of a being to live. This reason applies to animals and infants, but probably not to fetuses, although perhaps third-trimester fetuses have something like a desire to live. This is a more serious matter. We would each not want to have others go against this desire. It is a strong desire. We listen to each other when we say that it is wrong to kill someone who does not want to die (without good countervailing reason). That is a powerful moral argument.

The fact that the argument applies to pigs and cows — perhaps even to fish and chickens — may be reason to stop eating them. One might argue that abortion is morally acceptable because it is no worse than things that we already do, such as killing pigs, and we do that without much concern. But this is like saying that one wrong justifies another wrong. (There is a difference. We raise pigs to be killed, so they owe their brief existence to the fact that some people eat them. This may be better than their having no existence at all. The last thing that pigs would want, perhaps, is for the whole world to keep kosher.) If this argument applies to very late abortions, then we must demand very serious countervailing reasons in order to allow them, such as risk to the mother's life if the pregnancy is carried to term or the expectation that the fetus will not survive very long anyway. The question of who should make such decisions is not at issue here, except to say that it isn't clear that the law is the best instrument.

Peter Singer has pointed out another kind of reason for not killing adult humans (and perhaps adult chimpanzees and dolphins, and certainly human children after infancy).[16] This is that we have ongoing lives, plans and concerns that would be interrupted by our death. This goes beyond the biological desire to live, which we share with other animals. This is not an issue with fetuses, so it is not an argument against abortion. It is certainly a reason to care more about the mother's life when the choice must be made between that and the life of the fetus.

These are all easy reasons. It is clear that the things I have listed so far will be among the first things we think of as "wrong" in setting up a moral code. But none of them applies to early abortions. They give us no reason to think that early abortions are wrong. (And their application to late abortions may be overridden by other factors.)

At this point, people bring in another issue, actually an interesting one. Abortion cuts off potential adult life. This question is much more difficult to think about in terms of deciding what rules we would want for our moral code. Killing a fetus is not like killing a mosquito or even a pig, because neither will turn into a person if left to develop on its own. The question here is whether we want to include on our moral list a rule against preventing future adult life. Does our desire for the good of others extend to those who do not yet exist? (This is not the same as the anticipated murder argument discussed earlier, because that argument simply assumed that preventing life was equivalent to stopping it. We are now asking whether preventing life should be wrong in itself, whether or not it is equivalent to anything else.)

Before we get into the meat of this issue, notice that it has broader implications. Abortion cuts off potential life, but so does birth control. In fact, so do "natural" means of birth control such as abstinence. In general, any time we decide to do *anything* other than "be fruitful and multi-ply," we are making a decision that causes some person not to exist who might otherwise exist. This is true regardless of our intention. But in the case of abstinence — just in case you think intention matters — the very purpose of *abstaining* from sex is exactly to prevent someone's existence. Thus, if one opposes abortion on the grounds of potential life, then one should also opposed contraception (as the Catholic Church does) and also abstinence (as the Church does not).

It might be said that abstinence and contraception are different because contraception is an act while abstention is a failure to act. This distinction — the do-no-harm principle — is irrelevant if we accept the view of morality that I just sketched. If our moral rules arise only from our concern for each other's good, then the distinction between acting and not acting should not matter. If preventing potential life is harmful — if it goes against someone's good — then we must speak against it, whatever its cause.

Now, having seen that the question of potential life has implications that go beyond abortion, we can ask how we might even answer the question of whether this is something we want to add to our list of moral rules.

We can answer it by noting that we care about consequences for people because people have goals. They seek pleasure and avoid pain, and they have other goals, too. The things we put on our moral list have to do with the achievement of people's goals. When a new person comes into existence, that person's goals are added to the total set of goals that we care about. The question, then, is whether we want to view the adding of goals to the total set as something we want to promote.

Putting the question this way, we can see that it is the same question as whether we want to add new goals to those of a single person. This is a decision that we make even for ourselves. When we decide to pursue a career, get married, or take up a musical instrument, we add goals that were not there before: concern for the values of our chosen career, concern for a particular spouse, concern for the values of musical performance, and so on. These are not just ways of achieving goals that we already have. They are new goals, just like the goals that will come into existence when a person is born. Sometimes we think that it is good to add these goals, but sometimes we shy away from new commitments exactly because we think our plate is full. We worry that the new goals will interfere too much with the achievement of goals that we already have.

We can want to satisfy goals but not care whether the goals exist or not. We can even want them not to exist, although we will want to satisfy them if and when they exist. Bringing goals into existence and satisfying them once they exist are two different things. It is the latter that motivates our moral concern. We have other goals concerning the creation of new goals. When new goals arise from the creation of new people, they often impair the achievement of existing goals. From a social point of view, we may have reached a point at which we should perhaps even encourage each other to desire fewer new people.

In sum, then, stopping potential human life is something that does not belong on our list of moral prohibitions. Some people may have individual desires or ends concerning the creation of new people, but it is going to be hard for them to persuade others to add these to the moral list. If someone opposes abortion because of a desire to see new people born, that is just a personal preference, like saying, "Everybody should grow figs, because I like them." This does not mean the person's desire should be ignored. But it need not be elevated to the status of a moral rule. Of course, this applies to birth control and abstention too. These need not be considered wrong just because they prevent the existence of new people. (Again, this is just one argument, but it is a serious one, and my point is to show that the opponents of abortion do not *necessarily* have the high ground.)

It is still perfectly reasonable for us to say that we do not want the unborn to suffer *once they are born*. This does not mean that we want them to be born. Thus, for example, it is fully consistent for someone to think that it is a horrendous crime for a pregnant woman to abuse drugs *unless* she has an abortion, for without an abortion the drugs may seriously harm — subvert the goals of — a future person.

To summarize this argument, our reasons for moral praise or condemnation ultimately arise from our mutual concern for achieving each other's goals. We have examined all the reasons against abortion that arise in this way, and none of them applies to early abortion. If the moral case against abortion is to be made, it must be made in some other way. It must draw on some other principles than concern for each others' good. If someone does not already agree with these other principles, it is difficult to find any reason for supporting them. Moreover, if abortion is best in some cases, in terms of good or utility, then preventing abortion is a harm. We should demand a justification for such harm — the harm of preventing an abortion that increases good — in terms we can all accept, even if are we not yet convinced that abortion is necessarily wrong.

Abortion opponents also need to worry about the consistency of the principles they follow. If they oppose late abortions because they think that the fetus desires to live, then they need to think about the rights of animals. And if they oppose abortion on grounds of stopping potential life, they need to think about other ways of preventing births, including abstinence. If they think that these reasons are relevant only when they both apply together, they need to say why in a way that is relevant to those who do not yet agree.

We can thus seriously argue that abortion is not necessarily wrong. It would take at least another book to spell this argument out in a way that answered all the objections that people are likely to make to it. The relevance here is that the opponents of abortion do not necessarily occupy the high ground. If abortion is not morally wrong in itself, and if it has some benefit, then it is more than not wrong — it is right.

Abortion in Practice

When we look at the real world *with these considerations in mind*, it is easy to conclude that abortion is sometimes indeed a good thing. The clearest cases are those in which fetal testing indicates some serious abnormality, such as spina bifida. Someone faced with the possibility of such a seriously disabled child might well think that it is better to try again. Although both this child and its "replacement" would be loved, the replacement would have a better life and would be more likely to help others.

Fetal testing and abortion are also used for highly questionable purposes. In India, entrepreneurs travel the countryside with ultrasound machines, offering for a fee to determine the sex of a fetus. Girls are often aborted because boys are preferred. The Indian government has banned fetal testing for sex determination, but the law does not apply to those doing the bulk of it. Moreover, it is almost impossible to prevent such decisions without specifying in detail the legitimate reasons for abortion. As a practical matter, it would seem that the solution to this problem lies in greater rights for girls and women, and other changes in customs (such as those concerning dowrys) so that the bias toward male children will be reduced. Increased equality for women is surely desirable on other grounds, as well.

We are not far away from being able to test fetuses for IQ and other desirable traits. In principle, fetal testing and abortion could be used to select children with traits desired by the parents, even eye color. People will object to such uses on the grounds that this is unnatural. If we are concerned with consequences, though, this is only a sign, a reason to look harder. In some cases, when we look, we will find more serious reasons to discourage or ban some practice, reasons that grow out of our concern for each others well-being rather than out of our unreflective intuition. For example, selective abortions of girls, on a large scale, can increase the number of unmarried people, particularly males, because of not enough females to go around. In other cases, such as a preference for high IQ or blue eyes, there may be no harmful effects. We should look closely, but if we fail to find any bad effects, we should not assume they are there just because the process is unnatural.

Another good reason for abortion — perhaps the most important — is contraceptive failure. All contraceptives fail sometimes, so the only absolutely sure way to avoid pregnancy (virgin births aside) is sexual abstinence. Married and unmarried people want sex but may not want children. In an overpopulated world, we should certainly not frown on sexual desire. Sex within marriage can also be seen as an unadulterated good. Even if we ignore the fact that pleasure is a simple and straight-forward good in its own right, sex helps hold couples together. (Even Catholics recognize this function and thus do not hold that sexual plea-sure in marriage is wrong.) Thus, abortion for married people is a way of ensuring that they can enjoy sex without risk of pregnancy. If we are at all concerned with population control, access to abortion is almost necessary. (In this regard, the opponents of abortion who also oppose population control are correct. It is somewhat inconsistent to say that one is for population control but also in favor of stopping all abortion, although we might expect abortion rates to decline with increased use of more effective contraceptives.)

Sex outside of marriage is more controversial. Many cultures en-courage marriage by reserving sex as a reward for getting married (or at least engaged).[17] But denying abortion to unmarried people seems a poor way to do this, for the unmarried are also the least ready, in general, to care for children. From a social point of view, perhaps our concern should not be so much with promoting marriage but, rather, with discouraging childbearing outside of marriage. If so, then abortion should surely be available to the unmarried, even if we decide to use other means to discourage sex among them.

A final reason for voluntary abortion is failure to use contracep-tives at all, even though no pregnancy was desired. This is unfortunately all too common. In some countries, particularly in Eastern Europe, mod-ern contraceptives are difficult to obtain, and abortion has been used as a primary means of birth control. In the United States, adolescents sim-ply fail to think ahead, or they think "planning to have sex" as morally worse than having sex on impulse. In such cases, opponents of abortion often want to make the adolescents "pay" by suffering the consequences of their thoughtlessness. The intuition here seems still to be the idea that nature should run its course, combined with the idea that nature pro-vides its own justice. It would be easy to find other ways to make people pay aside from having them bear an unwanted child that they are poorly prepared to raise.

So, when we look at the consequences of abortion, we can find few cases where it is desired by the mother yet also wrong in terms of its effects. Making abortion legal seems on the whole to have more benefits than costs, although it does have costs.

The more difficult case is coerced abortion. Here, our intuition favoring autonomy is strong. We think of childbearing as a fundamen-tal right, perhaps because it is a natural function. Yet there may be cases where we can be sure that coerced abortion produces better con-sequences on the whole. In China, for example, women may have abortions in order to obtain the benefits from following the one-child policy. This may or may not be what China's critics refer to as coerced abortion, but it clearly involves the use of incentives to promote abortion, so that some abortions are being done that would not be done in the absence of the incentive. (There have also been abuses by local officials in which more forceful methods were used, but this is not government policy.) The same could be said of various U.S. proposals to limit welfare for children. These limits may cause some women to have abortions who otherwise would have had a child in the expectation of a subsidy from the state. Some of these measures may be justified by the need for population control or the need to discourage childbearing when the circumstances for child rearing are poor.

Opponents of abortion (and of euthanasia, and of some applications of genetic engineering) often bring up the slippery-slope argument. For example, "Life is indelibly marked by *a truth of its own*. By accepting God's gift, man is obliged to *maintain life in this truth* which is essential to it. To detach oneself from this truth is to condemn oneself to meaninglessness and unhappiness, and possibly to become a threat to the existence of others, since the barriers guaranteeing respect for life and the defense of life, in every circumstance, have been broken down."[18] As I argued earlier, however, the slope slips both ways. Prohibition of abortion could, just as arguably, lead to other kinds of moralistic state intrusion or to neglect of the need for population control. Slippery-slope arguments require no assumption about the rightness or wrongness of abortion itself. The fact that abortion opponents think of one slope but not the other is a form of my-side bias.

On the other hand, the relative slipperiness of the two possible slopes may depend on circumstances. The danger of loss of respect for life seems greater with late abortions than with earlier ones. The legal distinction made by many countries between early and late abortion seems well justified by this principle. This is not to say that late abortion should always be illegal, only that it should be regarded as a much more serious matter, as it is almost everywhere.

Ending Life

Both the proponents and the opponents of abortion rights see abortion as related to many other issues concerning human life, and their attitudes have a similar basis. This issue typically arises during two life stages, right after birth and in old age. The former cases are newborns with horrible disabilities, such as anencephaly (no brain or little brain) and spina bifida. Of course, there is a continuum between such extreme cases and normal babies, and the difficulty of drawing a line makes the issue especially difficult for everyone involved. The latter cases concern the conflict between prolonging the life of people who are near death and reducing their suffering or saving the resources needed to keep them alive. Recently a third, much smaller, category has received attention — namely, those who, because of their medical condition, do not wish to live but could live for quite a while unless active steps are taken. These people often request the help of doctors in committing suicide, and some doctors provide this help.

Opponents of abortion typically oppose euthanasia, in all its forms, as well. The concern is again that euthanasia interferes with the course of nature or (what amounts to the same thing) the will of God. As Pope John Paul II argued, criticizing contemporary culture with respect to euthanasia and abortion, "there exists in contemporary culture a certain Promethean attitude which leads people to think that they can control life and death by taking the decisions about them into their own hands."[19]

Just as the act-omission distinction — the do-no-harm principle — affects attitudes toward abortion, it also affects attitudes toward maintaining life. In most countries and states, it is legal to withhold life-sustaining treatment, even if the cost of the treatment is low and even if the purpose is to bring about death. Even when the courts try to ignore the distinction, its defenders use it to criticize them. For example, Dr. Kenneth M. Prager, reacting to a recent ruling by a federal appeals court that permitted physician-assisted suicide, argued, "A key concept in the court's opinion was its equating a physician's withdrawal or withholding of life support in a terminally ill patient with prescribing medication so that the patient could commit suicide. Most physicians who deal with critically ill patients would reject this logic outright. If death is imminent, then withholding or withdrawing life support is appropriate because it prevents the prolongation of the dying process. This is indeed more 'natural' and morally acceptable than prescribing a lethal dose of medication to a sentient, reasoning, albeit suffering, human being. The latter is morally reprehensible and emotionally repugnant to a large majority of doctors because it is an act that leads directly to suicide: the premeditated snuffing out of a human life."[20] Of course, Prager mixes several arguments here, some based on the naturalness of the dying process in cases of passive euthanasia, and the imminence of death. However, imminence of death may or may not be present in either case. In some cases, patients can live in a vegetative, not-quite-conscious state for years if only a simple medical procedure is done, and often such procedures are legally withheld so that the patient dies.

In some states, such as Pennsylvania, it is even legal to give large doses of painkillers such as morphine, knowing that the morphine will hasten death and knowing that one would not give the dose otherwise, so long as one has the additional purpose of relieving pain. The legality of such actions harkens back to the "doctrine of the double effect" in

Scholastic moral theory. By this doctrine, the goodness or badness of an act is determined by the intention behind it, even if the actor knows of some other consequences that are produced as side effects.[21] Thus, because of this doctrine, Catholic hospitals are allowed to carry out medical procedures that kill the fetus in order to save the mother's life, provided that the lifesaving effect of the procedure is not causally mediated by the death of the fetus — that is, the fetus must die as an unintended side effect of the procedure. If the death of the fetus is what saves the mother's life, then the procedure is not allowed, even if the doctor and mother fervently desire that they did not have to kill the fetus.

This puzzling doctrine does not fit into any of the categories I have listed. It is not an example of the do-no-harm principle, for example. But it does illustrate a similar kind of intuitive reasoning that has gained a foothold in Catholic moral theory and in the Anglo-American legal tradition at least. Clearly, my list of problematic intuitions is not complete.

Otherwise, this issue is a good example of where an intuitive rule leads to my-side bias in the selection of arguments. At issue is the distinction between active and passive euthanasia. People point out possible negative consequences of active euthanasia that could as well follow from passive euthanasia. Or at least they don't ask themselves why they worry in one case but not in the other. For example, if active euthanasia becomes legal, it is argued, sick people will feel an obligation to die in order to save money, and doctors won't try as hard to save lives, since respect for life in general will have been reduced. Increasingly, in many countries, doctors themselves are held responsible for holding down costs. Opponents of active euthanasia are afraid that doctors would err on the side of death in order to save money.[22] Why don't these arguments apply just as well to the current practice of withdrawing or withholding life-sustaining treatment?

An interesting contrast is the argument of Yoseph Thompson of the Lubavitch Organization for Jewish Development: "Life was blown into man by God. Every moment of a human life is of infinite value. The value of life itself is infinite. Any attempt to depreciate the value of any time segment of a life destroys the absolute value of the entire life. An attempt to shorten the life of a dying patient because that life is no longer considered to be worth living will destroy the infinite and inestimable value of all human life in the eyes of society." Although Thompson takes Jewish tradition to oppose withdrawal of life-sustaining therapy under most circumstances, he makes an exception: "There is an obligation to heal; there is no obligation to prolong the suffering. Invasive procedures, extraordinary treatments or highly suspect treatments may not be performed. It is a question of allowing the natural ebbing of life forces to leave the person. We are not attempting to retain this person for as long as possible. We are seeking to give the treatment that is available."[23] Here, it seems, the intuition of naturalness is used to undercut the claims of "infinite value" that prevent euthanasia or assisted suicide under any circumstances.

Again, I must point out that I am discussing the arguments here, not the ultimate question of how assisted suicide and euthanasia should be handled by the law. The typical conditions under which life-sustaining treatment is withdrawn and the typical conditions of euthanasia and assisted suicide are quite different, and this difference may justify a legal distinction, even though there will be exceptions to the typical cases that, taken by themselves, would make such distinction seem unfair.

Naturalism and Birth Control

I have already discussed the opposition of the Catholic Church to "unnatural" forms of birth control. Catholics are not the only ones who worry about birth control because it is unnatural. Consider a recent postcard campaign against a new method of birth control: a "vaccine" against sperm. The idea would be to immunize a woman against sperm, using her own immune system. The announcement of the campaign argued:

> Research on new contraceptives is mainly guided by the perception that population growth in countries of the South has to be stopped. Northern countries see population growth in the South as a threat. To cut down birth rates, new contraceptives have been developed which are long-acting and which cannot be controlled by women themselves. They are designed to be easily administered on a large scale to women in Third World countries.
>
> For 20 years contraceptive researchers all over the world have competed to develop a "vaccination" against pregnancy. Research teams have been set up for example by the World Health Organization (WHO), the Population Council (USA), the National Institute of Immunology/India, and others. The majority of the funding comes from the North.
>
> Anti-fertility "vaccines" have a completely new mode of action. Unlike vaccines against diseases, they do not prepare the body to react against harmful germs. Instead, they cause an immunological disorder. They reprogramme the self protection and force it to attack substances that are part of the reproductive process. To emphasize the difference between vaccination against disease and "vaccination" against pregnancy, women's health activists put the term between quotation marks. They do not share the view that pregnancy is seen as a disease that has to be fought immunologically.

Different kinds of anti-fertility "vaccines" are being re-
searched. The most advanced and the most "promising" type
for researchers is a "vaccination" against the female pregnancy hormone hCG. This vaccination triggers an immune reaction against the natural hCG and is supposed to prevent pregnancy for at least one year. The contraceptive's action cannot
be stopped in case adverse effects occur or the women want
to discontinue it for other reasons.[24]

As is typical of arguments on most issues, this is a mixture of good
points and appeals to unsupported intuition. The text is, of course, right
in raising questions about the ease of reversibility of the contraceptive.
The first paragraph implies that the vaccine could be used more easily
than other methods without the consent of the woman. It is, for example,
much easier to administer than is Norplant, Depo-Provera, or certainly,
sterilization. One of the supporters of the postcard campaign, whom I
shall call X, confirmed this in correspondence with me. She was indeed
concerned about the possibility that the vaccine would be used without
the woman's consent. X was also concerned about possible risks to the
mother and to the fetus (should the method fail), and about the possibility that researchers would minimize these risks because the method
would be so attractive to those interested in population control. These
arguments are real concerns. Whether their magnitude is sufficient to
outweigh the need for more contraceptive options and the attractive features of this one (mostly convenience, lack of expense, and, indeed, low
risk compared to the alternatives) is something that must depend on a
more complete analysis.

Other parts of the argument suggested a concern with the unnaturalness of the method. (This is aside from the complaint about the term
vaccine, which is at bottom a complaint that the advocates of the method
are appropriating a positive term to make the method more acceptable.)
This appears to be the source of the concern with the fact that most immune responses are against diseases. On further questioning, X said that
she was concerned about unnaturalness. In response to a question about
her personal concerns that she had not yet mentioned, she said, "Using
the immune system to fight a fetus as if it were a disease sounds weird to
me. It would be better to educate women and men to address contraception in a way that is 'soft' to the body. I know that the pill also 'tells' the
body something which is not true (namely that it is already pregnant).
But this is a state the body knows, meaning it is not something 'foreign'
to the body what prevents the pregnancy. This is the kind of argument
I would not name in the first place since it is very difficult to evaluate
correctly."[25]

It is interesting here that X did not spell out this argument until
probed. She seemed aware that it was a personal intuition that she felt

herself but could not convince others to feel unless they already felt it when confronted with the facts. Such is the nature of the kinds of intuitions that I discuss.

What may have happened here was that this intuition, on the part of many of those who participated in this postcard campaign, triggered the search for other evidence against the vaccine. It was then easy enough to find the other arguments, the potential violation of autonomy, the possible risks, and the possibility of excessive zeal on the part of researchers and population agencies. What makes me think that this happened is that most of the same arguments could be made against essentially any method of birth control. Only the particular ease of administration of this one made it stand out, and that was also one of its advantages. Once the naturalness intuition had taken hold, the ease of use was seen mainly as a disadvantage.

Tampering with Life

The Ethics Committee of Hospital X deals mostly with "tragic choices." One of its cases concerned a young girl who had little more than a year to live, and the only hope for saving her involved a bonemarrow transplant. There were no suitable donors, but there was a chance that a sibling could be born in time to donate marrow. The girl's mother and father were divorced, but they were both willing to have artificial insemination so that the mother would become pregnant again. The mother wanted to test the fetus to see if it was a suitable donor and, if not, abort it. The Ethics Committee had an advisory role only, and nobody had to ask its advice. The mother, if she wanted, could do all this herself: she could go to one clinic for artificial insemination, another for fetal testing, and another for abortion, if necessary. But she and her doctors wanted advice. Her obstetrician, whom she consulted first, was initially aghast at the idea, but after mulling it over, he decided that it might not be so bad. He was the one who brought the case to the committee.

The committee wondered about whether a child born to be a donor would be a means rather than an end, thus violating the philosopher Immanuel Kant's prohibition against using people solely as means. (It would, after all, be aborted if it were not a suitable donor.) In the end, the utilitarian view prevailed. It was clear to everyone that the mother would love and accept the second child if it were born, even though she would not want it if it could not be a donor. Her willingness to do anything to save her daughter was, in fact, an indication of the kind of parent she would be. So the second child would not suffer from being a means to save the first, and the first might be saved. Those members of the committee who took Kant seriously were also those who tended to consider the mother's autonomy. They pressed the argument that the committee should not put itself in the position of deciding what was and what was not a good reason for other people to have children. The members more inclined toward utilitarianism were perfectly happy, in principle, to make such decisions, but they felt that the reason for having the child was not so important as the child's fate.

Medical technology now allows us to tamper with nature for our benefit in ways that go beyond simply curing or preventing disease. Such cases as this present us with a clear choice between immediate utilitarian benefit and violation of perceived natural law.

Another recent case involves the patenting of human genes and genetically engineered animals by biotechnology companies. Patents on genetic engineering are the mainstay of the biotechnology industry, a high-risk enterprise that has already shown some successes such as genes that stimulate production of human growth hormone and production of red blood cells. Recently, a coalition of U.S. religious leaders issued a statement asking the government to prohibit such patents. Richard D. Land, head of the Christian Life Commission of the Southern Baptist Convention, thinks that "we are on the threshold of mind-bending debates about the nature of human life and animal life. We see altering life forms, creating new life forms, as a revolt against the sovereignty of God and an attempt to be God."[26] Bishop Kenneth Carder, head of the United Methodist Church's task force on genetic engineering, argued, "The patenting of life forms reduces life to its marketability. Gone is the fundamental principle that life is a gift that ought to be shared and nurtured." William Friend, a Catholic bishop, said, "Pope John Paul was clearest about this when he said that all activity, all interference in the genome, must absolutely respect the specific nature of the human species and the incomparable dignity of every human being."

Even the defenders of genetic engineering argue that its purpose is "not to play God . . . [but to] play doctor. . . . to fix those [genes] that through an error of nature are not working properly." The idea that nature can make mistakes allows some limited role for human intervention.

A related controversy concerns the use of fetal tissue in medicine and medical research. Such tissue, transplanted into a patient, may be useful in treating Parkinson's disease, diabetes, and other disorders. It must be obtained from aborted fetuses rather than miscarriages because of possible disease in the latter. Opposition to research has been based on the possibility that women would be more likely to have abortions if they thought that the tissue might be useful to others. "In our view, if just one additional fetus were lost because of the allure of directly benefiting another life by the donation of fetal tissue, our department [Health and Human Services] would still be against federal funding. . . . The issue is about whether or not the federal government should administer a policy that encourages induced abortions. However few or many more abortions result from this type of research cannot be erased or outweighed by the potential benefit of the research."[27] Note that this argument makes explicit the neglect of quantitative considerations that may have been implicit in the argument concerning the effect of the Mexico City Policy on abortions. Here, it is clear that what matters is the involvement of the government in the action, not the balance of costs and benefits.

Of course, nobody likes to make explicit comparisons of costs and benefits, especially when the outcomes are highly uncertain. Thus, the advocates of fetal tissue research like to argue that nobody will have an abortion that they would not otherwise have just because they know that they can help medical research.[28]

Just before the final draft of this book was completed, Ian Wilmut and his colleagues announced (in February 1997) that they had produced a sheep, Dolly, by cloning another sheep. This opens the way for cloning human beings, producing copies of fully developed people that are as close to the original as identical twins are to each other. This event produced an outpouring of pronouncements by editorial writers, ethicists, politicians, and scientists around the world. Most of these were opposed to the idea of cloning humans — ever, whatever the benefits. Wilmut himself has joined this chorus.

There may be cases in which the consequences argue for human cloning. Suppose a child will die without a bone marrow transplant, but there are no suitable donors, as in the case described earlier in this section. The chance of producing a suitable donor by having a natural child is small, hence the likelihood of an abortion in that case. If cloning were permitted, the new child — a younger "twin" of the first — would be a suitable donor for sure. Thus, a ban on cloning would remove the best means of saving children in this situation. Admittedly, this is rare kind of case, but there may be other cases in which cloning would have such clear benefits.

Against this, the opponents of human cloning have seized on the risk that clones would be in some way impaired. Given present techniques, this risk is apparently real, but the problem could be overcome through research on animals, and any ban on cloning would still apply. The supporters of such a ban — apparently almost everyone — may be in the grip of an intuition that cloning is wrong because it is unnatural. The risk of impairment is not their basic reason for their opposition. They enlist it to support a conclusion they have already formed, on the grounds of an intuitive response. They may speak of consequences, but thinking about consequences was not the origin of their view.

Conclusion

The intuition of naturalness combines with other intuitions to produce opposition to policies that might, on the whole, be beneficial. These other intuitions include the do-no-harm principle, which distinguishes acts from omissions without regard to consequences. When we base policies on such intuitions, we cannot be surprised that the consequences are not as good as alternative policies. Moreover, because some people are concerned about the consequences themselves, we cannot be surprised by continued conflict. When someone cannot get an abortion — despite believing in good conscience that it is morally right — or a fetal tissue transplant that might save his life or health, or a cloned second child to save the life of a first child — he will complain, or others will complain on his behalf. He will want to know by what authority he is prevented from achieving a better outcome. He will ask where the intuitions of his opponents get their power.

CHAPTER 10

What Is to Be Done?

People often make decisions about public issues on the basis of their intuitions rather than on the basis of expected future effects, and they are often overconfident in the correctness of these intuitions. These problems distort public policy so that, in the end, we have less good and more harm than the limits of nature would otherwise allow.

These problems are greatest in the case of our moral intuitions. When we act on these, we typically affect other people more than ourselves. Because of this, we do not have the same opportunity to learn from experience as we do when we make more self-interested decisions. We do not experience the effects of participating in a demonstration or writing our representative in the same way that we experience the effects of buying a box of breakfast cereal or a bottle of beer. Our moral intuitions are thus less attached to reality than are our intuitions about most other things.

Moreover, moral attitudes, by their nature, are inculcated by society. We all have an interest in ensuring that we all follow the moral rules, so we set up institutions to make sure that this happens: the family, religion, schools, and to some extent the state. The institutions that are most effective in this task are not necessarily the ones that have the most direct pipeline to the moral truth.

Problematic moral intuitions are even harder to correct because they are never drastically wrong. There is usually some sense to them. The principle of autonomy is a good one most of the time. Likewise, naturalism; when evolution has had a chance to perfect something, like a kidney or an eye, we'd best not monkey with it unless we know what we are doing or unless we have little to lose. Even the do-no-harm principle is a reasonable one for the law; it would be highly impractical to try to apprehend and prosecute people who committed harmful omissions, even if we limited ourselves to cases of intended harm.

These intuitions could be useful if people understood why they are useful. But most people do not try to understand the moral principles they follow, and those who try often misunderstand. In particular, they misunderstand the way in which moral principles evolved to produce good outcomes, but their evolution is imperfect and ongoing.

How can we improve the situation? In answering this question, we must not be too cynical, and we must also not expect perfection. All of the possible solutions involve people doing things more often than they do now. The glass is half full, and we need to try to make it more full. Success is a rising level, not necessarily a full glass. Even a little more consequential thinking might make a difference to the world, and bringing such a change about might be one of the easier things we can do to help. Such a change is typically left off the list of recommended actions, so we have not yet taken some of the easy steps we could take.

Thinking about Citizenship

The main thing to do is to improve our attitudes toward our roles as citizens. Each of us should try to use our limited power to do the most good possible. We should evaluate policies and candidates for office in terms of straightforward judgments of which policy and which candidate would do the most good.

Policy Wonks and the Need for Data

If we are individually unsure what is best, we should listen to those who advocate this approach to policy. There are many, and they sometimes disagree with each other because they disagree honestly about the facts. They are often called policy wonks, and are often interviewed by reporters as experts. They can be identified by their attraction to facts and figures, which are necessary if we are concerned with predicting outcomes, and — with greater difficulty — by their willingness to deal seriously with facts that contradict their views.

Policy wonks often find ways of simplifying decisions by finding some useful — if approximate — measure of consequences. We are familiar with such economic indices as gross national product, which can measure economic development. Although the measure is crude and misses a lot, it is sometimes useful. For example, it has been used in recent decades to ask what factors promote or impede the development of poor countries.[1] Decisions about medical policies, such as when to begin screening men for prostate cancer and what treatment to use if cancer is found, can sometimes be made by estimating the conversion of both beneficial and harmful effects to life expectancy. A finer-grained measure is the increase (or decrease) in "quality-adjusted life years" (QALYs), in which an increase in life expectancy may be discounted if the quality of that life is poor (e.g., if the therapy leads to impotence and incontinence, in which case a shorter life without the therapy might be better).

If nobody is sure about policies, we should support data collection that will give us the facts we need. We can even try social experiments, in which different people are given different treatments. This kind of concern with the facts about outcomes extends to all kinds of policies, from medical policies to those concerning social welfare. When we undertake such data collection, we must also give each other the benefit of any doubt about whether we will respond rationally to these facts. If the facts are ignored, the money spent on the research is wasted.

Limited Domains

We do not typically view our roles as trying simply to do the most good. Instead, we tend to think that our responsibility is limited to certain domains. When we vote in a national election, we think we should consider the good of the nation but not the good of other nations. When we vote in a state election, we consider the good of the state, and so on.

For example, state governments compete with each other in offering large packages of benefits to lure industrial plants to their states. Often, it is clear that the plant is going to go to one state or another, and the only decision is which. One state's loss is another state's gain. From a national perspective, it doesn't matter much where the plant goes. And the situation is worse because the state that gets the plant often depletes its treasury, to the detriment of its citizens. (Alabama is reported to have paid $200,000 per job for a Mercedes plant.) The interesting thing here is that the states that do this appeal to their own citizens as voters, who, presumably, appreciate the government's efforts. In order for this to happen, when they vote in state elections, most voters — except the very few who will actually benefit from the plants — must care more about the other citizens of their own state than about the citizens of other states. Very likely some of the same voters will think about the national interest when they vote in national elections. Why? What rule says that we cannot think about national interest in state elections, or world interest in all elections?

Of course, we are more affected by what happens in our own state or nation than by what happens elsewhere, but this gives us little reason to favor our own nation in our public behavior because the effect of that behavior on ourselves is essentially nil. Recall the example of the widget makers. If each widget maker thought only of her narrow self-interest, then the cost of political action would exceed the benefits. Only if she considers the benefits to others is the cost worth paying. If she is willing to consider this, why stop at just some others who are helped by a certain policy? Why not consider those who are hurt, too? The same goes for national voting. If we are altruistic enough to care about our fellow nationals, why stop there?

Local governments do have certain responsibilities. Nobody living outside my town knows about the potholes that need fixing here, so they are not going to take action to ensure that these get fixed. The local citizens must do it, or nobody will. The same goes for certain state and national problems that are generally seen as internal responsibilities. But we can be concerned with these things and still be concerned as well with the effects of our government on those outside its borders. Indeed, when outsiders visit my town, they experience the potholes. My concern for fixing the potholes is thus necessarily part of a larger concern for others outside of this particular domain of responsibility.

Self-interest and Public Choice

One of the reasons we find it difficult to think about consequences for everyone is that we are often taught that this is not our function as citizens. Many observers of political behavior assume that people pursue their own interests in the political sphere, even when these interests conflict with the interests of others. Moreover, these observers assume that this is enough, that the system can work if this is all we do. And indeed it can work this way, but the question is whether it would work better if we thought more broadly.

Because many people hold this attitude, politicians appeal for our support on the grounds of our self-interest, telling old people that they favor higher Social Security, rich people that they favor lower taxes, and so on.

James Buchanan won the Nobel Prize in Economics for a theory of political behavior based on the idea that citizens and politicians pursue their self-interest in the political sphere, which has come to be called the "public choice" view.[2] The main danger of democratic government, by this view, is that a majority will gang up and extract goods — money — from a minority, even though the minority might benefit more from keeping the goods. The examples that tend to worry the public-choice advocates are not so much the persecution of racial minorities, homosexuals, and so on, but, rather, excessive use of taxation to provide benefits to some at the expense of others. Social Security for older people is a prime example. Voters tend to support candidates who favor higher Social Security if the voters feel they will personally benefit from it. Since most people think that they will live longer than average,[3] they think they will benefit. Another example is roads for drivers. Most people drive, so they get the nondriving minority to pay taxes to build roads for themselves.

Voting has been likened to buying something in the market. If more people prefer Pepsi to Coke, then more Pepsi is produced in response to the demand. Voting is like demanding a certain product. The same goes for other kinds of political action. Just as consumers are supposed to choose what they like most in order for the market to work, so citizens should do the same, by this view.

The claim, then, is that individual citizens, acting rationally to secure their own individual safety and happiness, can make a government work. Really? The first problem with this idea is this: if citizens rationally pursued their self-interest, most of them would not participate at all. The cost of participation is usually higher than the *self-interested* benefits.[4] Rational political actors must consider more than their narrow self-interest if they want good reasons to do anything. They must consider either their moral intuitions or their interest in other people's good.

Moreover, despite the theory, lots of evidence indicates that people generally do *not* simply vote their economic self-interest.[5] Political behavior in general is determined more by ideological commitments — by moral intuitions, as I have called them here. People vote on behalf of property rights, aid for the poor, tax reduction, economic nationalism, or whatever, when it is consistent with their moral view of the world, almost without regard to how it affects their pocketbook. When there is some relation to money, it may even be explained in terms of people choosing their course of life so that their financial interests tend to coincide with their ideologies. Left-wingers usually do not become investment bankers, and right-wingers do not go into social work. Also, people who become investment bankers tend to take on the attitudes of their associates, even if it was not exactly these attitudes that led them into this line of work. These factors can account for such relationships between political behavior and self-interest that exist.

In sum, the theory that political behavior is motivated by the rational pursuit of self-interest is just not true. If it were, people would participate much less than they do now, and they would behave differently when they did participate. We should stop telling each other that our political behavior is self-interested. It is, in fact, moral. It is motivated either by a concern for others — if only others like ourselves — and by our moral intuitions. If changes are needed, it is within the different types of moral concern: less intuition, more altruism. The argument that voting is or should be a matter of self-interest is a distraction.

Counting Consequences

If we focused our moral concern on the interests of all other people, rather than focusing on people like ourselves or on our moral intuitions, our political behavior would lead to better consequences for all.

Our behavior matters. Politicians are sensitive to public opinion, in part because it is in their self-interest, but in part because they see it as their duty. They look at the sizes of votes, not just who wins, and they look at opinion polls, letters, and so on. Opinion matters, however it is expressed. Yet the effect of one person's opinion on each single person, including the person holding the opinion, is small for each affected person, but many people are affected. As the number of people increases, each person's opinion is a smaller part of the totality of opinion but the effect of the totality increases, just because there are more people. If I make decisions just for myself, my opinion is the totality and the effect is on one person. If I am part of a group of ten, my opinion is a tenth of the totality, but the total effect is ten times as great. So there is little change in the total effect of one person, as the size of the group increases. The same goes for 6 billion people. I contribute only one six-billionth of the total, but 6 billion are affected, so it balances out to about the same. It is difficult to conceive of this, but it is not unreasonable to think that this is approximately the way things are. Participation matters when we consider its effects on everyone, not just the person who participates; and the size of the group in which one participates does not matter much, despite appearances to the contrary.

This conclusion goes against a kind of fashionable cynicism, which holds that citizens are powerless, that politicians are liars, and that the news is boring. The idea that citizens are powerless focuses on the dilution of each citizen's influence from folding it in with the influence of others. This can be countered by focusing on the huge number of people affected by even a small effect. And the news need not be boring. Perhaps it is not so hard for people to start thinking of world events as an ongoing story, as interesting as any soap opera. Once people start paying more attention, they may come to think that they too can influence the course of events, if only as part of a great whole.

Thus, we must be well informed and ready to act when action is called for, if only during elections. We must also try, as individuals, to avoid some of the major biases. We should recognize our tendency to be unfair to the arguments of our opponents. We should bend over backward to be charitable in interpreting what they say, to try to make sense out of it even when it first sounds like nonsense. If we simply do not have the time to be fair, then we should not be so confident in our own views. It is perhaps best if each person takes an interest in a few issues at most and then tries to figure out whom to trust about the rest.

In thinking about what stance to take on public issues, we should be willing to adopt the cooperative attitude. That is, even when our current self-interest opposes the interests of others, we should be willing to support measures that would change the situation for everyone's good. For example, we should be willing to vote for increased taxes to reduce a budget deficit, even if we would not spontaneously make a charitable contribution to the government. It is not in the least hypocritical to be unwilling to contribute oneself but, at the same time, favor a change in the law that would make everyone contribute.

Trust

Trust is important in relations between citizens and government. Giving power to the government requires believing, or acting as if one believed, that the government officials involved will use the power correctly. Ultimately, this involves trust in one's fellow citizens. They must be trusted not only to do their jobs when they are government employees, but also to recognize and correct future errors of policy. Without such trust, change becomes difficult. People are afraid to risk giving power to the government, and they remain attached to the status quo.

Stephen Breyer (now a justice on the U.S. Supreme Court), in his book *Breaking the Vicious Circle*, described a circle resulting from mistrust of government, simplistic laws that tie the hands of government, government abuses as a result of trying to apply those laws, more mistrust, more laws, and so on.[6] So trust in government may also require trust in the ability of government officials to make wise judgments. Of course, the officials must deserve such trust, and Breyer discusses ways to bring about a situation in which they do deserve it (which I discuss shortly).

Trust is also important at an international level. We must trust people from other countries to negotiate honestly, to try to keep their commitments to treaties and other agreements, and not to use military force except in self-defense. International commerce clearly depends on trust in foreign business associates to be as honorable toward foreigners as toward compatriots. International trust will become more important as the world moves to solve environmental, population, and resource problems that affect many nations.

If trust is a good, and if we want to promote it, what exactly do we want to promote? In one sense, trust is a belief about the goodness or rationality of others. If we want person X to believe that others are good (or rational), and if X's beliefs about others are generally accurate, then either we must make sure that the other people *are* good or we must deceive X into having inaccurate beliefs. Of course, if X is cynical to the point of inaccuracy, then we can increase his trust by bringing his beliefs into line with the facts.

However, trust is not just a belief. It is also a behavioral disposition that is somewhat independent of belief. In this sense, we can make X more trusting by changing his behavior alone. We can promulgate a norm of trust as a behavioral disposition. Of course, such dispositions are affected by beliefs, and beliefs are affected by reality, but there is slippage at each of these links. Although the effort to influence beliefs independently of reality may require deception, the effort to influence behavior independently of beliefs requires nothing necessarily immoral or irrational.

We may thus speak of two kinds of trust. The first is believing something about others. The second is behaving as if you believed this. Although the second sense may be derivative, it is no less real or important. So trust is a virtue, not just a belief. The virtue of trust is the tendency to behave *as if* one believed that others will behave in the right way, and the tendency to value such behavior in oneself and others. A virtue is a kind of norm that we encourage in each other.

Such a norm *could* take the form of endorsing self-deception. It could tell us to change our belief so as to think well of others. Although some people could interpret it this way, I do not. I think that the norm tells us to give others the benefit of the doubt *in our behavior*, whatever we might think privately. It tells us to have courage, to lie down and bare our necks, even when we are trembling inside. Of course, like any Aristotelian virtue, trust must be practiced in moderation. We call it a virtue only because there is too little of it.

A competing norm might be called the norm of suspiciousness. It tells us to watch out, to avoid entanglements, to have everything in writing, to hire a lawyer. People who violate *this* norm are seen as saps or suckers, as weak. If the norm of suspiciousness is a virtue, then it is a personal virtue, not a moral one. It does us little good to have a society filled with people like this. It benefits only the individuals and, even then, only if others tolerate those who follow this norm. It is the kind of norm that parents might teach their children out of a concern for their children's good, but we don't hear preachers or commencement speakers telling us to watch our wallets. Perhaps this is because their audiences have already learned these lessons pretty well.

The distinction between trust as belief and trust as a norm of behavior may seem somewhat artificial. People, after all, adjust their behavior to follow their beliefs, and they adjust their beliefs to be congruent with their behavior — but not entirely. Moreover, thinking of trust as a norm leads us to think of different ways to increase it aside from deceiving people about what other people are likely to do, or aside from fomenting revolutions.

Following the norm of trust has an effect on both the beliefs and the norms of others. It creates a virtuous circle opposite to the vicious one I described. My evidence that this norm exists in society comes from my own experience. It was explicitly taught to me, over and over, by Leslie Cheek, the head of a school I attended in the eighth grade. He said that if we act as if we expect the best from others, they will often behave better as a result. I have tried to follow this principle when I remember it.

If trust in others is a norm, what form should this norm take? I suggest the following norm as something worth encouraging. We should think of each other as willing to sacrifice somewhat, but not excessively, for the common good. Thus, when we set up cooperative agreements, some enforcement mechanism may be needed, but it need not be Draconian. For example, spot audits of taxpayers, together with small penalties for violations, may be sufficient. We should also think of each other as willing to cooperate to set up such reasonable enforcement mechanisms. We should endorse such willingness as a social norm, and we should behave as if we expect it from each other.

Norms of good citizenship should also include trust in government and in the ability of democratic government to correct errors. We should discourage arguments based on mistrust in government, especially when these arguments are used to oppose an otherwise good solution to some social problem. Of course, it makes no sense to encourage trust when the government is completely untrustworthy, but the sins of government are frequently exaggerated by a fashion of cynicism that makes trust sound naive. This kind of argument should be just as much a part of education in civics as are the arguments that inspire mistrust, the stories of corruption, and so on.

Politicians may create mistrust when they feel forced to present one-sided recommendations. They may feel that they must indulge in belief overkill in order to satisfy the voters who think this way. It would sound strange for a politician to say, "I will recommend a tax cut if my economic consultants tell me that the overall benefits will exceed the costs." Better to talk about giving consumers more autonomy by cutting their taxes, and not mention any of the negative effects. Once in power, politicians sometimes go against their more simplistic policy promises when they learn more about the facts. They are then seen as untrustworthy. Intuitive thinking then becomes part of the vicious circle. If citizens were more tolerant of policy-wonk arguments from the outset, they would be more understanding of necessary adjustments.

Politicians and Government Officials

Citizenship is crucial because nothing else can happen without it. If government is to improve, then citizens must understand and support the improvements. Still, there are a few specific things that good citizens can expect their government to do.

Pick Good Policies

Often the trick here is to ask questions about underlying goals. Asking about goals can lead to novel solutions. This will happen if we think about consequences. In particular, we need to ask which consequences we really care about.

Senator Daniel Patrick Moynihan tells the story of an apparent impasse between the goal of auto-accident prevention and the goal of minimizing restrictions on drivers.[7] The critical insight came when it was understood that accident prevention was not the fundamental goal. Rather, the main purpose of accident prevention was to prevent death and injury to people. With this realization, emphasis shifted from traffic laws and their enforcement to seat-belt laws and the safe design of cars. Moynihan has recently urged a similar approach to the problem of guns in the United States, pointing out that restrictions on bullets designed to harm people could do more good more quickly than effective restrictions on guns (which are, in any case, politically impossible). In 1994, for example, he introduced a bill that would levy a 10,000% tax on Winchester hollow-tipped Black Talon bullets. The company got the message and stopped selling the bullets in question, which were specifically designed to harm people. But Moynihan has argued for extending this approach as a solution to the overall problem of guns. For example, bullets could be taxed more heavily.

Give Good Arguments

If policies are chosen in order to maximize the achievement of goals, then the best argument for them is that they do that. It is often possible to bypass questions of means and focus on ends. The advocates of NAFTA and GATT, for example, could say honestly that these agreements would (according to expert opinion) increase total employment in the United States as well as in other countries.

Use Relevant Numbers

Numbers can help us see issues in the proper perspective. When the EPA tells us that we have to pay more for gasoline to reduce air pollution, it should tell us the best estimate of what we are getting for our pennies per gallon in terms of reductions in colds, asthma, emphysema, and so on. Even better, it should tell us how these figures compare to other expenditures for reductions in health risk. Politicians running for office should do the same when they advocate policies.

Numbers are important because new policies generally have advantages and disadvantages. The honest argument for almost any policy is that the advantages outweigh the disadvantages. Wishful thinking in favor of a policy leads many to ignore the disadvantages, but then the critics quickly point them out and the proponents are exposed as untrustworthy. Most of the time, the only way to make an honest argument from the start is to provide the numbers, arguing that the advantages are larger. Sometimes this is done, as in the debates about the creation of the World Trade Organization in many countries. So it is not impossible.

Cost-benefit Analysis in Setting Government Policy

Cost-benefit analysis is the explicit attempt to quantify everything so as to get the greatest benefit for a given cost, or to minimize the cost for a given benefit, or to get the highest benefit-to-cost ratio. Although thinking in terms of consequences can often simplify decisions, providing a single common coin for weighing competing arguments and making the best choice more obvious, cost-benefit analysis is typically complicated and it must be done by experts.

Examples abound of waste that results from the failure to use such analysis.[8] Regulation of environmental pollution for the purpose of saving lives, for example, is sometimes extremely efficient and sometimes inefficient. Recent estimates range from $169 per year of life saved, for mandatory seat-belt laws, to $99 billion per year for certain chloroform regulations.[9] (Other regulations pay for themselves in purely economic terms, such as reducing expenditures on medical care.)

The advantages of cost-benefit analysis are obvious. It is a method designed to produce the best consequences. It is the policy embodiment of what I have advocated throughout this book. If these benefits can be realized, then citizens should accept this kind of analysis, and they should accept the role of government in basing policy on this sort of analysis.

Unfortunately, things are not this simple. One problem is that decisions must often be made in the absence of clear information about what the effects will be. This could, in principle, be solved by the use of expert judgments. For example, in dealing with global warming, we really do not know what the effects of various policies will be. We could rely on the best guesses of experts, however, and we could also take into account their uncertainties, not making commitments that we would have to reverse with new information. In order for this to work, however, the experts must be trusted. Political groups on both sides will find reasons to question the expertise and the motives of those who must provide relevant information.

There may be solutions to this problem. Justice Breyer has suggested a high-level corps of bureaucrats, chosen for expertise in several relevant areas and insulated from political pressure, as a way of building trust.[10] When experts disagree about best guesses, they often can agree on uncertainties. They can arrive at a best guess and translate their disagreements into a range of uncertainty. This was done in the case of the recent report on global warming by the Intergovernmental Panel on Climate Change.[11]

But this does not deal with the second major objection to the use of cost-benefit analysis, which is that it bypasses the democratic process because of its reliance on experts. Citizens do not get a chance to have their say about government regulation. One answer to this objection is that it doesn't matter. If the bureaucrats who do the cost-benefit analyses are ultimately accountable to an elected government, and if they are responsible for ensuring the best outcomes and are capable of doing this, perhaps this is the highest form of government — a combination of democracy and philosopher kings.

A second answer concerns the functioning of democracy itself. This can happen in a variety of ways, but in all of them citizens should find it helpful to have the results of a good cost-benefit analysis. Consider as an example the problem of urban air pollution, which is still not fully solved in the economically advanced countries and is a major health crisis in developing countries in Latin America, southern and eastern Asia, and Indonesia. (Some cities, such as Mexico City, suffer from bad luck because of local weather conditions, but that isn't the problem in most of them.) Most pollution comes from the burning of hydrocarbons, particularly gasoline. Ozone, which is produced by chemical reactions between sun and exhaust components, causes immediate health effects — sore throats and other irritations. Small particles contribute to premature death from many conditions, including heart disease and emphysema. Lead, now banned in developed countries but still used as a fuel additive in developing countries, causes reduced intelligence in large segments of the population and, in extreme cases, mental retardation.

Much of the pollution can be removed before it comes out of the tailpipe. In the United States, most pollution comes from a few vehicles, trucks as well as cars, so one reasonable strategy for reducing it is to inspect vehicles and require repairs in the high polluters. Such plans have been proposed in many U.S. cities, but few have been put into effect. Other plans to reduce pollution have involved efforts to increase the use of public transportation, telecommuting (working at home and communicating by modem and telephone), and staggered hours for commuting. (Staggering the hours reduces idling time from waiting in heavy traffic, but its effects are small.) Every time some plan is proposed, those who must make sacrifices complain to their representatives at all levels of government. Because all levels must cooperate to put a plan into effect, and because the complaints are taken seriously, the process slows down. Local governments refuse to cooperate with national mandates.

To solve this problem, many U.S. states and localities have instituted more democratic procedures to arrive at a pollution-reduction plan. These plans often involve the use of small groups of "stakehold-ers" — that is, interested parties — who discuss the problem in several meetings over a period of months. The idea is that a plan developed by representatives of all interested groups — motorists, auto mechanics, health and environmental officials, and political groups concerned with environmental protection — will be more acceptable.

It is difficult to see how these panels could do their jobs effectively without the facts and figures that would be part of any good cost-benefit analysis. For example, in deciding among alternative policies for vehicle inspection and maintenance, it would seem helpful to know how much pollution is reduced as a function of the amount of money spent on in-spections and repairs and as a function of various alternative policies concerning centralized or distributed inspection or inspection with vari-ous frequencies. And it would also seem helpful to know the health ben-efits of different amounts of pollution reduction. (It turns out that these benefits are relatively easy to estimate. The more difficult problems in-volve predicting compliance with various inspection policies, but these too can be estimated.)

In the absence of this information, members of the panels will have little choice but to rely on their intuitions. Undoubtedly, intuitions about autonomy are involved, since all effective programs are by their nature coercive. On this basis, many people will favor voluntary pro-grams, despite little evidence that such programs can reduce the more serious forms of pollution on a long-term basis. On the other side, envi-ronmentalists may bring to bear a belief in the goodness of nature and a consequent distaste for any unnatural pollution, despite the economic benefits (i.e., improvements in people's lives) of allowing some of it.

Of course, these panels can help the regulatory process by making regulators aware of details that they might otherwise miss — for exam-ple, how some regulation might be subverted or lead to bad side effects. On the other hand, if the panels are given what amounts to veto power, they may stagnate as did the fisheries council discussed in chapter 2. In general, though, the use of cost-benefit analysis is not an alternative to democratic participation. The question of whether cost-benefit analy-sis is done and the question of whether citizens participate in decisions can both be answered affirmatively. Perhaps the only real conflict lies in who makes the final decision. And perhaps the best answer to this is that those who are politically responsible — elected officials and their ap-pointees — should make the decision after considering input from both cost-benefit analysis and citizen panels. An interesting question for re-search is what kind of leeway the government will get from citizens to override the citizens' own preferences on the basis of an expert analysis of consequences.

Deal with Tradeoffs

Cost-benefit analysis by its nature deals with tradeoffs. It expresses the insight that almost no lunches are free. Despite what we would wish, any change in policy has costs as well as benefits. Political leaders could help by communicating this idea even without presenting a full analysis.

Suppose, for example, that you are a politician considering what position to take on a trade agreement. You understand that the agreement will cause some harm, but you think that the benefit is greater. In such a situation, most politicians say, "I support the agreement because of all the benefits," and then proceed to list the benefits. An opponent will list the harms, without mentioning the benefits.

What would happen if you told the truth in such cases? Perhaps nothing — that is, nothing would happen to *you*. Although some people would consider you to be wishy-washy, those who oppose you will understand that they have been heard. Perhaps they will even think that, in some future case, you are a politician who will listen to them about something else, or even make a different judgment about another trade agreement. This is a risk, of course, but taking it could elevate the level of political discourse. Rather than screaming matches in which one side says "harm" and the other says "benefit," the debate will focus on the relative magnitudes of the two.

Experiment, Don't Guess

Sometimes well-informed experts are quite unsure of the relative costs and benefits of alternative proposals. As I write, the U.S. government and many states are trying out various changes in the welfare system. Most of the proposed "reforms" will make life harder for poor people on welfare, who are mostly children. The hope is that, in the long run, these policies will lead to changes in attitudes of those who would otherwise wind up on welfare, leading to reductions in births to unmarried teenagers and increased use of educational opportunities. There is no rush to reform the system, and there is ample opportunity to find out what will happen with various changes. If we are concerned with the best consequences, and if we are open-minded, we will try to ensure that these experiments are done in a way that makes their evaluation possible in a few years, and then we can revisit the issue. This is the way government ought to work. Most of the changes are being done in such as way as to make evaluation impossible, however: they apply to everyone, so comparison is impossible.

Of course, the advocates of change are sure that their proposals will have the intended effects, and the opponents of change are sure that the immediate harm to the poor will be too great. Others may say that we should not make people into guinea pigs without their consent. But if we do not experiment, whether we change or not, we are testing one condition of two that ought to be compared. If we lack a basis for deciding between these two conditions (change or status quo), there is no reason to think that anyone in particular will suffer from being in the wrong one.

Take the Cooperative Attitude

We have seen examples throughout this book in which negotiations have broken down or dragged on too long because one side or the other felt it was being treated unfairly by the proposal on the table. Of course, negotiators should bargain hard, but they should also be aware of the costs of failure or delay. The cooperative attitude results from an awareness of how people distort their concept of fairness, so that in order to agree, each side needs to give the other, literally, the benefit of the doubt.

Negotiators also need to be honest about what they care about. It is not giving away too much to tell the person across the table that X is much more important to you than Y. If she thinks the opposite, then you can both gain by your taking X in return for Y, instead of bargaining hard over both.

Reporters and Interest Groups

Citizens get most of their information from the news media and from interest groups. This is a continuum between, at one end, the general news media that aim to summarize national and international news and, at the other end, the newsletters of organizations devoted to particular causes or interests.

These media are particularly important because, in a sense, they reduce the cost of acquiring information. Just as it is not in a person's self-interest to vote, it is also not in anyone's self-interest to spend a lot of time and effort becoming well informed about the issues, especially about the consequences of alternative policies. Mancur Olson refers to this fact as "rational ignorance."[12] Rational ignorance helps to explain the power of superficial political advertising. Advertising appeals to intuitions of the sort I have discussed. It is easier for people to base their political views on these intuitions and on appeals to them than on reflective consideration of consequences.

Good reporting can reduce the cost of acquiring information, but reporters must emphasize what advertizing does not emphasize — namely, analyses of consequences. Reporters can do this more easily than politicians just because reporters are *not* running for office. If the long-run good is served by a tax increase, an increase in the age for receiving retirement benefits, or a reduction in government spending, the reporter does not have to worry about being voted out of office as a result of bringing bad news.

Interest groups may find it difficult to focus on consequences when the fundamental ideology of the groups they serve is based on some intuitive principles other than those based on consequences. The general press can counteract this problem by reporting on the groups themselves and by examining the expected consequences of their proposals.

News media spend a great deal of time and effort covering public opinion itself. The arguments I have presented suggest that they have little value except in the raw poll numbers, which are sometimes relevant to policy formulation. Interviews, in particular, are typically full of the kind of intuitive arguments that cause the troubles I have discussed. This is not a criticism of the people interviewed. Even most policy wonks do not walk around with these facts and figures on the top of their heads, ready to spout them to a reporter who sticks a microphone in front of them.

The Rules of Campaigns

Part of the problem of electoral politics is the tremendous expense involved in political advertising. In the United States, senators and representatives must spend a large fraction of their total work time raising money to pay for such advertising. The need to raise money makes politicians generally beholden to the wealthy or to organized groups that can contribute large amounts. It also takes time away from the real job and makes the job less interesting, deterring many good people from political careers.

Proposals to reform this problem have generally focused on limiting campaign contributions, publicizing them, or providing free advertising. The arguments I have made imply that none of these proposals will help all that much. The main trouble with political advertising is its appeal to intuitive principles, distracting attention from the analysis of consequences. The simplest solution to all the problems would be to simply ban advertising, thus forcing campaigns to rely on news media for reporting of the campaign and the issues. If reporters did their job, this would work. The trouble is, there is no way of correcting bias or error on the parts of reporters, no way for a candidate to appeal directly to the voters. In sum, banning advertising is too much a violation of free speech. The main point of free speech is to allow exactly such direct appeals.

Still, we might usefully distinguish advertising from public argument. Politicians often debate through their advertisements, with each ad answering their opponent's last ad. But this is a very slow process. Instead of subsidizing advertising, government might subsidize argument.

It need not take the form of actual debate with the candidates present. A somewhat slower debate, in which candidates have time to look up facts, might be better. It might be possible to subsidize argumentation of this sort, on condition that those who accepted the subsidy would not produce ads of the usual sort.

Corporations

Some consider "business ethics" to be an oxymoron. Businesses have no choice but to maximize profit. Even breaking the law is seen as a risk of financial loss; if others can get away with something, then we'd better do it too or we will lose out in the competition. If a business sacrifices profit for the sake of doing good, it will be extinct before long.

This view is overstated. First, business operates within a framework of law that has the effect of protecting it: copyright and patent law, and truth-in-advertising law, for example. Without laws against misleading advertising, consumers would have less reason to believe any advertising. It is to the advantage of business to maintain this framework, even as individual businesses experiment to find its limits. The framework itself, however, is sufficiently ambiguous that its edges are difficult to find. Businesses end up getting sued for things that appeared at the time to be fully legal if questionably ethical. Perhaps the safest legal course is to be as honest as possible short of revealing trade secrets.

Second, businesses have flexibility within the constraints of maintaining financial viability. Profit is a necessary condition for continued existence; it is the business equivalent of sustainability. But companies have flexibility within that constraint. A pharmaceutical company can survive either by making the twenty-fifth medicine for unclogging the arteries of couch potatoes — and thus winning some percentage of the market — or by pursuing a riskier strategy of designing a new vaccine against some tropical disease, hoping that someone will figure out how to pay for it.

Third, reputation matters. If consumers care about the environment, for example, companies that go beyond legal requirements to preserve the environment can sell their products more easily. "Green marketing" has become a major part of business. Government can help by certifying the legitimacy of claims, and environmental organizations can help by supporting them, helping government officials identify incorrect claims, encouraging businesses to adopt good practices, and most important, alerting consumers to the significance of environmentally friendly products. Some scholars have argued that these mechanisms can replace a good deal of government regulation.[13]

DuPont earned this sort of respect from consumers when it decided to phase out the production of CFCs on its own, before the Mon-

treal Protocol insisted that all such ozone-destroying chemicals be eliminated. More important, Dow did not oppose the protocol itself. Such
corporate citizenship also affects what employees have to be paid: people will accept less money to work in a company or job that they view
as public-spirited.[14] The upshot is that corporations *can* play a role in
improving the world. They must also publicize what they do, if only to
get the maximum benefit from it, so they also play an educational role.

I have given reasons why companies need not see themselves as
profit-maximizing machines. But, of course, the need to make a profit
is an important constraint. The need for profit makes it unrealistic for
some fishermen to voluntarily restrain their fishing while others fish to
the limit. Like fishermen, though, corporations can ask government and
international agencies for regulations that will help them all in the long
run.

Education

The idea that policies should be evaluated by their expected consequences, and the more subtle idea that intuitions sometimes work against this
aim, should be part of every citizen's education. I am not asking for
indoctrination. Instead, students should know simply that this is a point
of view. It is disturbing that many college students in the United States
say that they have not heard of the idea of justifying punishment in terms
of deterrence, for example.[15] This is a standard argument that should be
part of any policy debate about punishment.

Much could be done in schools and colleges that is not now being
done. Some of the changes would involve new courses, either optional
or (at the pre-college level) required. Other changes would involve incor-
porating new material into existing courses (both optional and required).

An example of a new course that might be suitable at the secondary school level — as an option at first — is a course in social theory. Some schools now offer introductory economics at the college level,
leading to advanced placement in college. These courses serve some of
the purpose of the course I propose, since economics is a science based
on consequences. But a more general course might be better for other
students. (And the overlap would be low enough so that students could
take both economics and the course I would propose.) Such a course
— or other courses — could involve projects designed to help students
understand how knowledge can be brought to bear on public decisions.
For example, students could carry out a simplified cost-benefit analysis
of some air-pollution regulation, such as vehicle inspection and maintenance. What are the effects of pollution on health? How do people learn
these things? Does the number of saved lives and reduced respiratory
irritation justify the time and money?

This course would include many concepts from economics, such as the ideas of indifference curves as expressions of tradeoffs, incentive and deterrence in the form of elasticity, declining marginal utility as a justification for redistribution, and externalities (including social dilemmas) as a justification for regulation. It would also include the concept of expected utility as a way of justifying decisions made under risk, and the basic ideas of the free market and why it leads to efficient outcomes. Beyond these economic ideas, it would include enough psychology so that students could understand the nature of biases in judgment and decision making. Examples from foreign policy decisions such as those discussed by Robert Jervis[16] and Irving Janis[17] might be both interesting and relevant. And it would discuss basic social philosophy. Students should at least have heard of utilitarianism and other social philosophies. Some of this might be discussed in the context of issues in medical decision making and health policy. The (arguably irrelevant) distinction between acts and omissions is also relevant.

Other courses, at a more elementary level, could be developed for grades six through nine.[18] In general, students need to understand the basic idea of thinking about future consequences as a way of making decisions. This will conflict with intuitions that students and their parents have, but it is not the business of schools to force acceptance, just understanding. The view that future consequences matter is an important part of our traditions, so it should be taught and understood.

Schools need to help students understand the nature of expertise. Too much scientific knowledge is presented as simple dogma, without the students having any sense of where it came from or why it is different from astrology. Even attempts to teach "critical thinking" often result in students' learning to be critical of others to the point of cynicism. Instruction in thinking should help students understand how standards of thinking lead to knowledge in the scientific disciplines, especially those that help us predict consequences. If citizens think that science is no more than political prejudice disguised, then they will allow their own prejudices to have equal weight against the pronouncements of experts.[19]

We can teach students where expert knowledge comes from by walking them along the path that experts followed, at least a few times in each subject. True expertise comes from a process of critical inquiry in which ideas survive attacks by skeptics or else are modified or discarded. Science and other successful disciplines work because theories can be challenged and overturned according to standards of truth or rightness. The theories of science that we use and accept, including those in the social sciences, have value because they have survived this kind of criticism, not because they are old or because they are endorsed by important people. Astrology and religious dogma did not go through this process, so they do not have the same status. The teaching of science must help students understand this. They cannot hope to learn all that science offers, but they can learn what science is.

The teaching of social studies is particularly problematic because it derives ultimately from the social sciences, which are relatively new and still controversial. The tendency to water down the social studies curriculum is therefore great. In the 1960s, a group of scholars in the United States, funded by the National Science Foundation, developed "Man: A Course of Study" (MACOS), which, among other things, drew heavily on the social sciences as they were taught at the university level. It was too controversial to be implemented widely. Among other problems, it presented a view of culture as variable, with many possible options. Conservatives in the United States did not want their own culture presented as merely one option among many.

Understanding of the nature of knowledge in the social sciences (except history, perhaps) is thus largely limited to those who have been to college (at least in the U.S.). This is particularly unfortunate because the social sciences, especially economics, form much of the expertise relevant to government. To most citizens, the economists consulted routinely by government leaders might as well be astrologers and fortune-tellers who use the stars or tarot cards rather than computers to predict the future. Students need to go through miniature exercises in economics and the other social sciences in order to understand the origin of this kind of expertise.

In addition, students need to learn the geography of expertise. Even those who make it through graduate school are often ignorant of the fact that they are making statements about issues on which someone else is an expert. Psychologists, for example, frequently step into philosophy as if the discipline didn't exist, and economists do the same with psychology. As it is, the secondary curriculum in most countries is a watered-down version of the university curriculum of decades (or centuries) earlier, with no other particular justification. One way to remedy this problem is for universities to work harder, with the help of outside funds, to inform high school teachers and students of the full range of their activities.

Universities themselves could do more to teach students to understand expertise in fields outside of their own. In the United States, most college students are required to take courses in several different kinds of disciplines. Ideally, such "distribution requirements" should allow students to learn not only about the methods of inference in each discipline they study but also about how to learn the methods of other disciplines and how to ask good questions of experts in each discipline. Learning about these things will facilitate teamwork among members of different disciplines. If I am correct, what is central in all these types of learning are the kinds of evidence used to establish claims in a discipline and the kinds of inferences and criticisms that are made. If students focus on these, they will quickly learn what a discipline is about, even if they know little of its substance (although they must know *some* of the substance, if only to understand the methods of inquiry). Many current courses may actually do well at imparting this sort of knowledge.

In sum, we can provide a rationale for teaching the standards of actively open-minded thinking in terms of learning about the disciplines themselves. This rationale depends on the idea that an understanding of thinking is essential to an understanding of scholarship itself, which is what most education is (and should be) about. We need scholarship to predict the consequences of our decisions.

The Internet as a Forum

Several signs point to a decline in community in the United States and perhaps in other advanced capitalist countries as well.[20] This decline may be causing an increased sense of unease and reduced trust in social institutions of all sorts. Part of the decline may be the weakening of neighborhoods, clubs, and civic organizations. People are spending more time watching television and less time interacting with each other.

One symptom of these changes is a decline in discussion of public affairs. Reduced interaction combines with norms of politeness. If people spend less time with each other, they don't want to ruin it with political arguments. It is difficult to express an opinion strongly at a dinner party or a backyard barbecue.

The Internet now provides the major outlet for those who really like to discuss issues. The situation is very fluid, but as of now the main discussion takes place on news groups, discussion lists, and web pages. News groups distribute messages, or "postings," to subscribers, which now include most commercial on-line services and universities. Each newsgroup is devoted to a specialized topic. For example, the group called sci.environment is concerned with the environment, from abstruse technical questions and answers to discussions of politics and personalities (including attacks on those who post to the list). Each posting includes a subject heading, which allows the reader to skip it. The subject header indicates whether it is a reply to an earlier posting, and most news-reading programs now sort articles together, in chronological order, when they are replies to the same posting, so that readers can easily follow the "thread." Discussion lists work much the same way, except that the postings are distributed as electronic mail messages to individual subscribers rather than institutions. The lists tend to be much more specialized. Finally, web pages are used mostly for posting position statements, although some include provisions for readers to respond, with the responses posted much like a newsgroup.

The Internet has become an unregulated free marketplace for ideas. It is the place where people can talk back to politicians, newspapers, and each other. People who post to news groups ostensibly are arguing against someone who has posted earlier most of the time, but they do not expect to convince that person so much as the other readers of the group. This system can have tremendous benefits in restoring interest in public issues and in motivating people to inform themselves (if only so that they can better defeat their opponents). One benefit is that it is difficult to make arguments based on intuition alone because (typically) someone will reply who has an intuition that is just as strong on the other side. The system puts a premium on facts and figures that concern expected consequences.

The problem is to ensure the accuracy of these facts and figures, but that is not hard. Much more than news media, people who post to the Internet are used to giving their sources, just as scholars do. The reader who wants to check the source can go to the library or, with increasing frequency, to some site on the Internet. (Government reports, for example, are increasingly available on web pages.)

Some examples already exist. *Onco-link* (at http://cancer.-med.upenn.edu/ is now a web page with information about cancer. Started in 1994 by E. Loren Buhle, Jr., and Joel W. Goldwein, it is now accessed each month from over 90,000 different IP addresses (computers) on the Internet. It provides summaries, frequently updated, of information about diagnosis and treatment of various forms of cancer. Now it draws heavily on government sources, which contain similar information. It also contains information about clinical trials of new drugs, new research findings, and so on. Its accuracy is maintained in the same way that the accuracy of medical textbooks is maintained — by peer review.

Similar projects could be undertaken about many areas that affect public policy. For example, cost-benefit analyses of risk regulation and medical treatments[21] could be put onto a web site. Government funding may be necessary to get this started, but the cost is relatively low compared to the benefit of making this information easily available. The Internet is growing as the telephone once grew. In a few years, most people who have telephones will have Internet access. This means that information could be available to almost anyone who can understand it.

It is unfortunate that the use of the Internet in schools is being inhibited by the concern of parents and teachers that children will expose themselves to pornography. Although nothing can prevent the really eager viewer from seeing pornography, a few simple technical fixes can make it sufficiently difficult so that this is not a problem, yet fear of a few violations is leading to paralysis.

Parents

School officials would sometimes have us believe that parents' role is mainly to support them: to make sure that our children go to school fed and rested, nag them to do their homework, and come to parent-teacher conferences. Although all these things are important, the main role of parents is as ancillary teachers. Schools do not teach everything all that well, and they teach some things not at all.

It is primarily parents who create interest in public affairs through listening to the news, discussing it, participating in politics in various ways, and so on. In discussing the news, parents need not pretend to be teachers, using a nondirective tutorial method. Teachers are rightly limited in what they can do. Parents are free to set an example of the role of emotion in public life. They should not be afraid to express their anger at hypocrisy or stupidity in public officials or candidates for office. (This is a far more reasonable response than a cynical shrug, as if such behavior were to be expected.) Nor should they be afraid to express admiration.

Parents need not fear that interest in public affairs will go against the long-run interest of their children. When children come to choose occupations, they are only helped by having a thorough knowledge of the world and where it is going. Even as mundane a choice as what language to study in high school may require an understanding of world trends.

Parents should also try to ensure that their children develop an understanding of social and moral theory. As well as bringing their children to science museums, they might consider buying them various computer games such as Sim City or Sim Earth, which may create an interest in the complexity of economic and environmental effects. In helping children with science, parents should make sure that their children understand where the knowledge comes from.

Conclusion

Thinking about policy in terms of consequences requires facts, for it is the facts that tell us what consequences to expect. We can think of two styles of decisions. One, the older one perhaps, is suited to situations in which facts are difficult to get. Without facts at their disposal, people must fall back on intuitive principles such as those I have discussed. They can still think well. They can question the applicability of the principles and can think of alternative principles that might apply to the case.

As facts become — as the economists would say — less costly, a new way of thinking can emerge in which we use the facts to estimate the consequences. This is now pretty standard in large corporations and in many government agencies, but it is not well understood. People still hang on to the old ways. Yet with the Internet now making information cheaper than ever, we must not excuse ourselves for ignoring the facts as easily as did our ancestors. The recommendations I have made in this chapter will lead us in the direction of more reliance on the information that is available.

These are not utopian recommendations. Some of them are already followed by some people in each of the positions I have listed. I am just asking more people to follow them, and for all of us to hold people responsible for following their intuitions rather than thinking about the future. If a small percentage of people started thinking more effectively about the future, they could swing more decisions toward the options that are best on the whole.

The human population can — like fishermen who have succeeded in cooperating to restrain their catch — pull together and plan a sustainable future for ourselves. Or like those in the northwestern Atlantic, we can wait until it is too late, until overpopulation and neglect of our environment bring us to a crisis. We may be poised at a crucial point, like a pinball rolling toward one side or the other. A little shove may be all we need.

Notes

Chapter 1. Introduction

1. Asch et al. (1994); Meszaros et al. (1996).
2. Kahneman and Tversky (1984).
3. Passell (1995).
4. Svenson (1981); Weinstein (1980).
5. Gilovich (1991).
6. Spencer and Christy (1990).
7. Kempton, Boster, & Hartley (1995), pp. 173–174.
8. Jervis (1976), pp. 128–142.
9. Ellsworth and Ross (1983).
10. dos Santos (1996).
11. Kahneman, Knetsch, and Thaler (1990).
12. For defense of consequentialism and utilitarianism, and citations of other defenses, see Baron (1996a).
13. Baron and Ritov (1993).

Chapter 2. All the Fish in the Sea

1. Anthony (1993).
2. Safina (1994).
3. McGoodwin (1990), Weber (1995).
4. Kurien and Achari (1990).
5. Schmidtz (1990).
6. Hardin (1968).
7. Frank Mirarchi, a Scituate fisherman and president of the Massachusetts Inshore Draggerman's Association, quoted in *Boston Globe*, August 24, 1991, p. 27.
8. McGoodwin (1990), pp. 196–197.
9. Ostrom (1990).
10. Ostrom (1990); Ostrom, Gardner, and Walker (1994).
11. Baron (1997a).
12. Schneider (1993).
13. van Avermaet (1974; reported in Messick, 1985).
14. *National Fisher*, January 1982, p. 22.
15. *The Boston Globe*, March 9, 1992, p. 27.

16. Associated Press story, June 6, 1995.

17. *New York Times*, January 22, 1997, p. B4.

18. McGoodwin (1990).

19. McGoodwin (1990).

20. Lonnie Williamson, "Fish un-limited," *Outdoor life*, June 1992.

21. McGoodwin (1990).

22. Bob Holmes, "Biologists sort the lesson of fisheries collapse," *Science, 264* (1994); pp. 1252–1253.

23. Interview on *Frontline* (Public Broadcasting System), May 21, 1991.

24. Safina (1994); A. A. Rosenberg and others, *Science, 262* (1993); pp. 828–829.

25. Brian McGrory, "Studds bill provokes fishing industry wrath," *Boston Globe*, August 4, 1991, p. 27.

26. *National Fisher*, February, 1982, p. 3.

27. Joe Galgana, a fisherman, quoted in *Boston Globe*, August 4, 1991, p. 27.

28. Peter Hall, "Crisis in the Atlantic Fishery," *Canadian Business Review*, Summer 1990, pp. 44–48.

29. *Boston Globe*, May 9, 1989, p. 1.

30. Ludmilla Lelis, *USA Today*, June 21, 1993, p. 7a.

31. Brown (1994).

32. Baron (1997b).

33. Kerr (1996); Montzka and others (1996).

34. Hammitt (in press).

35. Parson and Greene (1996).

36. Alterman (1996).

37. Associated Press, May 1, 1995.

38. Limbaugh (1992, 1993).

39. Schelling (1992).

40. The British Thermal Unit is a measure of energy.

41. NBC Today, a TV show, February 18, 1993. See also Wald (1993).

42. Hearing before the Senate Finance Committee, April 22, 1993.

43. Kempton, Boster, and Hartley (1995), p. 151.

44. PR Newswire report, July 1, 1993.

45. "Nation," CBS TV, June 13, 1993.

46. Thomas L. Friedman, *New York Times*, May 19, 1996, p. 15.

47. W. Booth, "Ironing out 'greenhouse effect'; Fertilizing oceans is proposed to spur algae," *Washington Post*, May 20, 1990.

48. R. A. Kerr, "Iron fertilization: A tonic, but no cure for the greenhouse," *Science*, Feb. 25, 1994, p. 1089.

49. John W. Deming and 25 researchers from the University of Washington School of Oceanography, letter to the editor, *Seattle Times*, June 5, 1990.

50. Kempton, Boster, and Hartley (1995), p. 46.

51. Monastersky (1995).

52. Farhar (1977).

53. Spranca (1992).

54. A respondent quoted by Kempton, Boster, and Hartley (1995), p. 109.

55. Amato (1994).

56. Viggiano et al. (1995).

57. Easterbrook (1995); McGoodwin (1990).

Chapter 3. Benefits and Burdens

1. Ubel et al. (1996); Baron (1995).
2. Cohen (1997).
3. Victor D. Rudy, March 19, 1995.
4. Thomas M. Crawford, February, 1995
5. Kempton, Boster, and Hartley (1995), pp. 146–147.
6. *New York Times*, July 5, 1995.
7. J. V. DeLong, "It's my land, isn't it?" *New York Times*, March 15, 1994, p. A25.
8. Steve Schuck, on the McNeil/Lehrer News Hour, February 22, 1995.
9. Coase (1960).
10. Calabresi (1970).
11. *The T. J. Hooper*, 60 F.2d 737 (2d Cir. 1932).
12. Baron, Gowda, and Kunreuther (1993).
13. Baron et al. (1993).
14. Elster (1989).
15. Elster (1993).
16. Calabresi and Bobbitt (1978).
17. Clifford and Inculano (1987).
18. Dicke (1995).
19. Jake Minas, posted to bit.listserv.lawsch-l, May 4, 1996.
20. Kahneman and Lovallo (1993).
21. Mill (1859), chap. 5.
22. United Nations Development Program (1992, 1994).

Chapter 4. Nationalism and Group Loyalty

1. Buchanan (1995).
2. For example, Simon (1995).
3. AP dispatch, *New York Times*, August 11, 1993.
4. For example, Voices of Citizens Together (http://www.instanet.com/˜vct/).
5. Oberlink (1995).
6. Simon (1996).
7. FAIR (http://www.fairus.org/).
8. Oberlink (1995).
9. Gibbons (1992).
10. Maurice (1995).
11. Hanson (1991); Walsh (1986).
12. For example, see UNICEF (1995).
13. *New York Times*, December 26, 1993, p. 19.
14. Sachs (1997).
15. Buchanan (1994).
16. Conversely, support for foreign aid since 1949 has drawn largely on altruism and equality as motives for its support (Lumsdaine, 1993).
17. Goldwater (1961), p. 98.
18. Hoar (1995).
19. *New York Times*, August 5, 1995, p. 5.

Chapter 5. My-side Bias and Violent Conflict

1. Fischhoff, Slovic, and Lichtenstein (1977).

2. Koriat, Lichtenstein, and Fischhoff (1980).

3. Lord, Ross, and Lepper (1979).

4. Azzi (1992).

5. Many of these beliefs are recounted by Kelly (1995).

6. *Boston Globe*, January 6, 1995. Misspellings are Salvi's.

7. The historical account is from Kozlowski (1993), Khory (1993), and Varshney (1993), and several news accounts (e.g., *New York Times*, February 9, 1986, December 7 and 10, 1992, and September 17, 1993).

8. Syed Abdullah Bukhari, the Imam of India's largest mosque, quoted in *New York Times*, February 9, 1986.

9. Subhadra Butalia, quoted in *New York Times*, February 9, 1986.

10. Kozlowski (1993), p. 89.

11. Ramaswamy (1992).

12. Rosser (1995) and personal communication.

13. Jipendra Kumar Tyagi, a physician at a government hospital, quoted by Gargan (1992).

14. Agrawal (no date), capitals in original.

15. Mackay (1841).

16. Stanovich and West (in press).

Chapter 6. Do No Harm

1. See Baron (1996b) for details.

2. *New York Times*, February 28, 1994.

3. Baron and Jurney (1992).

Chapter 7. Risk

1. Stone (1992).

2. Harris (1993).

3. Harvard Medical School Health Letter (1989).

4. In fact, the cases of brain damage may not have been by the vaccine at all (Bowie, 1990; Howson & Fineberg, 1992). Infants unfortunately are subject to brain damage from various diseases, and sometimes these diseases occur right after the child is vaccinated. Even if some of these cases are caused by the vaccine, they are extremely rare.

5. Joint Committee on Vaccination and Immunization (1981); Smith (1988).

6. Cohen (1994); Johnson (1993).

7. Inglehart (1987).

8. Deber and Goel (1990). Recently, several authorities have recommended a mixture of both kinds of vaccines, in hopes of getting almost the full benefit of the Sabin vaccine but with less of the risk. The benefit is now largely in helping to annihilate the disease completely.

9. Marshall (1995).

10. Calle and others (1995); Ettinger and others (1996); Folsom and others (1995); Grady and others (1992); Newcomb and Storer (1995); Willis and others (1996).

11. Elstein and others (1986); Hershey and Baron (1987).

12. Wallis (1995).

13. Willis and others (1996).

14. Gladwell (1997).

15. Slovic (1987).
16. Cohen (1983).
17. Loewenstein and Mather (1990).
18. Breyer (1993).
19. Baron, Gowda, and Kunreuther (1993).
20. For example, Beckman (1995); Feldman (1994); Graves (1995); Gunter (1995); Mintz (1994).
21. Breyer (1993).
22. Ritov, Baron, & Hershey (1993); Baron, Gowda, & Kunreuther (1993).
23. Foster (1995).
24. Abelson (1993).
25. Ames and Gold (1990).
26. Easterling and Kunreuther (1995).
27. Stammer and Feldman (1991).
28. Stammer and Feldman (1991).
29. Easterling and Kunreuther (1995), p. 141.
30. Baron, Gowda, and Kunreuther (1993); Beattie and Baron (1995).
31. James Kotka, letter to the *Reno Gazette-Journal*, November 2, 1991, quoted by Easterling and Kunreuther (1995).
32. Easterling and Kunreuther (1995).
33. David (1986); Hinman (1986); Huber (1988); Inglehart (1987). The passage of a (partial) no-fault compensation law in 1986 may have reversed this trend (Hofmann, 1988).
34. Djerassi (1989), Huber (1988), Mastroianni, Donaldson, and Kane (1990), Service (1996).
35. Baron and Ritov (1993).
36. Huber (1991).
37. Sword (1994).

Chapter 8. Too Many People
1. Dyson (1994).
2. Postel, Daily, and Ehrlich (1996).
3. Naff (1997).
4. Ehrlich (1968).
5. Easterbrook (1995).
6. For example, Simon (1990).
7. Easterbrook (1995, p. 475).
8. Homer-Dixon (1995) discusses these questions with great insight.
9. Cohen (1995); Homer-Dixon (1995).
10. Easterbrook (1995).
11. Harlap, Kest, & Forrest (1991).
12. Sundström (1993).
13. Posner (1992).
14. Lamb (1984), p. 17 (quoted by Donaldson, 1990).
15. Donaldson (1990), p. 115.
16. Donaldson (1990), p. 115.
17. Graham-Smith (1994), p. 241.
18. Stein (1995), pp. 39–43, discusses this example and many more like those just listed, and provides a review of the situation in Tibet (chap. 9).

19. *People's Daily*, August 1949, translation from Stein (1995).

20. Hacker (1995).

21. See Green (1994), pp. 13–15, 234–236.

22. Simon (1990).

23. Pope John Paul II, *Evangelium Vitae*, 1995, section 91 (the quote from an address by John Paul II himself; italics in the original).

24. Stein (1995, chs. 7–8); Robey, Rutstein, and Morris (1993).

25. Graham-Smith (1994), p. 239.

26. Robey, Rutstein, and Morris (1993).

27. Pritchett (1994a,b).

28. Bongaarts (1994a,b).

29. Greenhalgh, Zhu, and Li (1994).

30. *International Planned Parenthood News, 168* (February), 3.

31. McIntosh and Finkle (1995).

32. See, for example, Cook (1993).

33. For example, Freedman and Isaacs (1993).

34. Freedman and Isaacs (1993), p. 19.

35. Kasun (1981).

36. Donaldson (1990), pp. 36–37.

37. Quoted by Robin Toner in *New York Times*, February 5, 1986.

38. For example, see McIntosh and Finkle (1995); Knodel and Jones (1996).

39. Donaldson (1990), chap. 4.)

40. Martine (1996), p. 72.

41. Donaldson (1990).

42. Simon (1980, 1990).

43. Charles S. Hammerslough, telephone conversation, March 26, 1995.

44. Hearing of the Senate Budget Committee, February 28, 1990.

45. Suggested by Charles S. Hammerslough, telephone conversation, March 26, 1995.

Chapter 9. Naturalism and the Sanctity of Life

1. For example, Finnis (1980).

2. *Humanae Vitae*, 1968, sections 11–12.

3. *Humanae Vitae*, 1968, section 16.

4. Rosenbaum (1995), p. 58.

5. Kuhn (1991).

6. Joanna Coles interview in *The Guardian*, August 10, 1996, p. 29; Reuters, August 11, 1996.

7. Kempton, Boster, & Hartley (1995), p. 90.

8. Tertullian, quoted in *Evangelium Vitae*, by Pope John Paul II, 1995, section 61.

9. Bernardin (1989).

10. *New York Times*, March 25, 1995, p. A1.

11. From the Vatican newspaper *L'Osservatore Romano*, quoted in an Associated Press dispatch, January 13, 1995.

12. *New York Times*, May 10, 1996.

13. *Evangelium Vitae*, 1995, section 61.

14. *Evangelium Vitae*, 1995, section 44.

15. For example, Baron (1996a); Hare (1975); Singer (1979).

16. In *Practical Ethics* (1975).

17. Posner (1992).

18. John Paul II, *Evangelium Vitae*, 1995, section 48 (italics in original); see also section 63.

19. *Evangelium Vitae*, 1995, section 15.

20. Letter to *New York Times*, April 5, 1996.

21. Kuhse (1987) provides an excellent discussion of this doctrine and many of the issues discussed in this section. See also Schick (1991), chap. 3.2.

22. These arguments and many others are found in the report of the Senate Special Committee on Euthanasia and Assisted Suicide (1995).

23. Testimony at Vancouver hearings, Senate Special Committee on Euthanasia and Assisted Suicide (1995).

24. At `http://w4.lns.cornell.edu/~staeck/action.html`, in summer 1996.

25. Quoted with permission.

26. E. L. Andrews, "Religious leaders prepare to fight patents on genes," *New York Times*, May 13, 1995.

27. Mason (1990).

28. Lafferty (1990).

Chapter 10. What Is to Be Done?

1. Sachs (1997).

2. For example, Buchanan and Tullock (1962).

3. Weinstein (1980).

4. Baron (1997a); Brennan and Lomasky (1993).

5. Brennan and Lomasky (1993); Brodsky and Thompson (1993); Sears and Funk (1991); Shabman and Stephenson (1994).

6. Breyer (1993).

7. Moynihan (1996)

8. Breyer (1993).

9. Tengs and others (1995).

10. Breyer (1993).

11. Watson, Zinyowera, and Ross (1996).

12. Olson (1982).

13. Orts (1995).

14. Frank (1996).

15. Baron and Ritov (1993).

16. Jervis (1976).

17. Janis (1982).

18. See Baron and Brown (1991) for some examples.

19. Baron (1993).

20. Putnam (1995); Lane (in press).

21. Tengs and others (1995, 1996).

References

Abelson, P. H. (1993). Pesticides and food. (Editorial.) *Science, 259,* 1235.

Agrawal, D. (no date). The Ayodhya debate: An introduction. http://-www.bjp.org (web page of the Bharatiya Janata Party, as of 1996).

Alterman, E. (1996). Voodoo science. Legislation to end the United States involvement with the Montreal Protocol introduced by Republicans Tom DeLay and John Doolittle. *The Nation, 262* (5), 6–7.

Amato, I. (1994). A high-flying fix for ozone loss. *Science, 264,* 1401–1402.

Ames, B. N., & Gold, L. S. (1990). Too many rodent carcinogens: Mitogenesis increases mutagenesis. *Science, 249,* 970–971.

Anthony, V. (1993). *Testimony before the Subcommittee on Fisheries Management, Committee on Merchant Marine and Fisheries, U.S. House of Representatives, Brooklyn, N.Y., September 10.* Washington, D.C.: Federal Document Clearing House, Inc.

Asch, D., Baron, J., Hershey, J. C., Kunreuther, H., Meszaros, J., Ritov, I., & Spranca, M. (1994). Determinants of resistance to pertussis vaccination. *Medical Decision Making, 14,* 118–123.

Azzi, A. E. (1992). Procedural justice and the allocation of power in intergroup relations: Studies in the United States and South Africa. *Personality and Social Psychology Bulletin, 18,* 736–747.

Baron, J. (1993). Why teach thinking? — An essay. (Target article with commentary.) *Applied Psychology: An International Review, 42,* 191–237.

Baron, J. (1995). Blind justice: Fairness to groups and the do-no-harm principle. *Journal of Behavioral Decision Making, 8,* 71–83.

Baron, J. (1996a). Norm-endorsement utilitarianism and the nature of utility. *Economics and Philosophy, 12,* 165–182.

Baron, J. (1996b). Do no harm. In D. M. Messick & A. E. Tenbrunsel (Eds.), *Codes of conduct: Behavioral research into business ethics* (pp. 197–213). New York: Russell Sage Foundation.

Baron, J. (1997a). Political action vs. voluntarism in social dilemmas and aid for the needy. *Rationality and Society, 9,* 307–326.

Baron, J. (1997b). The illusion of morality as self-interest: A reason to cooperate in social dilemmas. *Psychological Science, 8*, 330–335.

Baron, J., & Brown, R. V. (Eds.) (1991). *Teaching decision making to adolescents.* Hillsdale, NJ: Erlbaum.

Baron, J., Gowda, R., & Kunreuther, H. (1993). Attitudes toward managing hazardous waste: What should be cleaned up and who should pay for it? *Risk Analysis, 13*, 183–192.

Baron, J., & Jurney, J. (1993). Norms against voting for coerced reform. *Journal of Personality and Social Psychology, 64*, 347–355.

Baron, J., & Ritov, I. (1993). Intuitions about penalties and compensation in the context of tort law. *Journal of Risk and Uncertainty, 7*, 17–33.

Beattie, J., & Baron, J. (1995). In-kind vs. out-of-kind penalties: Preference and valuation. *Journal of Experimental Psychology: Applied, 1*, 136–151.

Beckman, B. (1995). The EPA on a witch hunt; Superfund: A hazard to innocent small businesses. *Atlanta Journal and Constitution,* July 17.

Bernardin, Cardinal J. (1989). Abortions: Catholics much change hearts as well as laws. *U.S. Catholic, 54*, 31–33.

Bongaarts, J. (1994a). Population policy options in the developing world. *Science, 263*, 771–776.

Bongaarts, J. (1994b). The impact of population policies: Comment. *Population and Development Review, 20*, 616–620.

Bowie, C. (1990). Viewpoint: lessons from the pertussis vaccine court trial. *Lancet, 335*, 397-399.

Brennan, G., & Lomasky, L. (1993). *Democracy and decision: The pure theory of electoral politics.* Cambridge: Cambridge University Press.

Breyer, S. (1993). *Breaking the vicious circle: Toward effective risk regulation.* Cambridge, Mass.: Harvard University Press.

Brodsky, D. M., & Thompson, E. (1993). Ethos, public choice, and referendum voting. *Social Science Quarterly, 74*, 286–299.

Brown, L. R. (1994). Population. In L. R. Brown et al. *State of the world 1994.* New York: Norton.

Buchanan, J. M., & Tullock, G. (1962). *The calculus of consent: Logical foundations of constitutional democracy.* Ann Arbor: University of Michigan Press.

Buchanan, P. J. (1994). Foreign aid: Ever with us. Speech, December 21. (http://www.buchanan.org).

Buchanan, P. J. (1995). Mexico BailOut Costs U.S. Billions. *Christian American,* February.

Calabresi, G. (1970). *The costs of accidents: A legal and economic analysis.* New Haven: Yale University Press.

Calabresi, G., & Bobbitt, P. (1978). *Tragic choices.* New York: Norton.

Calle, E. E., Miricale-McMahill, H. L., Thun, M. J., & Heath, C. W., Jr. (1995). Estrogen replacement therapy and risk of fatal colon cancer in a prospective cohort of postmenopausal women. *Journal of the National Cancer Institute, 87*, 517–523.

Clifford, K. A., & Iuculano, R. P. (1987). AIDS and insurance: The rationale for AIDS-related testing. *Harvard Law Review, 100*, 1806–1024.

Coase, R. (1960). The problem of social cost. *Journal of Law and Economics, 3*, 1–30.

Cohen, B. L. (1983). Risk and risk aversion in our society. *Ceramic Bulletin, 62*, 1285–1288.

Cohen, J. (1994). Bumps on the vaccine road. *Science, 265*, 1371–1373.

Cohen, J. (1997). Ethics of AZT studies in poorer countries attacked. *Science, 276*, 1022.

Cohen, J. E. (1995). Population growth and earth's human carrying capacity. *Science, 269*, 341–346.

Cook, R. J. (1993). International human rights and women's reproductive health. *Studies in Family Planning, 24*, 73–86.

David, A. B. (1986). DTP: Drug manufacturers' liability in vaccine-related injuries. *Journal of Products Liability, 94*, 361–405.

Deber, R. B., & Goel, V. (1990). Using explicit decision rules to manage issues of justice, risk, and ethics in decision analysis. *Medical Decision Making, 10*, 181–194.

Dicke, A. (1995). Genetic discrimination: Actuarial aspects. (Letter) *Science, 270*, December 1.

Djerassi, C. (1989). The bitter pill. *Science, 245*, 356–361.

Donaldson, P. J. (1990). *Nature against us: The United States and the world population crisis, 1965–1980.* Chapel Hill: University of North Carolina Press.

dos Santos, C. M. M. (1996). "Good reasoning: To whom? When? How? An investigation of belief effects on syllogistic and argumentative reasoning." Doctoral dissertation, University of Sussex.

Dyson, T. (1994). Population growth and food production: Recent global and regional trends. *Population and Development Review 20*, 397–411.

Easterbrook, G. (1995). *A moment on the earth: The coming age of environmental optimism.* New York: Viking.

Easterling, D., & Kunreuther, H. (1995). *The dilemma of citing a high-level nuclear waste repository.* Boston: Kluwer.

Ehrlich, P. (1968). *The population bomb.* New York: Ballantine.

Ellsworth, P. C., & Ross, L. (1983). Public opinion and capital punishment: A close examination of the views of abolitionists and retentionists. *Crime and Delinquency, 29*, 116–169.

Elstein, A. S., Holzman, G. B., Ravitch, M. M., Metheny, W. A., Holmes, M. M., Hoppe, R. B., Rothert, M. L., and Rovner, D. R. (1986). Comparison of physicians' decisions regarding estrogen replacement therapy for menopausal women and decisions derived from a decision analytic model. *American Journal of Medicine, 80*, 246–258.

Elster, J. (1989). *Solomonaic judgments: Studies in the limitations of rationality.* New York: Cambridge University Press.

Elster, J. (1993). Justice and the allocation of scarce resources. In B. A. Mellers and J. Baron (Eds.), *Psychological perspectives on justice: Theory and applications* (pp. 259–278). New York: Cambridge University Press.

Ettinger, B., Friedman, G. D., Bush, T., & Quesenberry, C. P. (1996). Reduced mortality associated with long-term postmenopausal estrogen therapy. *Obstetrics and Gynecology, 87,* 6–12.

Farhar, B C. (1977). The public decides about weather modification. *Environment and Behavior, 9,* 279–310.

Feeney, G. (1994). Fertility decline in East Asia. *Science, 266,* 1518–1523.

Feldman, L. (1994). Clinton proposals will rejig Superfund. *Christian Science Monitor,* February 1.

Finnis, J. (1980). *Natural law and natural rights.* Oxford: Clarendon.

Fischhoff, B., Slovic, P., & Lichtenstein, S. (1977). Knowing with certainty: The appropriateness of extreme confidence. *Journal of Experimental Psychology: Human Perception and Performance, 3,* 552–564.

Folsom, A. R., Mink, P. J., Sellers, T. A., Hong, C., Zheng, W., & Potter, J. D. (1995). Hormonal replacement therapy and morbidity and mortality in a prospective study of postmenopausal women. *American Journal of Public Health, 85,* 1128–1132.

Foster, K. R. (1995). Review of *Cancer from Beef. DES. Federal food regulation, and consumer confidence,* by Alan I. Marcus (Baltimore: The Johns Hopkins University Press, 1994).

Frank, R. (1996). Can socially responsible firms survive in a competitive environment? In D. M. Messick & A. E. Tenbrunsel (Eds.), *Codes of conduct: Behavioral research into business ethics* (pp. 86–103). New York: Russell Sage Foundation.

Freedman, L. P., & Isaacs, S. L. (1993). Human rights and reproductive choice. *Studies in Family Planning, 24,* 18–30.

Gargan, E. A. (1992). The hatreds of India; Hindu memory scarred by centuries of sometimes despotic Islamic rule. *New York Times,* December 11, p. 10.

Gibbons, A. (1992). Researchers fret over neglect of 600 million patients. *Science, 256,* 1135.

Gilovich, T. (1991). *How we know what isn't so: The fallibility of human reason in everyday life.* New York: The Free Press.

Gladwell, W. (1997). The estrogen question. *New Yorker, 73* (15), June 9, 54–60.

Goldwater, B. (1961). *Conscience of a conservative.* New York: McFadden Books.

Grady, D., Rubin, S. M., Pettti, D. B., Fox, C. S., Black, D., Ettinger, B., Ernster, V. L., & Cummings, S. R. (1992). Hormone therapy to prevent disease and prolong life in postmenopausal women. *Annals of Internal Medicine, 117,* 1016–1037.

Graham-Smith, F. (Ed.). (1994). *Population — The complex reality: A report of the population summit of the world's scientific academies.* London: The Royal Society; Colden, Colo.: North American Press.

Graves, R. (1995). Viewpoints: Get Superfund off backs of small business. *Buffalo News,* December 5.

Green, E. C. (1994). *AIDS and STDs in Africa: Bridging the gap between traditional healing and modern medicine.* Boulder: Westview.

Greenhalgh, S., Zhu, C., & Li, N. (1994). Restraining population growth in three Chinese villages, 1988–93. *Population and Development Review, 20,* 365–395.

Gunter, B. (1995). True polluters often escape while innocents pay. *Tampa Tribune,* July 24.

Hacker, A. (1995). The crackdown on African Americans. *The Nation, 261* (July 10), 45 ff.

Hammitt, J. K. (in press). Regularoty impact analysis and stratospheric-ozone depletion: U.S. policy and the Montreal Protocol. In R. D. Morgenstern (Ed.), *Regulatory impact analysis at EPA: Lessons learned.* Washington, D.C.: Resources for the Future.

Hanson, K. (1991). We must find our business heroes. *Executive Excellence, 8,* 5–6.

Hardin, G. R. (1968). The tragedy of the commons. *Science, 162,* 1243–1248.

Hare, R. M. (1975). Abortion and the golden rule. *Philosophy and public affairs, 4,* 201–222.

Harlap, S., Kest, K., & Forrest, J. D. (1991). *Preventing pregnancy, protecting health: A new look at birth control choices in the United States.* New York: Alan Guttmacher Institute.

Harris, S. B. (1993). *The Right Lesson To Learn From Thalidomide.* Document distributed on the Internet. Compuserve 71450,1773.

Harvard Medical School Health Letter. (1989). Whooping cough: the last gasp? *15* (2), 3 ff.

Hershey, J. C., & Baron, J. (1987). Clinical reasoning and cognitive processes. *Medical Decision Making, 7,* 203–211.

Hilts, P. J. (1990). Plan is offered for stable birth rate. *New York Times,* February 26, p. 9.

Hinman, A. R. (1986). DTP vaccine litigation. *American Journal of Diseases of Children, 140,* 528–530.

Hoar, W. P. (1995). UNICEF: Behind the mask. *The New American,* April 3, 1995 (http://www.execpc.com/~jfish/na/).

Homer-Dixon, T. (1995). The ingenuity gap: Can poor countries adapt to resource scarcity? *Population and Development Review, 21,* 587–612.

Howson, C. P., & Fineberg, H. V. (1992). Adverse events following pertussis and rubella vaccines: Summary of a report of the Institute of Medicine. *Journal of the American Medical Association, 267,* 392–396.

Huber, P. W. (1988). *Liability: The legal revolution and its consequences.* New York: Basic Books.

Huber, P. W. (1991). *Galileo's revenge: Junk science in the courtroom.* New York: Basic Books.

Huber, P. W., and Robert E. Litan (Eds.). (1991). *The liability maze: The impact of liability law on safety and innovation.* Washington, D.C.: Brookings Institution.

Inglehart, J. K. (1987). Compensating children with vaccine-related injuries. *New England Journal of Medicine, 316,* 1283–1288.

Janis, I. L. (1982). *Groupthink: Psychological studies of policy decisions and fiascos.* Boston: Houghton-Mifflin.

Jervis, R. (1976). *Perception and misperception in international politics.* Princeton: Princeton University Press.

Johnson, C. (1993). New vaccine technologies boost children's health. *The Reuter Library Report,* July 15.

Joint Committee on Vaccination and Immunization. (1981). The whooping cough epidemic 1977–1979. In *Whooping cough.* London: Her Majesty's Stationary Office.

Kahneman, D., Knetsch, J. L., & Thaler, R. H. (1990). Experimental tests of the endowment effect and the Coase theorem. *Journal of Political Economy, 98,* 1325–1348.

Kahneman, D., & Lovallo, D. (1993). Timid choices and bold forecases: A cognitive perspective on risk taking. *Management Science, 39,* 17–31.

Kahneman, D., & Tversky, A. (1984). Choices, values, and frames. *American Psychologist, 39,* 341–350.

Kasun, J. (1981). The international politics of contraception. *Policy Review,* Winter, pp. 135 ff.

Kelly, M. (1995). The road to paranoia. *The New Yorker,* June 19.

Kempton, W., Boster, J. S., & Hartley, J. A. (1995). *Environmental values in American culture.* Cambridge, Mass.: MIT Press.

Kerr, R. A. (1996). Ozone-destroying chlorine tops out; atmospheric chlorine levels beginning to decline; atmospheric chemistry. *Science, 271,* 32.

Khory, K. R. (1993). The Shah Bano case: Some political implications. In R. D. Baird (Ed.), *Religion and law in independent India* (pp. 121–137). New Delhi: Manohar.

Knodel, J., & Jones, G. W. (1996). Post-Cairo population policy: Does promoting girls' schooling miss the mark? *Population and Development Review, 22,* 683–702.

Koriat, A., Lichtenstein, S., & Fischhoff, B. (1980). Reasons for confidence. *Journal of Experimental Psychology: Human Learning and Memory, 6,* 107–118.

Kozlowski, G. C. (1993). Muslim personal law and political identity in independent India. In R. D. Baird (Ed.), *Religion and law in independent India,* pp. 75–92. New Delhi: Manohar.

Kuhn, D. (1991). *The skills of argument.* New York: Cambridge University Press.

Kuhse, H. (1987). *The sanctity of life doctrine in medicine: A critique.* Oxford: Oxford University Press.

Kurien, J., & Achari, T. R. T. (1990). Overfishing along Kerala coast: Causes and consequences. *Economic and Political Weekly, 25,* 2011–2018,

Lafferty, K. J. (1990). Should the fetal tissue research ban be lifted? *Journal of NIH Research, 2,* 16–18.

Lamb, D. (1984). *The Africans.* New York: Vintage Books.

Lane, R. E. (in press). The joyless market economy. In A. Ben-Ner and L. Putterman (Eds.), *Economics, values, and organization.* New York: Cambridge University Press.

Limbaugh, R. H. (1992). *The way things ought to be.* New York: Pocket Books.

Limbaugh, R. H. (1993). *See, I told you so.* New York: Pocket Books.

Loewenstein, G., & Mather, J. (1990). Dynamic processes in risk perception. *Journal of Risk and Uncertainty, 3,* 155–175.

Lord, C. G., Ross, L., & Lepper, M. R. (1979). Biased assimilation and attitude polarization: The effects of prior theories on subsequently considered evidence. *Journal of Personality and Social Psychology, 37,* 2098–2109.

Lumsdaine, D. H. (1993). *Moral vision in international politics: The foreign aid regime, 1949–1989.* Princeton: Princeton University Press.

Mackay, C. (1841). *Memoirs of extraordinary popular delusions.* London: Richard Bentley.

Marshall, E. (1995). Tamoxifen's trials and tribulations. *Science, 270,* 910.

Martine, G. (1996). Brazil's fertility decline, 1965–95: A fresh look at key factors. *Population and Development Review, 22,* 47–75.

Mason, J. O. (1990). Should the fetal tissue research ban be lifted? *Journal of NIH Research, 2,* 17–18.

Mastroianni, L. Jr., Donaldson, P. J., and Kane, T. T. (1990). *Developing new contraceptives: Obstacles and opportunities.* Washington, D.C.: National Academy Press.

Maurice, J. (1995). Malaria vaccine raises a dilemma. *Science, 267,* 320–323.

McGoodwin, J. R. (1990). *Crisis in the world's fisheries: People, problems, and policies.* Stanford, Calif.: Stanford University Press.

McIntosh, C. A., & Finkle, J. L. (1995). The Cairo conference on population and development: A new paradigm? *Population and Development Review, 21,* 223–260.

Messick, D. M. (1985). Social interdependence and decision making. In G. Wright (Ed.), *Behavioral decision making* (pp. 87–109). New York: Plenum.

218   REFERENCES

Meszaros,Meszaros, J. R., Asch, D. A., Baron, J., Hershey, J. C., Kunreuther, H., & Schwartz-Buzaglo, J. (1996). Cognitive processes and the decisions of some parents to forgo pertussis vaccination for their children. *Journal of Clinical Epidemiology, 49,* 697–703.

Mill, J. S. (1859). *On Liberty.* London.

Mintz, B. (1994). Losing your shirt; federal rules for environmental cleanup trouble even the smallest of businesses. *Houston Chronicle,* January 30, Business, p. 1.

Monastersky, R. (1995). Oceanographers cautiously explore a global warming therapy. *Science News, 148,* 220.

Montzka, S. A., Butler, J. H., Myers, R. C., Thompson, T. M., Swanson, T. H., Clarke, A. D., Lock, L. T., & Elkins, J. W. (1996). Decline in the tropospheric abundance of halogen from halocarbons: Implications for stratospheric ozone depletion. *Science, 272,* 1318–1322.

Moynihan, D. P. (1996). *Miles to go: A personal history of social policy.* Cambridge, Mass.: Harvard University Press.

Naff, T. (1997). The long, dark shadow: Population, water, and peace in the Middle East. In R. K. Pachauri & L. F. Qureshy (Eds.). *Population, environment, and development* (pp. 123-151). New Delhi: Tata Energy Research Institute.

Newcomb, P. A., & Storer, B. E. (1995). Postmenopausal hormone use and risk of large-bowel cancer. *Journal of the National Cancer Institute, 87,* 1067–1071.

Oberlink, R. (1995). The case for shutting the door. *Los Angeles Times,* Op-Ed, November 3, part B, p. 9.

Olson, M. (1982). *The rise and decline of nations: Economic growth, stagflation, and social rigidities.* New Haven: Yale University Press.

Orts, E. W. (1995). Reflexive environmental law. *Northwestern University Law Review, 89,* 1227–1340.

Ostrom, E. (1990). *Governing the commons: The evolution of institutions for collective action.* New York: Cambridge University Press.

Ostrom, E., Gardner, R., & Walker, J. (1994). *Rules, games, and common-pool resources.* Ann Arbor: University of Michigan Press.

Parson, E. A., & Greene, O. (1996). The complex chemistry of the international ozone agreements. *Environment, 37,* 16 ff.

Passell, P. (1995). A mystery bankers love: How do credit cards stay so profitable? *New York Times,* August 17, D2.

Posner, R. A. (1992). *Sex and reason.* Cambridge, Mass.: Harvard University Press.

Postel, S. L., Daily, G. C., & Ehrlich, P. R. (1996). Human appropriation of renewable fresh water. *Science, 271,* 785–788.

Pritchett, L. H. (1994a). Desired fertility and the impact of population policies. *Population and Development Review, 20,* 1–55.

Pritchett, L. H. (1994b). The impact of population policies: reply. *Population and Development Review, 20,* 621–630.

Putnam, R. (1995). Bowling alone: America's declining social capital. *Journal of Democracy, 6,* 65–78.

Ramaswamy, C. S. (1992). Ayodhya is not the problem: It is a warning. *Hindustan Times,* December 20. (From the BJP web page: http://-www.bjp.org/rjb/ayodhya.html).

Ritov, I., Baron, J., & Hershey, J. C. (1993). Framing effects in the evaluation of multiple risk reduction. *Journal of Risk and Uncertainty, 6,* 145–159.

Robey, B., Rutstein, S., & Morris, L. (1993). The fertility decline in developing countries. *Scientific American* (December), 31–37.

Rosenbaum, R. (1995). Staring into the heart of the heart of darkness. *New York Times Magazine,* June 4, pp. 36 ff.

Rosser, Y. C. (1995). "Acronyms and oxymorons." Manuscript, Department of Asian Studies, University of Texas, Austin.

Sachs, J. (1997). Nature, nurture and growth. *The Economist, 343* (8021), 19–22.

Safina, C. (1994). Where have all the fishes gone. *Issues in Science and Technology, 10,* 37–43.

Schelling, T. C. (1992). Some economics of global warming. *American Economic Review, 82,* 1–14.

Schick, F. (1991). *Understanding action: An essay on reasons.* New York: Cambridge University Press.

Schmidtz, D. (1990). When is original appropriation required. *The Monist, 73,* 504–518.

Schneider, P. (1993). Breaking Georges Bank; controversy over fishing problems in the Atlantic Ocean off of the New England coast. *Audubon, 95,* 84 ff.

Sears, D. O., & Funk, C. L. (1991). The role of self-interest in social and political attitudes. *Advances in Experimental Social Psychology, 24,* 1–91.

Senate Special Committee on Euthanasia and Assisted Suicide (1995). *Final report.* Ottawa: Government of Canada (http://www.island-net.com/~deathnet/senate.html).

Service, R. F. (1996). Contraceptive technology: panel wants to break R&D barrier. *Science, 272,* 1258.

Shabman, L., & Stephenson, K. (1994). A critique of the self-interested voter model: the case of a local single issue referendum. *Journal of Economic Issues, 28,* 1173–1186.

Simon, J. L. (1980). Resources, population, environment: An oversupply of false bad news. *Science, 208,* 1431–1437.

Simon, J. L. (1990). *Population matters: People, resources, environment and immigration.* New Brunswick, N.J.: Transaction Publishers.

Simon, J. L. (1995). *Immigration: The demographic and economic facts.* Washington, D.C.: The Cato Institute (also http://www.cato.org/-pr-immig.html).

Simon, J. L. (1996). Public expenditures on immigrants to the United States, past and present. *Population and development review, 22,* 99–109.

Singer, P. (1979). *Practical Ethics.* Cambridge: Cambridge University Press.

Slovic, P. (1987). Perception of risk. *Science, 236,* 290–285.

Smith, M. H. (1988). National Childhood Vaccine Injury Compensation Act. *Pediatrics, 82,* 264–269.

Spencer, R. W., & Christy, J. R. (1990). Precise monitoring of global temperature trends from satellites. *Science, 247,* 1558–1662.

Spranca, M. (1992). "The effect of naturalness on desirability and preference in the domain of foods." Unpublished masters thesis, Department of Psychology, University of California, Berkeley.

Stammer, L., & Feldman, P. (1991). Nuclear dump denounced at state hearings. *Los Angeles Times,* July 23, p. 3.

Stanovich, K. E., & West, R. F. (in press). Individual differences in rational thought. *Journal of Experimental Psychology: General.*

Stein, D. (1995). *People who count: Population and politics, women and children.* London: Earthscan.

Stone, R. (1992). Controversial contraceptive wins approval from FDA panel. *Science, 256,* 1754.

Sundström, K. (1993). *Abortion: A reproductive health issue.* Working paper, Women's Health and Nutrition Work Program, Department of Population, Health, and Nutrition. Washington, D.C.: The World Bank.

Svenson, O. (1981). Are we all less risky and more skillful than our fellow drivers? *Acta Psychologica, 47,* 143–148.

Sword, D. (1994). Midwesterners jump at quake insurance. *Rocky Mountain News,* September 11, p. 34A.

Tengs, T. O., Adams, M. E., Pliskin, J. S., Safran, D. G., Siegel, J. E., Weinstein, M. E., & Graham, J. D. (1995). Five-hundred life-saving interventions and their cost-effectiveness. *Risk Analysis, 15,* 360–390.

Tengs, T. O., Meyer, G., Siegel, J. E., Pliskin, J. S., Graham, J. D., & Weinstein, M. C. (1996). Oregon's medical ranking and cost-effectiveness. *Medical Decision Making, 16,* 99–107.

Tversky, A., Sattath, S., & Slovic, P. (1988). Contingent weighting in judgment and choice. *Psychological Review, 95,* 371–384.

Ubel, P. A., DeKay, M., Baron, J., & Asch, D. A. (1996). Cost effectiveness analysis in a setting of budget constraints: Is it equitable? *New England Journal of Medicine, 334,* 1174–1177.

UNICEF. (1995) *The Progress of Nations 1995.* New York: UNICEF (also http://www.iisd.ca/linkages/un/pon/progtoc.html).

United Nations Development Program. (1992, 1994). *Human Development Report.* New York: Oxford University Press.

van Avermaet, E. (1974). "Equity: A theoretical and empirical analysis." Doctoral dissertation, University of California, Santa Barbara.

Varshney, A. (1993). Battling the past, forging a future? Ayodhya and beyond. In P. Oldenberg (Ed.), *India briefing, 1993* (pp. 9–42). Boulder, Colo.: Westview Press.

Viggiano, A. A., Morris, R. A., Gollinger, K., & Arnold, F. (1995). Ozone destruction by chlorine — The impracticality of mitigation through ion chemistry. *Science, 267,* 82–84.

Wald, M. L. (1993). Pondering and energy tax that can't please all the people. *New York Times* (Business), January 31, p. 10.

Wallis, C. (1995). A tonic for the mind. *Time,* June 26.

Walsh, J. (1986). River blindness: A gamble pays off. *Science, 232,* 922-925.

Watson, R. T., Zinyowera, M. C., & Moss, R. H. (1996). *Climate change 1995 — Impacts, adaptations and mitigation of climate change: scientific-technical analysis.* New York: Cambridge University Press.

Weber, P. (1995). Protecting oceanic fisheries and jobs. In L R. Brown et al., *State of the world 1995: A Worldwatch Institute report on progress toward a sustainable society.* New York: Norton.

Weinstein, N. (1980). Unrealistic optimism about future life events. *Journal of Personality and Social Psychology, 39,* 806–820.

Willis, D. B., Calle, E. E., Miricale-McMahill, H. L., & Heath, C. W., Jr. (1996). Estrogen replacement therapy and risk of fatal breast cancer in a prospective cohort of postmenopausal U.S. women. *Cancer Causes and Control, 7,* 449–457.

Index